LAW AS AN INSTRUMENT

How can the law be employed pragmatically to facilitate development and underpin illiberal principles? The case of contemporary China shows that the law plays an increasingly important role in the country's illiberal approach to both domestic and China-related global affairs, which has posed intellectual challenges in understanding it with reference to conventional, Western legal concepts and theories. This book provides a systematic exploration of the sources of Chinese law as pragmatically reconfigured in context, aiming to fill the gap between written and practised law. In combination with fieldwork investigations, it conceptualises various formal and informal laws, including the Constitution, congressional statutes, supreme court interpretations, judicial documents, guiding cases and judicial precedents. Moreover, it engages a theoretical analysis of legal instrumentalism, illuminating how and why the law works as an instrument for authoritarian legality in China, with international reflections on other comparable regimes.

Shucheng Wang is an Associate Professor at the School of Law, City University of Hong Kong. He was a Fulbright Scholar (Emory University) and a Clarendon Scholar (Oxford University). He has authored three books and over fifty articles. He is also an affiliated researcher of the Law and Religion in the Asia Pacific Region program at The University of Queensland, Australia.

LAW AS AN INSTRUMENT

Sources of Chinese Law for Authoritarian Legality

SHUCHENG WANG
City University of Hong Kong

CAMBRIDGE
UNIVERSITY PRESS

CAMBRIDGE
UNIVERSITY PRESS

University Printing House, Cambridge CB2 8BS, United Kingdom

One Liberty Plaza, 20th Floor, New York, NY 10006, USA

477 Williamstown Road, Port Melbourne, VIC 3207, Australia

314–321, 3rd Floor, Plot 3, Splendor Forum, Jasola District Centre, New Delhi – 110025, India

103 Penang Road, #05–06/07, Visioncrest Commercial, Singapore 238467

Cambridge University Press is part of the University of Cambridge.

It furthers the University's mission by disseminating knowledge in the pursuit of education, learning, and research at the highest international levels of excellence.

www.cambridge.org
Information on this title: www.cambridge.org/9781009152563
DOI: 10.1017/9781009152556

First published 2022

A catalogue record for this publication is available from the British Library.

Library of Congress Cataloging-in-Publication Data
Names: Wang, Shucheng, 1982- author.
Title: Law as instrument : sources of Chinese law for authoritarian legality / Shucheng Peter Wang, Associate Professor, School of Law, City University of Hong Kong.
Description: Cambridge, United Kingdom ; New York, NY : Cambridge University Press, 2022. | Includes bibliographical references and index.
Identifiers: LCCN 2021061909 (print) | LCCN 2021061910 (ebook) | ISBN 9781009152563 (hardback) | ISBN 9781009152570 (paperback) | ISBN 9781009152556 (epub)
Subjects: LCSH: Law–China–Philosophy. | Law–Political aspects–China. | Rule of law–China. | Law and socialism. | Authoritarianism–China.
Classification: LCC KNQ464 .W364 2022 (print) | LCC KNQ464 (ebook) | DDC 340/.1150951–dc23/eng/20220331
LC record available at https://lccn.loc.gov/2021061909
LC ebook record available at https://lccn.loc.gov/2021061910

ISBN 978-1-009-15256-3 Hardback

To my family

哀公问曰："何为则民服？"孔子对曰："举直错诸枉，则民服；举枉错诸直，则民不服。"（《论语》二章十九节）

The Duke Ai asked, saying, "What should be done in order to secure the submission of the people?" Confucius replied, "Advance the upright and set aside the crooked, then the people will submit. Advance the crooked and set aside the upright, then the people will not submit."

The Analects, 2:19 (English translation: James Legge)

Owe no one anything, except to love each other, for the one who loves another has fulfilled the law. For the commandments, "You shall not commit adultery, You shall not murder, You shall not steal, You shall not covet," and any other commandment, are summed up in this word: "You shall love your neighbor as yourself." Love does no wrong to a neighbor; therefore love is the fulfilling of the law.

Romans 13:8–10 (English Standard Version 2016)

CONTENTS

FIGURES

TABLES

PREFACE AND ACKNOWLEDGEMENTS

The American writer John Steinbeck once confessed at the beginning of his book *Travels with Charley: In Search of America* that:

> In America I live in New York, or dip into Chicago or San Francisco, but . . . I discovered that I did not know my own country. I, an American writer, writing about America, was working from memory, and the memory is at best a faulty, warpy reservoir. . . . I knew the changes only from books and newspapers . . . I was writing of something I did not know about. (1962: 11)

This statement resonates to some extent with my own experience. When I was first granted the opportunity to study outside mainland China, I soon realized that there may be two or even more contrasting imaginations of "China" in the minds of people from different parts of the world. China, as a super-economy in the twenty-first-century global order, is rapidly becoming more relevant to world affairs than ever before. Nonetheless, it seems that understanding China has not been intellectually easy in many respects for those both inside and outside the country. In particular, at one point in history, China's law largely comprised penal codes; today, however, after over four decades of legal transplantation and codification, a relatively comprehensive legal system has been established in the country. More importantly, the increasingly key role of law in China's society can be clearly distinguished from the situation in developed liberal democracies. This may further present an intellectual challenge when attempting to understand the functions of "Chinese law" in its sociopolitical context, and in a global context more broadly, due to China's unprecedented integration into the global economy, although it still seems to exist in a state of increasing tension with the liberal world.

Undoubtedly, I owe a great deal to the many people who made it possible for me to continue my academic career and finally complete this book in Hong Kong. First, I would like to thank the Chinese judges I spoke with (who have opted to remain anonymous) for their assistance in facilitating my ethnographic fieldwork in China's courts, as well as the many judges I interviewed; the information they provided was invaluable, of the kind frequently inaccessible to the public, and formed an essential part of this book. I also wish to sincerely thank the University Grants Council of Hong Kong for its generous awarding of three research grants (Projects: CityU 11635116, 21605915, 11601419) in support of my interdisciplinary study of Chinese and comparative law (as partly presented in this book). Moreover, I had the great pleasure of working with my colleagues at the School of Law at City University of Hong Kong, which allowed me to pursue my studies in a very supportive research environment, in particular through its Centre for Chinese and Comparative Law (CCCL). At the same time, the university provided generous staff development funds in support of organizing various academic activities, as well as many overseas presentations of the early drafts, without which this book would not have been possible.

I owe an enormous debt of gratitude to Kwai Ng and He Xin for their detailed and constructive comments on the earlier version of Chapters 4 and 6 of this book. Moreover, relevant theoretical discussion, in particular that contained in Chapter 7, was presented and tested at an international symposium ("Sources of Law, Authoritarian Legality and Chinese Jurisprudence") held online by CCCL in May 2021. I am also immensely grateful to Hualing Fu, Taisu Zhang, Sida Liu, Samuli Seppänen and Jiangyu Wang for their critical and constructive engagement. Furthermore, the relevant early drafts of several book chapters have been presented in some way at numerous conferences and institutions, including the Chinese University of Hong Kong, National University of Singapore, Academia Sinica in Taiwan, Seoul National University in South Korea and Jilin University in mainland China. I would like to express my sincere thanks to the conference organizers and participants for their helpful comments and discussions, including Xi Chao, Björn Ahl, Cai Lidong, Michelle Miao, Yu Xiaohong, Yang Fan, Liu Xiaoping, Andrew Harding, Fort Fu-Te Liao, Yu-Jie Chen, Yun-Chien Chang, Jeong Hoon Park, Guangwen Jiang and Woo-Young Rhee. I additionally wish to extend my sincere thanks to Joe Ng for his kind help and practical suggestions on the publication of this book, as well as to the anonymous reviewers for their insightful expert comments. Thanks should also go to Daniel Pascoe and Charles Qu for offering their valuable advice on relevant matters of publishing the book.

In conducting the relevant critical analysis of common law and comparative law perspectives presented in this book, my previous studies and experience in the common law jurisdictions of the USA, the United Kingdom and Hong Kong have been of great benefit. I am deeply indebted to my mentor Michael J. Perry for his invaluable guidance and unwavering support all these years. I still remember with profound gratitude the moment at which I received his offer to be a supervisor in support of my application for the Fulbright Chinese PhD Dissertation Research Program, and I was fortunate enough to be finally selected to join the program in the USA. I would also like to extend my heartfelt gratitude to Andrew Shacknove for providing me with unconditional support during my studies at Oxford; there, I had the privilege of mingling with a cohort of exceptional professionals and professors who have made significant advances in various jurisdictions throughout the world, which has further pushed me to think outside the box about many of the issues discussed herein. In addition, my special thanks to both the Fulbright and Clarendon scholarships for their generous financial support for my studies in the USA and United Kingdom.

Furthermore, I very much appreciate the many hours of outstanding research assistance provided by Chen Minhui, Xiong Zhanglin, Kit Tin Lok Pau and Huo Xiaobin.

Most of the chapters in this book draw to some extent on my previous studies, whether published or forthcoming, which have been rewritten or revised appropriately to make them fit coherently with the book's structure. Chapter 2 drew from a previous study with a substantial revision ("Emergence of a Dual Constitution in Transitional China", *Hong Kong Law Journal* 45(3): 819–850, 2015). A different version of Chapter 4 has been published as an article entitled "The Judicial Document as Informal State Law: Judicial Lawmaking in China's Courts", *Modern China* 48(3): 617–649, 2022. An earlier version of Chapter 5 was published as "Guiding Cases as a Form of Statutory Interpretation", *Hong Kong Law Journal* 48(3): 1067–1096, 2018. Chapter 6 drew from a previous study published as an article entitled "Guiding Cases and Bureaucratization of Judicial Precedents in China", *University of Pennsylvania Asian Law Review* 14(4): 96–134, 2019. Finally, an earlier version of some parts of Chapter 7 has been published with the title "Authoritarian Legality and Legal Instrumentalism in China" in *The Chinese Journal of Comparative Law* (https://doi.org/10.1093/cjcl/cxac012).

Finally, my deepest gratitude goes to my family – in particular, my wife Sophie Hu, for her selfless love, patience and encouragement, and my children Andrey and Jadon, for tolerating my incessant disappearances into my office. They paint my world with bright colours. I cannot truly express the extent of my gratitude to them in words, and I am genuinely amazed by every day I get to spend my life with them.

ABBREVIATIONS

CCP	Chinese Communist Party
CIAJ	China Institute for Applied Jurisprudence
CMC	Central Military Commission
DIC	Discipline Inspection Commission
LPC	Local People's Congress
MPA	main points of adjudication
NJC	National Judges College
NPC	National People's Congress
NPCSC	Standing Committee of the National People's Congress
PCLRAD	Provisions on Citation of Laws, Regulations and other Normative Legal Documents in Adjudicative Documents
PLC	Political-Legal Committee
PRC	People's Republic of China
PWGC	Provisions Concerning Work on Guiding Cases
SC	Supervision Commission
SPC	Supreme People's Court
SPP	Supreme People's Procuratorate

1

Introduction

Emergence of Chinese Law?

Background: China's Turn against or towards the Law?

Throughout the twenty-first century, China has played an important role in the changing world order that cannot be easily ignored, both before and after the beginning of the Sino-US trade war, given its unprecedented integration into the global economy. In parallel with its economic development, China has also made tremendous efforts to build up an instrumentalist legal system ever since 1978, when Chinese leader Deng Xiaoping realized the importance of law for the country's economic revival and political stability. Interestingly, after Xi Jinping came to power in 2012, there has been some scholarly debate over the dynamics of China's legal order. One side argues that China is turning against or away from law with an attempt to revive pre-1978 court mediation practice, in contrast to its previous legal reforms emphasizing the role of formal law and court adjudication in resolving civil disputes (Minzner 2011). Other scholars contend that China's efforts to deepen its dictatorship in the Xi Jinping era have been to a large extent highly legalistic, empowering legal institutions and developing legal measures to combat traditional bureaucratic corruption; in short, harnessing the organizational and legitimizing capacities of the law rather than circumventing it (Zhang and Ginsburg 2019). To some extent, this debate is like focusing on two sides of the same coin. On the one hand, in recent years, China has witnessed a "litigation explosion": in short, a rapid increase in the number of cases filed with courts, largely due to the ups and downs of China's economic development, as well as the introduction of the "registration system for case dockets" (立案登记制 *lian dengji zhi*) in 2015, which requires courts to docket all case applications according to the law. This represents a significant departure from previous practice, in which courts had wide discretion to review and reject a case filed with the court. In addition, in order to improve the professionalism of Chinese judges, the Supreme People's Court (SPC) adopted a "judge quota" system (法官员额制 *faguan yuan'e zhi*) in 2015; as a result, the number of quota judges with better remuneration packages, as distinct from other categories of court staff (i.e. judicial assistants and administrative staff), dropped by over 40 per cent according to the SPC's report (Sohu.com 2017). These reforms signal China's turn towards law through professionalizing court personnel; this is true despite the fact that, in reality, the increasingly heavy caseload has put judges in a difficult position, with judges in many courts being required to deal with an average of more than 300 cases per year. This heavy workload has led many judges to leave the courts (Lubman 2015).

Central authorities are certainly aware of the dilemma resulting from these judicial reforms, and have been attempting to revive the Maoist approach to dispute resolution, called the "Fengqiao Experience" (枫桥经验 *fengqiao jingyan*), which focuses on "small matters not leaving the village, and larger matters not leaving the township" as indicated in the Chinese Communist Party's (CCP) plan to revitalize the countryside (Central Committee of the Chinese Communist Party and State Council 2018). In order to implement the CCP's revival of the Maoist approach to social management, the SPC has specified a series of measures designed to integrate courts into this Maoist model of dispute resolution, led by the Party committee and government, which insists on engaging in non-litigation dispute resolution mechanisms wherever possible and prioritizing mediation, as well as overcoming difficulties and solving conflicts in a timely manner at the grassroots level (Supreme People's Court 2019). In this model, the court as a political actor plays a significant facilitatory role in the non-litigation dispute resolution network, led by the Party committee and government; for example, through setting up "judge liaison points" (法官联络点 *faguan lianluo dian*) in grassroots communities to provide periodic or even door-to-door consultation, or indoctrination, in order to resolve the dispute without litigation as early as possible. At this point, as one grassroots official said, it is much easier to resolve a dispute if a judge is involved in the mediation process, because the parties concerned are more willing to accept a proposal facilitated or offered by a judge (Interview 66-19-ZJWZ01). Clearly, apart from the state actors involved, a basic idea behind the Maoist approach to dispute resolution (i.e. the Fengqiao Experience) is to mobilize the masses through a politically selected group of people, usually with a certain (monetary and/or non-monetary) incentive – such groups include the "Chaoyang Masses"

(朝阳群众 *chaoyan qunzhong*) and "Xicheng Aunties" (西城大妈 *xicheng dama*) in Beijing city, or the "Wulin Aunties" (武林大妈 *wulin dama*) in Hangzhou city – to target and indoctrinate the parties concerned in order to resolve the dispute or other issue within the community. This political approach is primarily rooted in the CCP-led grassroots community in which the party concerned resides. This approach is also likely to impose peer pressure on those who are targeted, who may be politically labelled and treated as "troublemakers" or even "lawbreakers". In the Mao era, in extreme situations, in order to purge these political opponents, the idea of "class struggle" was even raised by the CCP via political movements, such as the Socialist Education Movement (社会主义教育运动 *shehui zhuyi jiaoyu yundong*) launched in 1963, to remove "reactionary" elements with the CCP's bureaucracy (Baum 1969). It is clear that the revival of the Maoist approach to dispute resolution indicates a definite shift towards stressing the importance of mediation in various forms, such as court mediation, societal mediation and administrative mediation. In this sense, it may be understood as a turn "against" law.

Nonetheless, this is only one side of the coin. On the other side, tremendous efforts have been made at the same time to build up a more professional judiciary. In fact, there is no inherent contradiction between these two sides of the coin, as both work to solidify China's authoritarian regime by strengthening authoritarian legality and increasing the resilience of the CCP's authoritarian politics.[1] It has been observed that the revival of pre-1978 court mediation practice represents an attempt to resolve disputes at early stages, particularly if the fault (as concluded from the court's fact-finding) cannot simply be assigned to one party, in such a way as to "mitigate at least to some extent the kinds of adversarial excesses"; this is then followed by a verdict of right or wrong, determining the winner or loser in a similar way to a formalist Western-style legal system (Huang 2006b: 297, 306). This is in fact largely compatible with China's traditional legal culture of Confucianism, with its emphasis on dispute resolution as its foremost concern rather than the protection of rights via formalist reasoning (Huang 2006b: 278). Furthermore, different from the traditional ideal of settling disputes by societal mediation (Huang 2006a), the Maoist approach to mediation expands the role of the court to the masses in the community, in accordance with the

[1] Mary E. Gallagher (2017) is a pioneer of exploring the theory of authoritarian legality in China.

ideology of the "mass line", which means that "judges do not just sit at court but must go down to the village to investigate the truth with the help of the 'masses' and then resolve or 'mediate' a case" (Huang 2006b: 286).

In the era of Xi Jinping, due to the establishment of the "grid management system" (网格化管理 *wanggehua guanli*) that divides the territory of a local government into a number of segments, each monitored by an officially designated agent (Cai 2018), judges are now designated to each of these grids to resolve the disputes arising there. Judges' engagement in the Maoist approach has in fact caused mediation to develop adjudicative features, as judges – constitutionally designated as adjudicators – have been playing a facilitative *political* role in the CCP-led grid management system. This political role of judges in the community, as arguably different from its constitutionally designated adjudicative role in court trials, is in reality politically pragmatic and influenced by practical political needs. For instance, judges may engage in propagandizing these newly enacted laws, or the CCP's achievements pertaining to the "Chinese rule of law", by propagandizing a number of selected judgements throughout the community. Moreover, in political movements or activities, certain political tasks may be assigned to them (e.g. in targeted poverty alleviation programmes) in the same way as they are to other political subordinates of the CCP in order to achieve specific political goals. All of this clearly shows the application of the CCP's mass line – "from the masses, to the masses" – to the courts (Huang 2006b: 286). Given the both implicit and explicit involvement of state actors in the mediation process, as Huang observed, "mediation" in China's context has "taken on a far more adjudicatory, aggressive, and interventionist meaning than the mediatory ideal of voluntary settlement of differences through third-party facilitation" (2006b: 287). The extent to which courts may expediently intervene in the dispute resolution process depends largely on the complexity and severity of the dispute, as well as the potential threat it poses to social security and political stability. The court may play a role in such a process: either at a very early stage, as a facilitative actor outside the courtroom, or in the final stages, acting as an adjudicator and making a judicial decision if early efforts to resolve the dispute (including mediation) are unsuccessful. Before a dispute goes to the court, various soft and/or hard measures may be employed by relevant state actors in order to effect reconciliation, such as through "moral-political education, through political pressure (applied also by the local party leadership), and social pressure (applied also by relatives and neighbors), and even through positive material inducements" (Huang 2006b: 288). In this vein, it would be unsurprising for a judge to conduct on-site visits in order to persuade and educate the disputants into a voluntary compromise (Huang 2006b: 278). Moreover, political indoctrination may be readily integrated into such a didactic dispute resolution process by various state actors, either consciously or unconsciously.

To say this, however, is not to say that law is absent from these processes. Rather, given the development of formalist Continental law in China during the reform era since 1978, law has indeed come to play an increasingly important role in Chinese society, as indicated by the government's periodical nationwide propaganda efforts to stress the importance of the law with the goal of building up a (rhetorically so-called) rule-of-law order with Chinese characteristics. This approach somewhat downplays – at least domestically – the more authoritarian features of the regime, which are often exaggerated or blamed by its liberal counterparts for political purposes.

In this vein, given the importance of law for solidifying China's authoritarian governance, every effort has been made since 1978 to develop a positive system of law through law codifications, which represents a complete break from the period of the Cultural Revolution from 1966 until 1976, during which time legal nihilism prevailed across the entire country. Of course, in the process of codification, it is inevitable that China has been required to import a large amount from foreign jurisprudence. For example, private law was underdeveloped in the Chinese law tradition, meaning that conflicts arising from business deals and contracts were largely handled by customs and local traditions through non-official channels (Fairbank 1983: 122–123). After decades of the development of law codification in the areas of both public and private law, China has made tremendous efforts and achievements in this field, as partially evidenced by its promulgation of the Civil Code of the People's Republic of China (PRC) (中华人民共和国民法典 *zhonghua renmin gongheguo minfa dian*) in 2020. Nonetheless, these codified laws, the underlying concepts of which are largely imported from Western jurisprudence, may have distinctive meanings and logic in the context of Chinese society. For instance, from a historical and cultural perspective, the Western formalist legal tradition emphasizes principles of the protection of rights; by contrast, Chinese law in the Confucian tradition comprises *qing* (compassion based on Confucian humanness), *li* (moral principles governing both nature and society) and *fa* (the laws of the state), while law occupies an instrumental position in maintaining social order (Huang 2006b: 279). An intellectual inquiry that identifies these sources of Chinese law in action, along with their functions in the country's sociopolitical context, is accordingly merited.

Thesis: Sources of Chinese Law

As China's legislative enterprise has developed, its positive law system has been comprehensively codified in a specific law: that is, the Legislation Law of the PRC (中华人民共和国立法法 *zhonghua renmin gongheguo lifa fa*), enacted in 2000 and amended in 2015, which provides various statutes normatively and with binding force that enable the government to govern its territory, various actors to gain its authority with legitimacy and judges to have a legal basis for making judicial decisions (National People's Congress 2015). Keller (1994: 726) has divided the statutes therein into three categories: primary, secondary and tertiary legislation. At the top of this pyramid is the primary legislation, which ranks just below the Constitution in terms of legal authority and is often narrowly categorized as "*falü*", a term usually translated as "law". The secondary legislation is "*fagui*", a term usually translated as "regulations", which are made by the State Council (which possesses the highest executive power according to the Constitution) and regional people's congresses (including their standing committees as executants) at the prefectural level and above. The tertiary legislation is "*guizhang*", a term usually translated as "rules", which are produced by central government ministries and local government at the prefectural level and above.

Moreover, there is a special category of laws applicable to ethnic autonomous areas, usually translated as "autonomous and separate regulations" (自治和单行条例 *zizhi and danxing tiaolie*), which are issued by the people's congresses of ethnic autonomous areas to modify relevant higher-level statutes in light of the political, economic and cultural characteristics of the area in question (Keller 1994: 726). However, these laws only come into force after obtaining approval not only from the higher-level Congress but also from the CCP (Feng 2017: 59). This approval system, which lacks specific criteria, has in fact undermined the legislative autonomy in practice. It has been found that although ethnic autonomous regions have made efforts to make autonomous regulations, which are usually deemed to be the most important form of autonomous legislation, none of the five provincial-level autonomous regions have passed them with formal approval.[2]

Nonetheless, such a conceptualization, the process of which contains legal concepts such as "primary legislation" and "secondary legislation" that are largely used in Western parliamentary and presidential systems, can only indicate the hierarchical status of various positive laws, which are in turn based on the hierarchical authority of the lawmaking bodies in China's context; it can by no means reflect the practical functions of various positive laws in categories of this kind. Obviously, China, as a communist state that has adopted a people's congress system, is substantially different from – although perhaps on the surface similar to – liberal democracies, with their congressional legislative system that usually consists of primary and secondary legislation. In this regard, it has been pointed out that the Chinese legal terms discussed earlier, such as those translated as "law", "regulation" and "rule", are very likely to give rise to considerable confusion in foreign accounts of Chinese law if no specific definition or explanation is provided for them (Keller 1994: 726). For instance, it is a general rule-of-law requirement that a law should be certain, stable and predictable. However, distinctively, according to an important Chinese doctrine of lawmaking referred to as the policy of "preferring the coarse to the fine" (宜粗不宜细 *yicu bu yixi*), ambiguity is considered a key quality of national legislation – in particular, those of the National People's Congress (NPC) and the Standing Committee of the National People's Congress (NPCSC), which in principle are not intended to be certain or predictable with reference to the "plain meaning" of language as understood in Western legal formalism (Keller 1994: 749). Therefore, in practice, primary legislation often does not function as a source of law of chief importance to judges when making judicial decisions. Instead, it is the SPC's specific judicial interpretations and documents (as discussed in Chapters 3 and 4) that constitute the de facto primary source of law relied on by judges for adjudicating disputes. As one senior judge stated, without specific judicial interpretations or documents that provide an interpretation of relevant national legislation, a

[2] It has been pointed out that the autonomous legislative power is mostly underused and that, in the reform era, there has been no significant expansion of the amount of autonomous legislation. At the subregional level, autonomous regulations of twenty-five out of thirty autonomous prefectures were passed within six years of the passage of the Regional National Law in 1984. The five autonomous prefectures that did not pass their autonomous regulations are all located in the Xinjiang Uyghur Autonomous Region (Feng 2017: 65, 72).

judge usually can do almost nothing with the adjudication by the national legislation of the NPC/NPCSC. This shows that, given the lack of case law in China, the national legislation of the NPC/NPCSC can hardly act as a stand-alone legal basis for judges to make judicial decisions if no relevant judicial interpretations and documents are invoked. This clearly indicates a unique structure of China's positive law in which the SPC's specific judicial interpretations and documents, rather than the statutes of the NPC/NPCSC, are the primary sources of positive law relied on by judges in making judicial decisions.

In this vein, a further avenue of scholarly inquiry concerns *how* and *why* the SPC's judicial interpretations and documents have become a primary source of law in adjudication, which can in fact only be understood in China's sociopolitical context, rather than from some other perspectives. Moreover, as far as the Constitution – which ranks highest in the hierarchy of legislation – is concerned, its function and logic in Chinese law is effectively ignored due to the lack of an effective constitutional review system such as those in liberal democracies. Notably, this should not be interpreted to mean that the Constitution has no position in China's positive law. Rather, its importance has been stressed constantly, particular in the Xi era, as exemplified by the establishment of National Constitution Day in 2014, the goal of which was to increase awareness of the Constitution, promote its spirit, and strengthen its implementation (South China Morning Post 2014). Subsequently, establishing an effective constitutional review system that is suitable for China became a priority on the CCP's reform agenda. In response, the NPCSC (2019) has made significant efforts to establish a limited form of constitutional review system, of a kind that is suitable for its authoritarian regime, by enacting a specific statute – the Working Measures for the Recording and Review of Regulations and Judicial Interpretations (hereinafter "Working Measures") in 2019. Although courts are largely excluded from China's current model of constitutional review, the Constitution undoubtedly occupies an indispensable position in the structure of China's positive law, the dynamics of which also need to be intellectually examined in China's sociopolitical context.

Of course, apart from these positive laws, one element that cannot be ignored in the discussion of the sources of law is case law, which may either have a binding force (as in the common law tradition) or an increasingly persuasive force (as in the civil law tradition). Although China has no case law system with binding force based on judicial independence, it is interesting to note that in order to achieve consistency in the application of laws – as officially claimed – in practice, the SPC has made efforts to build up a so-called "guiding case system" that can be distinguished from all other judicial precedents. In addition, it has been a common practice for China's courts to select and periodically publish a certain number of judicial precedents as "typical cases" (典型案例 *dianxing anlie*) or "reference cases" (参考案例 *cankao anlie*). This kind of hybrid judicial precedent system is unprecedented in the family of legal systems. Apart from the existing literature, which pays attention to the guiding case system largely at the descriptive level, there is still a need to examine the nuances of various judicial precedents in the entire picture of sources of Chinese law regarding its practical function and position in China's sociopolitical context, which are discussed in Chapters 5 and 6.

Arguments and Implications

As already mentioned, given the emergence of sources of Chinese law with an increasing importance in China's legal order, which are quite different from those in both the civil law and common law traditions, it is intellectually desirable to explore the structure, function and logic of sources of Chinese law in the Chinese context. It has been perceived that these legal concepts in Chinese law, such as "rights" and "courts," are largely transplanted from foreign laws, but may have a distinct meaning in China's context that cannot be easily understood in the context of the Western tradition. This means that the understanding of Chinese law may even be misleading if taken outside of the Chinese context. For example, the conceptions of "rights" in China's political discourse have significantly different meanings from the Anglo-American tradition, while protests about "rights" in China seem less politically threatening (Perry 2008). Moreover, it has recently been argued that the conventional language of Western jurisprudence (such as that pertaining to laws and judges) may be misleading if used to discuss the Chinese legal system. Given China's integration into – while often being in a certain amount of tension with the world order, as Donald Clarke (2020) pointed out, "we should not derogate difference just because it is different, but we should not be biased against finding difference in the first place."

Having realized that it is often inappropriate to understand Chinese law in contrast with these "Western rule of law" concepts, it is intellectually imperative for scholars to explore the dynamics of Chinese law in a Chinese context, without relying excessively on concepts and theories imported from the West, as a way to respond to both theoretical and philosophical interest, as well as the practical realities in China. This has been categorized as the "third wave" of Chinese law scholarship and represents an attempt to reconceptualize the academic study of Chinese law (Minzner 2011: 975). This differs substantially from the previous scholarship conducted before the mid-twentieth century, when there was no existence of "Chinese law" as a discrete field of research in the scholarly narrative of the West; at this time, imperial law was largely considered as penal, and imperial legal institutions were mostly ignored in the scholarship (Minzner 2011: 975). The emphasis on the relative unimportance of Chinese law continued until the 1960s, when scholars began to explore imperial legal institutions and legal cases and even researched contemporary Chinese law in Communist China by investigating its processes and models of its application; however, as admitted by contemporary Chinese law research pioneer Jerome Cohen, due to outside observers' limited access to that Chinese legal system, it could be difficult for these observers to fully grasp the meaning assigned to certain legal terms (1968: vii–viii). Needless to say, there has increasingly been a turn in the scholarship towards seeing PRC legal institutions and practice as intelligible objects of study (Minzner 2011: 976), particularly after China – as a single-party state – became a global economic superpower in the twenty-first century.

During the "third wave" of Chinese law scholarship, characterized by the development of China's legal codification and ongoing judicial reforms, abundant descriptive research has been conducted on various specific subjects of Chinese law, such as Chinese company law, land law, civil law and criminal law. Moreover, due to the gap between the law on the books and in action, particularly in an authoritarian regime, some Chinese law scholars have attempted to conduct fieldwork in China through various access channels in order to explore relevant issues of Chinese law and legal institutions from a socio-legal perspective, thereby deepening scholarly understanding of these aspects in a specific socio-political context in a manner that differs from the assumptions made from some other (e.g. Anglo-American) perspectives.[3] However, as far as the sources of law – a fundamental issue for any legal order – are concerned, and despite the scholarly attention paid to some of them (such as the SPC's judicial interpretations and guiding cases), they tend

[3] For example, Kwai Hang Ng and Xin He have done a lot of fieldwork to research China's court system (Ng and He 2017).

to be largely fragmented, and a comprehensive and systematic examination of them in China's socialist context has not yet been completed.

As an exercise in the "third wave" of Chinese law scholarship, this book aims to make a contribution by systematically examining various sources of Chinese law and illustrating the dynamics of their sociopolitical logic employed in the applications. In addition to descriptive, theoretical and comparative analysis, it conducts an interdisciplinary exploration of various sources of Chinese law in the Chinese context through my fieldwork in China, with a particular focus on ethnographic observations within China's courtrooms and interviews with judges. A detailed discussion of the research methodology and data collection has been included in the Appendix.

More specifically, it examines several important common sources of law, i.e. the Constitution, statutes and judicial precedents, in China's sociopolitical context. In addition, three other significant sources of Chinese law – the SPC's judicial interpretations, judicial documents and the SPC's guiding cases – are thoroughly investigated with reference to the ways in which they have been involved and applied in practice. It further theorizes about relevant issues regarding these sources of law in China's context. For instance, it points out that the SPC's judicial interpretation has become a de facto primary source of law for adjudication, which is well suited to China's authoritarian regime. It further attempts to reconceptualize Chinese law in the Chinese context, as it is difficult or even impossible for many existing legal concepts imported from Western jurisdictions to explain the dynamics of various sources of Chinese law in this context. For example, China's constitutional law is conceptualized as a "dual constitution" in a way that provides stronger explanatory power regarding the function and logic of China's constitution in its socialist order, which goes beyond these normative statements, particularly from the standpoint of liberalism. This theorization and reconceptualization of Chinese law aims at deepening the understanding of sociopolitical logic employed by these law enforcers in the application of Chinese law, which goes beyond, and seems more sensible and durable than, these normative statements in various legislations.

Furthermore, a significant component of the book's narrative is the paradigmatic significance of understanding the structure of positive Chinese law, which has not yet been comprehensively addressed in the scholarship. Based on the systematic examination of various important and seemingly fragmented sources of law in China's legal system, it provides an integrated framework of positive Chinese law that is embedded into its socialist legal order and illustrates the dynamic relations between these sources of law in China's authoritarian regime. As discussed in the book, apart from these judicial precedents, which typically have only limited persuasive force as a reference for judicial decision-making, China's positive law system practically incorporates five categories of law with distinct practical functions: (1) the Constitution; (2) various statutes; (3) the SPC's judicial interpretations; (4) judicial documents; (5) the SPC's guiding cases. This dynamic structure differs substantially from those in the existing family of legal systems elsewhere in the world.

It is clear that the emergence of China's positive law system is not accidental, but rather has emerged from China's sociopolitical context, which (as the book discusses) has made it possible to propose a theory for Chinese law – that is, instrumentalism – explaining the formation, evolution and application of Chinese law in China's authoritarian regime. This particular theory of instrumentalism, as distinct from the debates over this theory in the Anglo-American tradition, reflects the dynamic function of law as an instrument in the political, economic, cultural and historical aspects of Chinese society. Moreover, instrumentalism of this kind may shed light on the academic study of the legal systems of other socialist states or, more broadly, other authoritarian regimes or illiberal democracies.

Chapter Outline

This book is an attempt to systematically examine various sources of law in contemporary China in order to develop and present a paradigmatic framework of Chinese law in context, and, on this basis, propose a theory of instrumentalism for Chinese law. It offers a detailed analysis of significant components of positive law in China's legislative system, as presented in the following chapters.

Chapter 2 considers the Constitution, the highest law in the legislative hierarchy, and (inescapably) its relationship with the CCP. Due to China's economic development over recent decades, it has been difficult for traditional theories, either communist or liberal ones, to accurately reflect the constitutional reality in China. Concepts such as the "unwritten constitution" or "living constitution" in the Western context are unable to provide a holistic view of China's Constitution, especially after

1978. China's Constitution, centred on the CCP and the state, has been largely transformed since this time. This chapter goes beyond the liberal approach and argues that a dual constitution has developed in China, within which the Party's Constitution attempts to keep pace with that of the state. More specifically, the Party has been endeavouring to integrate itself into the state through political conventions and "intraparty regulations" (党内法规 *dangnei fagui*). This dual constitution is unique in the sense that it departs from the model articulated by Mao Zedong, as well as from that of the Soviet Union, and does not follow the formalistic approach adopted by Western countries in defining the nature of a constitution.

Chapter 3 examines the SPC's judicial interpretation, which has been formally legalized as a source of law for adjudication, as well as its relationship with various other statutes in China's legislative system. It points out that the inner logic of China's legislation with different hierarchical status, as distinct from those of democratically elected parliamentary systems, is determined by the de facto distribution of legislative power within its authoritarian regime, where the SPC has become a significant player in exercising legislative power in a way that has largely evolved beyond its constitutional settings. In particular, it investigates the unique inner logic of the SPC's judicial interpretations, which have become a de facto primary source of law for adjudication in practice.

Chapter 4 explores the unique function and role of judicial documents – a significant form of informal state law, as distinguished from formal statutory laws – in China's legislative enterprise. In particular, it examines *why* and *how*, with no explicit statutory delegation, the judicial lawmaking practice of producing judicial documents has become embedded in the adjudication of China's courts. It accordingly proposes a twilight theory of China's judicial documents that explains why the practice of judicial lawmaking through producing documents exists in a twilight zone between legal and illegal, and is suitable for China's politically resilient authoritarian regime. Moreover, it demonstrates how the judicial document can be referred to effectively by judges in adjudication. It further investigates the extent to which the judicial document has enabled the court, under the dual leadership of the superior court and the local Party committee, to efficiently and effectively respond to the subnational diversity and the differences of local politics.

Chapter 5 focuses on the guiding case system, which is distinctive and cannot be simply explained by current case law theories. More specifically, it first explores the distinctiveness of the guiding case system in the specific context of China, as opposed to other types of case law in liberal democracies, then goes on to explain why the SPC has been able to expand its judicial lawmaking authority in the sense of being able to interpret the law through guiding cases. Furthermore, it illustrates that the Main Points of Adjudication (MPA) (裁判要点 *caipan yaodian*), as a part of a guiding case, has essentially become a form of statutory interpretation that enables the SPC to independently perform a legislative function to a certain extent without routine surveillance by the NPCSC. This stands in contrast to the previous practice, where the SPC performed the legislative function merely through having it delegated by the NPCSC. It is further suggested that, under China's authoritarian regime, the effectiveness of the SPC's lawmaking function through the guiding case system depends largely on the extent to which the courts could be independent in the context of China.

Chapter 6 investigates judicial precedents in China's instrumentalist legal system and finds that judges are generally reluctant to refer to a judicial precedent, including a guiding case, in the process of making a judicial decision. It further reveals that the guiding case system has effectively crystallized a bureaucratic system of judicial precedents with guiding cases at the top of the pyramid. A bureaucratic system of this kind is grounded primarily in the political hierarchy of the courts and a nationwide typical-case-selection movement, in which the lower courts are politically responsible for submitting a certain number of typical cases selected from within their respective jurisdictions to the SPC every year. Finally, it attempts to develop a bureaucratic theory of judicial precedents centred on guiding cases that fits into China's authoritarian context and that differs substantially from any other type of case law in a liberal context.

Chapter 7, which centres around the discussion of previous chapters, proposes a theory of instrumentalism – contextually, a more explanatory framework than either Marxist or Confucian legal theories – to explain the function and role of law in Chinese society. This kind of instrumentalism, which differs from the debate over this theory in the Anglo-American tradition, is situated in China's authoritarian regime, where a primary concern is the maintenance of political stability through strengthening authoritarian legality for the ruler. On this premise, economic development, as well as other social goals – such as efficiency of the government – for which the law can undoubtedly be placed in an instrumental position may become a priority in the ruler's political agenda. When it comes to dispute resolution, the primary matter of concern is not the achievement of the formalist justice of Western tradition via either a formal or informal process, but rather the settlement of disputes for which the law primarily plays a facilitative role as a tool, regardless of what strategies it may use. Instrumentalism of this kind, which is suitable for Chinese society both culturally and historically, shows that law is visible and does matter in China, although it cannot be completely understood through the lens of other legal traditions, particularly those from the West.

2

A Dual Constitution with Illiberal Characteristics

> The National People's Congress of the People's Republic of China is the highest organ of state power. Its permanent body is the Standing Committee of the National People's Congress.
>
> *Article 57 of the Constitution of the People's Republic of China 1982*

> The Communist Party of China leads the people in promoting socialist democracy ... It upholds and improves the system of people's congresses, the system of multiparty cooperation and political consultation under its leadership.
>
> *Excerpted from the General Program, the Constitution of the Communist Party of China*

Alongside China's economic development since 1978, it has been witnessed that China has embarked on a distinctive road towards its so-called constitutionalism with Chinese characteristics. It is clear that the importance of the Constitution has been stressed significantly in the official discourse. However, there is no doubt that the function of the Constitution in China's Party-state can never be understood from the standpoint of a liberal state. It is true that scholars once fiercely debated the model of China's constitutional development. Some Chinese left-wing thinkers, who celebrate state power, have argued that constitutionalism is an idea that belongs only to the West and is inapplicable to China, as its intention is to subvert the leadership of the CCP and socialist sovereignty (Yang 2013; Zheng 2013). By contrast, Chinese liberals hold that constitutionalism is the common achievement of liberal civilisation and should be viewed as a goal for the CCP to pursue in the future (Han 2012). At the very least, the existence of such debate indicates that the CCP, as the single ruling party, *is not* ruling the country on the basis of liberal constitutionalism in the eyes of either its advocates or opponents (Zheng 2013a).

Since Xi Jinping came to power, the official ideology has made clear that China's constitutional development shall not follow the liberal model of Western countries but will instead continue to follow its own model centred around the CCP's absolute leadership. As China's constitution has evolved in an illiberal way over the past decades, it has been difficult for traditional theories, whether communist or liberal ones, to accurately reflect the constitutional reality in China. It has been noted that, although the concept of the Party-state may be readily used to convey the CCP's deep penetration into state institutions, this framing may bring about more confusion than convenience when scholarly inquiry is directed towards deeper questions, such as the structural conflicts usually assumed to have beset the Party organization and the state institutions, and the ways in which these have been resolved or alleviated to the extent that a stable authoritarianism has been maintained thus far (Zheng 1997: 11; Wight 2015: 195). In particular, given the increasing importance of law – including the highest law, the Constitution – as emphasized by the Party-state, significant intellectual efforts have been made to explain China's constitution in its context in order to construct a suitable constitutional theory for China that exists beyond Western standards (Jiang 2014; Backer 2014). A typical example is the concept of the "unwritten constitution" used to describe China's political regime, since it is evident that the Constitution as written does not adequately describe the reality within China (Jiang 2009). In addition, some early scholarship attempted to explore China's constitutional development from a non-liberal perspective, with a particular focus on the development of the NPC as a way of tracking the emergence of China's constitutionalism (Dowdle 2002). Furthermore, the concept of a "living constitution" has been used to move beyond an analysis of the Constitution as a formal text and shed light on the de facto constitutional order in China (He 2012b; Peerenboom 2012). It is clear that this kind of theorization has recognized and incorporated the great importance of the CCP and/or NPC in China's constitutional development from a non-liberal perspective. Nonetheless, more detailed analysis is intellectually desirable regarding the interdependence of the CCP and the state, a relationship that has evolved for decades in line with a vision that differs from that of the traditional Party-state, which simply implies that the Party commands, controls and integrates all other political organizations and institutions in China (Zheng 1997: 12).

An Unwritten Constitution in China?

The concept of the "unwritten constitution" was first proposed by Dicey in an attempt to interpret the situation in the British state, which at present does not have a formal written constitution. However, in the context of China, it is well understood that the Chinese legal system does not function completely according to the current Constitution as written, and that there is moreover a wide gap between the Constitution on paper and actual constitutional practice (Jiang 2009: 13). In this regard, if the written Constitution is unable to describe the Chinese legal system, then by what constitutional rules does the regime operate? To answer this question, the concept of an "unwritten constitution" has been elaborated. This argument is mainly grounded in the two types of rules elaborated by Dicey. The first is "the law of the constitution", in the strictest sense, since these are rules that are enforced by the courts; the second is the "conventions of the constitution", which comprise conventions, understandings, habits or practice (Jiang 2009: 18). In particular, Wheare's statement is referred to as collateral evidence:

> [W]e are thinking of the distinction between those rules regulating a government – mostly rules of law – which are written down either in a Constitution or in some act of parliament or other legal document, and those other rules, mainly the customs and convention and usages regulating the government, which have usually not been precisely formulated and put in writing.
>
> (1951: 19)

Consequently, it can be inferred that the existence and functioning of China's Constitution can be illustrated by different unwritten forms, such as the Party's Constitution, constitutional conventions, constitutional doctrine and constitutional statutes (Jiang 2009: 22). However, as illustrated later in this section, use of the term "unwritten constitution" in China's context can be quite misleading.

Although Dicey (1915: 26–27) puts forward two types of rules that make up constitutional law in England, it is clear that the "conventions" discussed here are not formal laws, even if they may regulate the conduct of some members of the sovereign power. For example, "the King must assent to, or (as it is inaccurately expressed) cannot 'veto' any bill passed by the two Houses of Parliament"; "the House of Lords does not originate any money bill". One point in common is that if any or all of these conventions were broken, no court would take notice of their violation. Moreover, the difference between laws and conventions is not the same as the difference between "written law" (or statute law) and "unwritten law" (or common law). Thus, some laws of the constitution that were at one time unwritten or common law may at some point be legislated into written or statute law. On the other hand, the conventions of the constitution cannot be recorded in the statute book, even if they are formally written down. Constitutional conventions could be considered a part of constitutional law in a broad sense, which implies that their status is equal to the laws of a constitution. However, as stated by Dicey (1959: 470–472), constitutional conventions must be subject to the laws of the constitution (Freeman 1876: 87, 109, 112), according to the principles of the sovereignty of Parliament and the "rule of law" in Britain as guiding principles truly underlying the English polity. Dicey clearly states that:

> [T]hree such guiding principles gradually become apparent. They are, first, the legislative sovereignty of Parliament; secondly, the universal rule or supremacy throughout the constitution of ordinary law; and thirdly (though here we tread on more doubtful and speculative ground), the dependence in the last resort of the conventions upon the law of the constitution.
>
> (1982: cxlviii)

Nonetheless, China's written Constitution, in practice, is often dismissed as merely a "rubber stamp" that does not fulfil its prescribed function (Jiang 2009: 23; Cho 2002). Jiang states that:

> The Constitution of the PRC clearly stipulates a system of people's congresses based on the Soviet model, which is itself similar to the British parliamentary system. The NPC and its Standing Committee, as the organs that exercise sovereign power, are to possess a wide range of powers and the highest political authority ... Thus, what constitutes China as a nation-state is not the system of people's congresses established by the written constitution, but the leadership of the CCP within the system of multiparty cooperation that was formed during the revolution, promulgated in the preamble of the written constitution, and affirmed in political practice.
>
> (2009: 23)

Hence, it is further argued that the CCP leadership could be considered the "unwritten constitution" in China, given that the written Constitution does not function in practice. Here, however, the concept of an "unwritten constitution" is used misleadingly (Zhou 2011). First, its reference to Dicey's work is made out of context. As already mentioned, Dicey strictly refers to the "constitutional convention" and "unwritten law", not an "unwritten constitution". Evidently, a constitutional convention, subject as it is to the laws of the constitution, differs from the "unwritten constitution" in China, which holds that the CCP's leadership can prevail over the written Constitution. Second, when considering constitutional conventions, Dicey (1982: 286) suggests that these consist of "customs which (whatever their historical origin) are at the present day maintained for the sake of ensuring the supremacy of the House of Commons, and ultimately, through the elective House of Commons, of the nation". By contrast, in the context of China, the CCP's conventions can to a certain extent prevail over the "people's sovereignty" as entrenched in the written Constitution (Jiang 2009: 24). Third, it is evident that the "unwritten law" is a concept elaborated in common law jurisdiction; it is accordingly doubtful whether it can be appropriately applied in China's context. In particular, at the institutional level, the evolution of the "unwritten constitution" is grounded in Britain's parliamentary sovereignty and the "rule-of-law" principle, in which the courts are the cornerstone for the development of common law. China's courts, by contrast, are subject to CCP leadership and still struggling to gain judicial independence (Peerenboom 2010). As it is widely accepted that China remains an authoritarian country under the rule of the CCP, it would not be fair to simply analyse China within such a narrow scope, purely based on a "similarity" with the British parliamentary system in terms of form.[1]

In order to describe the holistic theoretical framework of China's illiberal constitutional order, the concept of a small-c "constitution" is employed in the following discussion to illustrate that China has in fact formed a "dual constitution" structure comprising the Party and the state interdependently since 1978. Such a small-c dual-structured constitution goes beyond traditional constitutional theories focusing on the written Constitution, as well as those that focus substantially on the CCP, and contains extensive reflections on how the state under the dual constitution has been strengthened, how the Party under the dual constitution has been normalized in practice and how the two evolve interdependently in reality.

[1] Jiang argues that the Constitution of the PRC clearly stipulates a system of people's congresses based on the Soviet model, which itself resembles the British parliamentary system (2009: 23).

Emergence of a Dual Constitution

It is widely acknowledged that China's Constitution is not judicially enforceable, as it stipulates that only the NPC exercises the power to amend the Constitution and supervise its enforcement, while only the NPCSC can interpret the Constitution and supervise its enforcement, according to the Constitution (宪法 *xianfa*) (article 62, 67). Moreover, in 2009, the SPC issued the Provisions on Citation of Laws, Regulations and Other Normative Legal Documents in Adjudicative Documents (PCLRAD) (关于裁判文书引用法律、法规等规范性法律文件的规定 *guanyu caipan wenshu yinyong falü fagui deng guifanxing wenjian de guiding*), which excludes the Constitution as a basis for judicial decisions. In this regard, in order to understand China's constitutional regime, it is necessary to move beyond the traditional judicial review model with its focus on the written Constitution and instead shift attention to the CCP's substantial involvement in the constitutional enterprise, since the CCP is not simply a general party in the sense of a political association but rather a political cornerstone in China's polity.

Therefore, a true understanding of the dynamics of China's constitutional law must reveal the substantial relationship between the CCP as the single ruling party and the NPC as the highest organ of state power in the constitutional sense, and moreover, under what conditions this dual mechanism operates in practice. Methodologically, there may be no substantial difference when considering the small-c constitution of a regime beyond the written Constitution. Taking the United States as an example, as Tushnet states:

> [I]n the context of the US, a constitutional order is more like a small-c British constitution than it is like the document called the United States Constitution. Moreover, just as scholars of constitutionalism have found it productive to think about the British constitution, it is productive to think about a constitutional order that goes beyond judicial doctrine and the written Constitution to encompass relatively stable political arrangements and guiding principles.
>
> (2003: 1)

Similarly, it will be more productive to think about China's small-c constitution, which is incapable of being fully disclosed by the written Constitution with normative expressions, and particularly how the dual constitution has emerged and evolved in an illiberal context.

Strengthening of the State Constitution

Historically, China largely transplanted the political system of the Soviet Union following its establishment in 1949, after which it adopted a system characterized primarily by legal nihilism in the era of Mao (Tsou 2012: 2). The former vice president of China, Liu Shaoqi, once remarked to a constitutional scholar that "it is meaningless to study constitutional law in China" (Shen and Wang 2011: 78). However, this statement is particularly ironic given that Liu later sought to claim his constitutional rights when he was persecuted during the Cultural Revolution. Needless to say, the People's Congress system and the state Constitution at this time were merely "rubber stamps" to serve the empire or tools to strengthen the leader's charismatic authority. The case was similar at the turn of the twentieth century, when a parliament was implanted in China in an attempt to save the empire at a point when imperial rule was in jeopardy due to invasion from abroad, as well as the threat of revolution and the rise of the constitutionalism movement from within (Yang 1936). Thus, under Mao's totalitarian regime, there was no doubt that society was subject to the strict and all-encompassing political control of the CCP. It was also no surprise that the Third NPC fell into a state of paralysis for almost ten years, which meant that the provisions – embedded in the Constitution but subject to the will of the CCP – could not be implemented in practice, even at a surface level.

As is evident, over the past four decades, China has undergone unprecedented economic and legal reform and has taken a different road towards modern constitutionalism. Learning from previous lessons, the Party has realized the importance of the law and its capacity to be used pragmatically for China's development. The Constitution adopted in 1982, despite declaring the socialist system as the basic system (article 1), has come to play an increasingly significant role in this process, as may be reflected by the literal incorporation of many components of a modern democratic state in the form, such as a parliamentary system (i.e. the People's Congress system) (article 2), democratic elections (article 3), term limits for significant leadership positions (such as the vice president, the premier and vice premiers and the president of the SPC), the independence of the courts (article 126) and various fundamental rights as declared in chapter II of the Constitution. Although no effective constitutional review mechanism based on the liberal model of separation of powers exists in China, it is fair to say that the normative constitutional framework has been practised to some extent without a serious breakdown since 1978, notwithstanding sporadic political challenges or even crises (e.g. the Tiananmen Square protests in 1989).

However, the Constitution has been condemned as simply a "facade" because it lacks any meaningful judicial mechanism for implementation and is left unprotected against official violations (Zhang 2010: 952). This is especially so after the rise and fall of *Qi Yuling* v. *Chen Xiaoqi et al* (齐玉苓诉陈晓琪等以侵犯姓名权的手段侵犯宪法保护的公民受教育的基本权利纠纷案 *qi yuling su chen xiaoqi deng yi qinfan xingmingquan de shouduan qinfan xianfa baohu de gongmin shoujiaoyu de jiben quanli jiufen an*) (hereinafter "*Qi Yuling*"), which appears to remove all hope for the future of the judicial enforcement of China's Constitution (Shandong High People's Court 2001; Tong 2010). In 2001, the SPC's interpretation of constitutional provisions in relation to *Qi Yuling* opened up the possibility – greeted enthusiastically – for the judicial application of China's Constitution in deciding cases. By the end of 2008, however, this path was foreclosed by the SPC itself when it announced that judicial interpretation had lost its legal effect. It has been argued that judicial implementation of the Constitution was viewed as a potential threat to the Party leadership, and there were rumours that the SPC had circulated an internal directive forbidding the courts from following the *Qi Yuling* decision. This might explain the de facto demise of that decision's potential for judicializing the Constitution (Zhang 2010: 962). In December 2008, the SPC published a document that officially and retroactively voided the legal effect of several judicial explanations, among which *Qi Yuling* was the only one for which not even a brief explanation was provided (Supreme People's Court 2008). Thus, the critique of China's Constitution as merely existing to maintain the government's image is understandable (Zhang 2010: 952). This conclusion, however, is drawn primarily from a "court-centred" approach; it overlooks the fact that the Constitution has also been strengthened and enforced by other state actors. In particular, the NPC, as the highest organ of state power stipulated by the Constitution (article 57), has not ceased its operations since 1978. During this time, the functions and powers exclusively possessed by the NPC in accordance with the Constitution (article 62) are as follows: to amend the Constitution; to elect the president and the vice president of China; to confirm the choice of the premier of the State Council upon nomination by the president; to elect the chairman of the Central Military Commission (CMC) (中央军事委员会 *zhongyang junshi weiyuanhui*); to elect the president of the SPC; and to elect the Procurator-General of the Supreme People's Procuratorate (SPP). None of these powers have ever been exercised by any other state actor. In this regard, to say that China's Constitution is not justiciable does not mean that the Constitution cannot be enforced in other ways. As China's

Constitution adopts the People's Congress system as its foundation, unlike Western political systems (such as parliamentary sovereignty in Britain or the separation of powers in the United States), it will be more effective to assess the implementation of the Constitution through the operation of the People's Congress system rather than focusing only on the judicialization of the Constitution.

Having said this, it should by no means be concluded that China has practised the electoral parliamentary system in a liberal way. On the contrary, it indicates that China has been able to maintain its illiberal system (including the CCP's leadership) through the People's Congress system, which has been progressively strengthened over the past four decades. The congresses at both national and local levels have been held routinely in accordance with the Constitution of 1982: specifically, they meet in session once a year and are convened by their respective standing committees. As noted by O'Brien (1990: 157), it would be a mistake to conclude that the NPC and the Chinese political system after 1978 still closely resemble their predecessors under Mao. A review of legislative and other activities will reveal that the NPC has come to occupy an essential position in China's authoritarian regime (Zhao 2012).

First, since legal drafting resumed in 1978, the NPC along with the NPCSC as national lawmaker have built up a comprehensive legislative system in China with a distinctively Chinese quality, including seven categories of law subjects (constitutional laws, civil and commercial laws, administrative laws, economic laws, social laws, criminal laws and procedural laws) covering all major aspects of political, economic, cultural and social life (S. Chen 2010). As of 24 February 2021, the NPC and NPCSC had passed 275 national laws currently in force (including the Constitution), while the State Council had passed 609 administrative regulations currently in force. Meanwhile, the SPC had passed 637 judicial interpretations currently in force. Moreover, more than 16,000 local regulations and rules currently in force had been passed by various local statutory authorities (Npc.gov.cn 2021). In particular, the NPC established the Database of Laws and Regulations (国家法律法规数据库 *guojia falü fagui shujuku*) in 2021, which includes all types of statutes accessible to the public.[2] Clearly, the NPC and NPCSC have come to occupy a crucial position at the centre of a horizontally and vertically integrated legislative system, linked sideways to relevant national

[2] The database is available at https://flk.npc.gov.cn/fl.html, accessed 28 April 2021.

lawmaking authorities (including the State Council, ministries and SPC) and downwards to regions via local congresses (O'Brien 1990: 164).

Second, normative frameworks for the NPC's institutional supervision and the role of deputies have been established. The supervision may be conducted by the full NPC, its committees or individual deputies, and may be directed at state functionaries or the institutions they head. Supervision may be personal and sporadic or institutional and regular.[3] Furthermore, in 2006, the NPCSC adopted the Law on the Supervision of Standing Committees of People's Congresses at Various Levels (各级人民代表大会常务委员会监督法 *geji renmin daibiao dahui changwu weiyuanhui jiandu fa*). This law provides more details about the functions and powers of Local People's Congresses (LPCs), which include (1) hearing and deliberating on Special Work Reports of the People's Government, the People's Court and the People's Procuratorate; (2) examining and approving Final Accounts, hearing and deliberating the Plans for National Economy and Social Development and the Reports on the Implementation of Budgets and hearing and deliberating on Audit Reports; (3) inspecting the implementation of laws and regulations; (4) examining the archival filing of regulatory documents; (5) inquiry and interrogatory; (6) investigating special issues and (7) deliberating on and deciding cases concerning dismissals from office (Standing Committee of the National People's Congress 2006). This undoubtedly demonstrates the indispensable role played by LPCs in China's authoritarian regime, regardless of the ways in which it has been played. In practice, for instance, the LPC may sometimes veto the Work Report of a People's Court due to unsatisfactory performance (such as miscarriages of justice), as occurred for example in Hengyang city in 2007. It has also vetoed Work Reports of Local Government, for instance, in Zhengzhou city in 2006 (Ju 2007; You 2008). Another example is that the LPC Standing Committee did not approve the appointment of the chief procurator at Bingzhou city according to Article 101 of the Constitution (Du 2009). At the same time, LPCs may sometimes even pioneer "new forms" of strong measures that are not clearly provided for in laws rather than simply grumbling

[3] There are several forms of supervision in practice: (1) criticism of ministry or State Council officials by deputies in small-group meetings, (2) inspection of local government organs and economic enterprises by groups of NPCSC or NPC deputies and (3) institutional oversight of subordinate administrative agencies by NPC committees (O'Brien 1990: 164–165).

about problematic systems. These new measures include examination and appraisal of the "responsibility system of department law enforcement" (部门执法责任制 *bumen zhifa zerenzhi*), "law supervision papers" (法律监督书 *falü jiandushu*) and "individual case supervision" (个案监督 *gean jiandu*) (Cho 2002).

Furthermore, some deputies may play an active role in the NPC session, particularly if the political atmosphere at that time is relatively liberal. It has been perceived that, since 1979, incisive interpellations and angry deputy speeches may occur at NPC sessions under the current People's Congress system. For example, deputies at the 1988 convening criticized Premier Li Peng's suggestion that academics could take on second jobs to supplement their incomes, saying that this was an "improper measure" that would interfere with teaching and research and would "damage long-term national interests". Moreover, several deputies openly disagreed with General Secretary Zhao Ziyang's assessment that such a policy was "necessary and possible". In the meantime, deputies in small-group meetings at plenary sessions could also criticize state officials for immorality, incompetence and mistaken priorities (O'Brien 1990: 165). The deputies may even argue as they please in their speeches and votes, provided that they "[seek] truth from facts" and serve the public interest and are able to speak for regions or occupational groups and press for "allocation responsiveness" in order to draw the attention of leadership to their claims and nudge policies in a desired direction (O'Brien 1990: 170). Thus, as Vice Chairman Zhang of the NPC Law Committee[4] once put it, "some deputies are dissatisfied with the status quo on work outside meetings . . . and would like to do even more. They ask to intervene directly in government, judicial, and procuratorial work, or to directly handle mass appeals, complaints, and proposals" (1983: 5). In fact, it is possible that the established normative framework of the NPC may create some opportunity for the operation of the People's Congress system to be opened up further to broader society. In particular, when the Party Centre gives legislators fewer and more ambiguous signals regarding its wishes, and has in any case substantially lowered the penalties (whether explicit or implicit) for disobeying those wishes, the legislators may – to a certain extent – feel free to perform their functions (Lin 2015; Tanner 1994). Therefore, if the political atmosphere has been relatively liberal over a certain period of time, even

[4] The Law Committee (法律委员会 *falü weiyuanhui*) was renamed the Constitution and Law Committee (宪法和法律委员会 *xianfa he falü weiyuanhui*) in 2018.

in an authoritarian context, it is possible for some delegate(s) to question officials during sessions of the NPC. For example, in 2009, delegates from Henan Province questioned the minister of education regarding the unequal distribution of education resources nationwide (Chu 2015). As a result, the voting of deputies may become more effective – albeit *limited* – than otherwise. Legalistically, in accordance with the state Constitution, it is the NPC deputies who decide whether to approve reports on the work of the government by voting to reflect the degree of satisfaction. For example, due to the poor performance of the SPC, 605 negative votes – the highest yet – were cast in the NPC session of 2013. However, in 2017, 180 negative votes, far fewer than before, were cast in the NPC session of 2017; to some extent, this signals greater satisfaction with the improving performance of the SPC under the then new presidency of Zhou Qiang, who had endeavoured to enhance legal professionalism through in-depth legal reforms and strengthen judicial independence as much as possible in China.

Moreover, in some areas, single-candidate elections have been replaced by what appear to be "competitive" elections, which has seemingly given deputies more freedom with regard to their right to vote. For instance, 161 NPCSC members were elected from 174 nominees during the 2013 plenary session. Sometimes, CCP nominees may not even be approved for senior positions. For example, in the 1995 Plenary Session, more than a third of the deputies failed to support the CCP's nominee, Jiang Chunyun, for the vice-premier position. Over a quarter of the deputies also failed to support State Council proposals for a draft Banking Law and a draft Education Law (Dowdle 1997).

However, this is by no means to suggest that the CCP has made efforts to shift China's reforms towards a liberal constitutional order: all the cases mentioned – which sometimes may occur in practice under the normative framework of legislation – are very rare and absolutely not routine in practice. In an illiberal context, the normative framework of the NPC is practised on the premise that the single ruling party system is not challenged. On the surface, the NPC clearly has an arguable representation mechanism based on a sort of politically controllable election system. A mechanism such as this differs from that of liberal democracies, where the executive may strive to manipulate the legislature by lobbying, political canvassing, etc.

It is true that, in essence, such representation, as Pitkin (1967: 221–234) puts it, "entails regular, institutionalized responsiveness and can only be discussed in reference to the overall structure and functioning of a political system". It has been recognized that representation in the legislature, like decision-making influence, is not as clear-cut as it may first appear. This is based on the observation that representatives are not the constituency's puppets but rather human beings with their own consciousness. Such consciousness will decide (at least potentially) their role or function. It thus stresses the deputy's role orientation rather than the relationship between decision-making, roll-call voting and the views of the constituency (Eulau and Karps 1977; Alexy 2005). Hence, the legislator's sense of representation and willingness to represent clearly has a part to play in the legislature's potential capacity to have real influence (Zhao 2012; Hu 1993). Thus, in having a broad horizon beyond the Western paradigm of representation through a multiparty system, the representation of the legislature is by no means a dichotomous variable. Rather, as Hu points out, we should be able to assign "points" to the various legislatures and place them on a continuum of representation, or at least arrange them in a broad topology according to their representation levels (1993: 16). As such:

> [T]he existence of certain representation in non-democratic legislature becomes understandable, and can be explained, and compared. It is the configuration of the component aspect of representation that might yield viable theories of representation other than representative government only, in the modern complexity of society.
>
> (1993: 16)

Therefore, it is argued that even though the forms of representation may differ and the activities do not resemble legislative supervision as found in liberal democracies, they do serve similar ends in a weakly institutionalized system with a very strong executive (O'Brien 1990: 165). Of course, there is no doubt that the representation as approached in an illiberal context is largely premised on the dominance of the single ruling party, although there may be a possibility of allowing other political parties to compete for elections constitutionally speaking. Nonetheless, the competition of other political parties is subject to the dominance of the single ruling party, which has in fact been institutionalized in the sense that the constitutional system is substantially controlled by and can be adjusted by the single ruling party to ensure its dominance in elections, while there is no substantial threat from other political parties. One example of this could be Singapore (Tushnet 2015). At the extreme end, this kind of competition of a political party with the single ruling party in elections is not allowed in practice. This means that the election, from nomination to final voting, is essentially manipulated by the single ruling party, whether either implicitly or explicitly. China stands as an example of this. In any event, elections in illiberal regimes are politically manipulated by the single ruling party. Although there may be a certain degree of responsiveness from therein, the elections, as well as the so-called representative legislature, are largely performative due to the dominance of the single ruling party throughout the political process.

Undoubtedly, the NPC, being composed of deputies, has a unique paradigm of representation, and it is a fact that the People's Congress with its formal election mechanisms has continued to operate routinely. Nonetheless, an important lesson for an authoritarian regime is that of learning how to manipulate the people's congresses at different levels politically, so as to make sure that the so-called representative system can be reconciled with the single-party system and does not challenge the authoritarian regime in any fundamental way. In practice, important decisions usually go through two stages of deliberation: first the Party, then the state. The first, by its nature, is actually a political process inside the Party. The second works to legalize the political decision through the state organs according to the law. Taking the election of deputies as an example, it is understandable that the prospective candidates may be first deliberated and screened either implicitly or explicitly by the Party and, if appropriate, subsequently formally recommended as nominees. However, in order to ensure that preselected nominees favoured by the Party can be elected by the voters, who have the right to vote and are free to choose among the Party-screened nominees according to the election laws, the Party must first seriously deliberate and evaluate its favoured nominee(s) in terms of their reputation in the society, professional competence, etc. Otherwise, the nominee who is favoured by the Party may lose the election or get an unsatisfactory voting result (although this rarely happens in practice); to a certain extent, such occurrences have been a signal of the political incompetence of the governmental authorities (particularly the responsible leader) in charge of electoral affairs, as the election has escaped the Party's tight political control.

In practice, however, the Party generally uses various methods to gain sufficient information about the prospective candidate and assess whether he or she is suitable for the nomination before making a decision (Interview 55-17-JMGD01). It is possible that a proposal – for example, the Amendment of Special Equipment Safety Law ("特种设备安全法"修正案 *tezhong shebei anquan fa xiuzheng an*) – may be objected to and terminated for review by the members of the NPCSC, naturally on the premise of adhering to the CCP's leadership (Caixinglobal.com 2017). It can be seen that the legal mechanisms of election through which voters can cast their vote freely, particularly in direct elections where citizens have the right to do so under the law, does in fact impose a kind of political responsibility on the Party if it wishes its predecision to be "confirmed" by sufficient votes, although for indirect elections, it normally just goes through the motions, as these selected political officials or representatives are largely submissive and loyal to the Party.[5]

Due to the CCP's leadership over state apparatuses, the NPC are to some extent performing a performative rather than a deliberative function, in the sense that all major issues have been deliberated and decided by the Party before the annual plenary session occurs. The extent to which such a performative function can be performed is critical, because, on the one hand, it can indicate the extent to which these borrowed democratic institutions can operate in an illiberal context with relative political stability, thereby bequeathing a sense of mass legitimacy. On the other hand, it can serve as an indicator of the Party's governing capacity in controlling these nominally democratic institutions to bolster their own rules and, more importantly, in mobilizing and engaging people with these nominally democratic processes under the Party's leadership (Gallagher 2017: 43–44). In other words, it could be a signal of the Party's governing capacity as regards maintaining the authoritarian system under its political leadership.

Having said this, it can be seen that referring to China's Constitution as merely a facade is mainly based on liberal perspectives that assume democratic institutions to be important for democratic functions in liberalizing or opening up politics, and that the courts are politically independent in performing a judicial review function according to the Constitution (Zhang 2010: 957). As already illustrated, constitutionally speaking, the real foundation of the state Constitution in China is the People's Congress system, due to its fundamental role in creating and maintaining other state actors (including the courts) in accordance with the Constitution.[6] More importantly, in an illiberal context, these nominally democratic institutions are evidently operating and even

[5] In practice, the Party may use various tactics to ensure these preselected nominees can gain enough votes.

[6] Some scholars have attempted to illustrate the development of China's constitutionalism from a non-court-centred perspective (Dowdle 2002).

strengthened under the leadership of the single ruling party. Of course, due to China's status as a single-party regime, it would be difficult to understand China's Constitution without looking at the other side of the coin, i.e. the workings of the CCP.

Normalization of Party Constitution

Originally, the establishment of the CCP was facilitated by the Soviet Union. However, as Lubman states, this changed after the Cultural Revolution:

> China attempted to employ legislation and administrative rules as essential tools in governing China. The Chinese leadership, departing from their previous reliance on policy declarations and their disregard of formal legal rules, has moved to elevate such rules into primary sources of authority.
>
> (1999: 138)

In fact, since 1978, the CCP has been transformed from a revolutionary party to a governing party, embracing the notions of socialist democracy and the rule of law (Chen 2008: 508). In this way, it has departed from the Soviet Union. It has been noted that this occurred because Deng and his associates were seeking to build up the NPC, which largely comprises individuals with social prestige who would wholeheartedly support Party policy and work to secure its implementation. Through the NPC, the Party sought to integrate itself into the polity and to organize it around the principle of one-party rule (Lin 2015; Zhao 2012). The CCP's controlling role over the NPC is crucial, since its deputies give voluntary assent and support to the CCP in this ultimate goal (Hu 1993: 19). However, as already noted, with the development of the People's Congress system, the CCP may sometimes have some trouble maintaining discipline, while the most important leaders may encounter some difficulty in maintaining their full authority. It might be seen as ironic that, in its quest to legitimize its own authority through the operation of nominally democratic institutions, the CCP has planted something of a "thorn" in its own side that cannot be readily removed (Hu 1993: 29). Given the adoption of the open-door policy, it is a fact that society has become more open and that Party discipline may be more difficult to maintain, as more opportunities are available to climb the social ladder other than through a career in the cadre or as a government employee. Party membership, which was previously very valuable owing to its connection to a successful political career, thus substantially if not completely lost its appeal in many areas of society (Dickson 2014). In this regard, it is understandable that given the growing challenges or even threats to the CCP's legitimacy, the Party may begin to move backwards by reinforcing the imposition of Party discipline on its members who are members of government cadres but subject to strict Party control, in such a way that CCP members will be submissive to the Party and lend political support to its policies, work and decisions. President Xi Jinping's tremendous emphasis on the reinforcement of Party discipline and leadership is a typical example of this. During his presidency, ideology has come to play an increasingly important role in the assertion of communist power; this represents a departure from previous periods, which have been marked by a laissez-faire open-door policy under which Western technology and investment, along with "Western bourgeois liberalism", was brought in. To a certain extent, the CCP's emphasis on ideology is a means of achieving an ideological consensus and preventing an ideological crisis, given that the CCP's coherent ideology can further underpin its ultimate vision, goals and concrete strategy in terms of Marxist concepts (Hu 1993: 20).

Given that the CCP intentionally prioritizes and maintains the high profile of the People's Congress system as enshrined in the state Constitution, the NPC – as the highest organ of state power – has formal constitutional legitimacy, grounded in the way it allows for some sense of representation. Interestingly, the CCP previously had no formal constitutional position in the state Constitution and only received a mention in the relevant statement in the Preamble: "The victory in China's New-Democratic Revolution and the successes in its socialist cause have been achieved by the Chinese people of all nationalities, under the leadership of the Communist Party of China." Of course, this kind of historical statement had been unable to provide substantial legitimacy for the CCP's rule over the country since the Revolution. Therefore, the NPC's legitimacy, based in the state Constitution, was able to prevail over that of the CCP in the constitutional sense. For this reason, it is understandable that in regard to certain incidents, people could appeal to the NPC to challenge the CCP's rule by invoking relevant constitutional provisions under the banner of the state Constitution, a situation that could even potentially lead to a constitutional crisis. Of course, in 2018, the CCP unambiguously constitutionalized its leadership in the constitutional amendments (article 36) as follows: "The defining feature of socialism with Chinese characteristics is the leadership of the Communist Party of

China" (National People's Congress 2018a).[7] More importantly, over the past decades, the CCP has been attempting to normalize its mechanisms of political control over the People's Congress in practice, in such a way that the people's congresses operate in the service of authoritarianism while at the same time underpinning the legitimacy of the state and its political leadership.

The CCP's Conventions

A highly innovative and important institutional arrangement devised by the CCP was to combine itself with, and adhere to, the People's Congress system. At the central level, the chairman of the NPCSC (legislative branch), the premier (executive branch) and others, appointed in accordance with the state Constitution, are members of the Standing Committee of the CCP's Politburo.[8] In order to reconcile the Constitution of the CCP (中国共产党党章 *zhongguo gongchandang dangzhang*) with the state Constitution, it is now a political convention for the Party to hold its plenary session of the National Congress of the CCP first in order to decide the composition of the Central Committee of the CCP (e.g. 204 members and 170 alternate members were elected by the 19th CCP National Congress) and the Central Commission for Discipline Inspection of the CCP (e.g. 133 members elected by the 19th CCP National Congress); only then will it select the Politburo of the Central Committee (e.g. twenty-five members elected by the 19th CCP Central Committee), Party's CMC, Standing Committee of the Politburo (e.g. seven members elected by the 19th CCP Central Committee) and the general secretary of the Central Committee. It has been a political convention that the general secretary of the CCP must serve concurrently as the chairman of the Party's CMC. This is because the chairman acts as commander-in-chief, in that he can deploy troops, controls the country's nuclear weapons and uses the budget after it is approved by the NPC or NPCSC (Mackerras et al. 2001: 74). This is compatible with the CCP's convention, which states that "the Party commands the gun" (党指挥枪 *dang zhihui qiang*). This has further been legalized by the

[7] Similarly, in Vietnam, the leadership of the Communist Party of Vietnam was incorporated into the constitutional amendment in 2013 following decades of Party and state reform (Sidel 2009: 131).

[8] Xi Jinping, as the general secretary of the Standing Committee of the CCP's Politburo, was elected in accordance with the Party Constitution.

Law on National Defence (国防法 *guofang fa*) (article 21), which stipulates that the armed forces of the PRC are subject to the leadership of the CCP (Standing Committee of the National People's Congress 2020).[9]

During the session of the National Congress of the CCP, issues of national importance – including those relevant to the personnel structure of the state organs to be finally confirmed by the NPC – that have been prepared, discussed and decided by the Party leadership are confirmed in accordance with the Party Constitution. To some extent, the session of CCP National Congress is a kind of rehearsal for the subsequent session of the NPC months later; this is because these fundamental issues decided upon by the Party will then be followed up with a formal constitutional decision by the NPC, most deputies of which are CCP-screened Party members, in accordance with the state Constitution. There may, however, be some – albeit very rare – unexpected behaviours during this process, as already discussed; this, in turn, may in fact be a politically beneficial signal or even cause for alarm for the CCP, prompting it to discern and self-examine its capacity to exert political control in the changing sociopolitical context.

To procedurally streamline the CCP's leadership over the NPC, at the beginning of the NPC's plenary session, it is the CCP that suggests the nominees, initially to the NPC Presidium, which then submits the list to the deputies for final discussion and decision. These nominees are intended to assume the posts of the new NPC, president, vice president and chairman of the CMC of the state. At the initial stage of the NPC election, the CCP's general secretary will be elected by deputies to assume the posts of president and chairman of the CMC of the state. This is considered a constitutional convention in China. In addition, it is recognized that the general secretary of the Party should assume the offices of state president and chairman of the CMC concurrently (the so-called "trinity system") in order to maintain political stability. This occurs because it has been argued that, historically, political tragedies such as the Cultural Revolution had their origins to a certain extent in the division of offices. For example, Mao Zedong was chairman of the Party and chairman of the Military Commission of the Party, while Liu

[9] In addition, the People's Liberation Army is subject to the CCP's absolute leadership, and the highest authority is headed by the CMC of the CCP and the CMC of the state. These two in fact exist in the form of "one body with two names" (Central Committee of the Chinese Communist Party, and Central Military Commission of the Chinese Communist Party 2010).

Shaoqi was the president of the state according to the state Constitution (Jiang 2009: 27–31). Even so, it should be noted that the context in the era of Mao differed substantially from that of the subsequent era with its institutionally strengthened NPC.

In the second stage of the plenary session of the NPC, it is the general secretary of the CCP, with the new status of state president and chairman of the CMC of the state, who nominates the premier and vice chairman and members of the CMC and presents these to the NPC for a decision. Meanwhile, the president of the SPC, procurator-general of the SPP and director of the National Supervisory Commission (NSC) are nominated under the leadership of the NPC Presidium and presented to the NPC for a final decision. The final stage of the election is to form a cabinet according to the premier's nominations (Cai 1998: 358–359).

Such conventions – though sometimes perhaps with some slight adjustment – have largely reconciled the Party with the state without hindering the operation of the NPC. All other state organs, including the SPC, SPP and NSC, have been created by the NPC according to the state Constitution. On the one hand, the CCP's involvement in the state Constitution has been normalized by its earlier Party Congress and the incorporation of state cadres into the Party. For instance, the premier (the leader of the highest organ of executive power) and the chairman of the NPCSC (the highest organ of legislative power) are both members of the Politburo's Standing Committee. On the other hand, the CCP has learned how to convert its Party's leadership into the state's leadership through the NPC according to the state Constitution. For example, the exercise of military power by the CCP before 1982 was not grounded in the state Constitution but rather in the Party Constitution, in that the CCP at that time was an omnipotent authority. However, in the process of building up an enterprise of authoritarian legality,[10] the state Constitution of 1982 established the chairmanship of the CMC of the state. This allowed the CCP to transfer its Party's role in exercising military power into a constitutional one by means of the political convention that the chairman of the Party's CMC is concurrently the

[10] It is argued that China has adopted the "thin theory" of the rule of law. As analysed by Peerenboom (2002: 673; 2003), whereas a "thick" or substantive theory of the rule of law would incorporate elements of political morality (such as the forms of government, the economic models or the various conceptions of human rights), a thin theory would put forward formal or instrumentalist aspects of the rule of law, which would rest on a system of laws that are general, published, prospective, clear, coherent, applicable, stable and implemented.

chairman of the state's CMC; in practice, these two bodies are usually collectively referred to as "CMC", with no substantial distinction between them.

More importantly, the CCP has played a dominant role in the establishment and amendment of the Constitution. This was seen in practice as early as 1954, where it was the CCP that first initiated a proposal to establish a Constitution. According to this proposal, the central government decided to establish a Constitution-drafting Committee (宪法起草委员会 *xianfa qicao weiyuanhui*) and proceeded accordingly. At the same time, the CCP established a Constitution-drafting Team (宪法起草小组 *xianfa qicao xiaozu*) to draft the Constitution. In essence, it was the CCP's Constitution-drafting Team that drafted the constitution exclusively, after which it submitted the draft to the Constitution-drafting Committee for a procedural follow-up (Tong 2014). By analogy, in terms of constitutional amendments, in 2004, it was the Standing Committee of the Politburo that first decided the general principles on constitutional amendments. In the meantime, the chairman of the NPCSC, politically subject to the Politburo, was appointed as the head of the Central Constitutional Amendments Group (中央宪法修改小组 *zhongyang xianfa xiugai xiaozu*). After seeking advice from the opinions and recommendations of local governments, non-communist parties' communities, experts etc., the draft proposal was first adopted at the plenary session of the 16th CCP's Central Committee. It was then adopted by the sixth plenary session of the NPCSC based on the proposals by the CCP Central Committee, and ultimately voted on at the NPC session (Xinhua News Agency 2004). It would appear that the CCP has played a dominant role by exercising its exclusive authority on drafting and amending the Constitution before it enters into legal procedures. As regards other statutes, due to the reinforced role of the state Constitution, national legislatures under the CCP's leadership have become more autonomous and assertive since the CCP issued Central Document 8, providing a guidance on strengthening its leadership over lawmaking, in 1991 (Central Committee of the Chinese Communist Party 1991). The document clearly indicates that Party leadership over the NPC should henceforth be rather general and not involve micromanagement (Tanner 1994: 397). Subsequent to this, there has been a broad retreat by the party from the NPC's actual legislative drafting process, as well as from many other aspects of the NPC's constitutional operations (Dowdle 1997: 14). Certainly, this is not to deny that the CCP can still exercise political control over legislatures through its Party organ, which is established within all public organs, as well as the Party's membership of most cadres or representatives working therein. For example, the chairman and some vice-chairmen of the NPCSC are members of and subject to the Politburo, as well as the *nomenklatura* system, namely the Party Centre's list for NPC appointments which includes all members of the NPCSC Party Group (党组 *dangzu*), plus all NPCSC members, along with the leaders of all the Special Committees under the NPCSC. The Politburo pre-approves the final list of all candidates for the NPCSC (Tanner 1994: 389; Sun 2004: 64–65).

Furthermore, at the local level, it has been common practice for the Party secretary to assume the chairmanship of the LPC Standing Committee during his/her term. It has also been common practice that, at the provincial level, the Party secretaries of all twenty-four provinces – apart from some with extremely important political and/or economic status in China's governance, including four municipalities under the direct administration of the central government (i.e. Beijing, Shanghai, Tianjing and Chongqing), as well as the Xinjiang Uygur Autonomous Region, Tibet Autonomous Region and Guangdong – assume the chairmanship of the LPC Standing Committee in the same way. Such a practice effectively integrates the Party with the local government. On the one hand, this could strengthen the Party's prevailing leadership over the government at the local level; on the other hand, it maintains the operation of the LPCs according to the state Constitution (The Beijing News 2013).

In addition, the CCP created a consultative body, the People's Political Consultation Conference (PPCC), to "receive societal feedback on governance, to improve the quality of public service and to incorporate influential social leaders into the establishment through limited political empowerment and controlled participation" (Yan 2011: 70). By involving non-communist social elites and societal leaders in the PPCC, the CCP is able to create patron–client networks, allocate preferential treatment and consolidate its ties with elites and leaders in society. Currently, it is a political convention that the NPC holds each plenary session immediately following the PPCC's meeting; these are always discussed in parallel as "the two meetings" (两会 *lianghui*). In this regard, the PPCC plays a supplementary but essential role to that of the People's Congress through its participation in Party and state mechanisms (Yan 2011: 73).

CCP Intraparty Regulations

In addition to the political conventions, the CCP as a ruling party also endeavours to strengthen its political leadership through the building up of a systematic intraparty regulation system. In particular, in 2019, according to the Party Constitution (National Congress of the Chinese Communist Party 2017), the CCP promulgated the new Regulation on the Formation of Intraparty Regulations (中国共产党党内法规制定条例 *zhongguo gongchandang dangnei fagui zhiding tiaolie*) in order to systematize the party rules (Central Committee of the Chinese Communist Party 2019). In addition, in order to maintain the consistency of the entire intraparty regulation system, the CCP issued a new specific regulation for the filing and reviewing of intraparty regulations and other normative documents (General Office of the Central Committee of the Chinese Communist Party 2019a). The development of this intraparty regulation system is still law-based both logically and rhetorically, as the CCP's regulation clearly states that the enactment of Party rules must be in accordance with the state Constitution and national laws (Central Committee of the Chinese Communist Party 2019). Nonetheless, the CCP maintains its prerogative *within* the law; this is because the intraparty regulations are only reviewable by the Party in itself, rather than any state authority (including the NPCSC and courts). In 2019, the NPCSC enacted the Working Measures for the Recording and Review of Regulations and Judicial Interpretations (法规、司法解释备案审查工作办法 *fagui sifa jieshi beian shencha gongzuo banfa*) for reviewing relevant statutory regulations and judicial interpretations, which excludes the intraparty regulations from the scope of NPCSC review. It states in article 26 that, for the recommendations filed with the NPCSC for the review of intraparty regulations and regulatory documents enacted by the Party organizations, these shall be transferred to the Bureau of Regulations (法规局 *fagui ju*) of the General Office of the CCP Central Committee for handling (Standing Committee of the National People's Congress 2019).

Moreover, the CCP has been endeavouring to strengthen Party self-discipline, as well as improve the Party's art of leadership and governance capacity, through disclosure within the Party or outside the Party of relevant matters concerning Party leadership activities and strengthening the Party-building work carried out by Party organizations. The principles pertaining to open party affairs have been prescribed in a CCP regulation enacted in 2017 – Regulation on Open Party Affairs (党务公开条例 *dangwu gongkai tiaolie*). Evidently, the CCP's efforts to increase transparency in Party affairs have enabled Party members, as well as the public, to understand more about and even participate in affairs of the Party (Central Committee of the Chinese Communist Party 2004). This represents a marked difference from previous practice, as the Party was largely secretive about its composition and operations before this point (McGregor 2010: 15). Now, the public can gain access to more resources on the Party than before, for example through specific CCP websites that disclose greater amounts of relevant information about the Party. Nonetheless, all this is done on the premise of the CCP's absolute political leadership remaining unchallenged while also representing an attempt to further strengthen the CCP's unified political leadership and advance the CCP's governance capacity, particularly as regards the implementation, oversight and improvement of Party affairs at the local level. In addition, it is a basic principle that open party affairs shall not endanger political security in whatever sense in the eyes of the CCP. Furthermore, the CCP's Regulation on Open Party Affairs (article 7) excludes disclosure of "matters involving party and state secrets or that are not suitable for disclosure" (Central Committee of the Chinese Communist Party 2017). In practice, of course, the content and scope of disclosure is determined entirely by the CCP itself, as it is in effect the CCP's self-enforcement of its regulations.

Undoubtedly, in practice, the CCP has never been a party in the ordinary sense of a political association. In fact, CCP organizations have been given essentially equivalent status to the government. Some CCP departments are separate, but with equivalent status to the government, while others are merged with the government, such as the CCP Taiwan Affairs Office under the Party Constitution and the Taiwan Affairs Office of the State Council under the state Constitution. Both fall within the term, "one body with two names" (一个机构，两块牌子 *yige jigou, liangkuai paizi*). The personnel of CCP departments also fall under the category of those who perform public duties in accordance with law and have been included as part of the state administrative staff whose wages and welfare are borne, in practice, by the state. Moreover, according to the Civil Servant Law (公务员法 *gongwuyuan fa*) (article 4), it is the CCP that assumes the administration of cadres (Standing Committee of the National People's Congress 2018b; Organisation Department of the Central Committee of the Chinese Communist Party 2019).

As already illustrated, both political conventions and the CCP's endeavours to systematize its intraparty regulations reveal the normalization and integration of the Party Constitution into the state Constitution, on the premise of maintaining the single-party regime and the CCP's absolute leadership over the state.

Evolution of a Dual Constitution

Due to the emergence of the dual constitution, comprising the Party Constitution and the state Constitution, it would be unfair and even biased to evaluate China's Constitution while overlooking either one of these. More importantly, four dimensions of duality have formed in the evolution of this dual constitution: dual congresses, dual judiciaries, dual executives and the military system.

Dual Congresses

The dual constitution institutionally comprises the two highest representative authorities, one for the Party and the other for the state. Of course, coordinating and combining the functions of the Party Congress and the state Congress is crucial if a balanced internal structure of the dual constitution suitable for China's authoritarian regime is to be maintained.

As far as the CCP National Congress is concerned, the CCP has been attempting to adopt some form of intraparty democracy or competitive mechanisms within the Party since 1987 (Zheng 2013b: 15). Regarding the election of the Party Congress, the Party Constitution (article 11) states that:

> The election of delegates to Party congresses and members of Party committees, at all levels, shall reflect the will of the voters. Elections shall be held by secret ballot. Lists of candidates shall be fully deliberated and discussed by Party organizations and voters. The method of nominating a greater number of candidates than the number of persons to be elected may be adopted to directly carry out a formal election, or this method may first be used in a preliminary election to generate a list of candidates for the formal election that is to follow.

It is important to note here that multicandidate elections, known as a "more candidates than seats election" (差额选举 *cha'e xuanju*), have been held by the CCP since 1982. For instance, the 2002 Party Congress had 5.1 per cent more candidates than available full-membership seats of CCP Central Committee, and 5.7 per cent more candidates than alternate-membership seats. In 2007, the 204 full members of the CCP Central Committee were elected from a total of 221 candidates on the ballot (C. Li 2010). Of course, the CCP's approach to elections is not to adopt a liberal model but rather an illiberal one, which is undoubtedly premised on the fundamental principle of CCP's absolute political leadership over the state; this is evidenced by official claims, bluntly made by CCP leaders such as former NPCSC Chairman Wu Bangguo (among others), that Western models of democracy emphasizing multiparty competitive elections, the separation of powers system and bicameralism are not suitable for China's single-party regime (C. Li 2010). Therefore, on the one hand, imagining the CCP as intending to develop a liberal electoral system would be largely incorrect in China's context. On the other hand, however, the practice of elections in an illiberal context has to a certain extent indicated the usefulness of electoral mechanisms for improving the stability and governing capacity of the regime.

Moreover, under the state Constitution, the current legal system has provided a framework for the CCP's integration with the People's Congress system. According to the Organic Law of the Local People's Congresses and Local People's Governments (地方各级人民代表大会和地方各级人民政府组织法 *difang geji renmin daibiao dahui he defang geji renmin zhengfu zuzhi fa*) (article 21), there are two channels available through which persons can be nominated for leadership position elections (members of the Standing Committee of the LPC, the chairmen and vice-chairmen of the people's congresses, governors and deputy governors, presidents of the People's Courts and chief procurators of the People's Procuratorates, etc.): nomination by the presidiums of the people's congresses at the corresponding levels, and joint nomination by deputies (Standing Committee of the National People's Congress 2015). For the latter nomination mechanism, the law states that thirty or more deputies to the People's Congress at the provincial level, or twenty or more deputies to the People's Congress at the prefecture level, or ten or more deputies to the People's Congress at the county level, may nominate, with joint signatures, the candidates mentioned above (Standing Committee of the National People's Congress 2015). Here, it appears that the law does provide a seemingly liberal channel for democratic elections, which could be interpreted as a means of incrementally activating democracy in China. Nonetheless, it has been perceived that these electoral mechanisms in authoritarian regimes operate very differently from those in their democratic counterparts, particularly as regards participation incentives and resulting electoral behaviour for example (Gandhi and Lust-Okar 2009). For instance, in 2011, the influential Chinese writer Cao Tian announced that he would run for mayor of Zhengzhou city as an independent candidate. Legalistically speaking, such an action is consistent with the Constitution and relevant laws in China. However, he was deterred, in practice, by tax inspections and other measures. Moreover, for example, as of 7 June 2011, it is estimated that more than 127 independent candidates in local elections had declared their candidacies in China (Lam 2011). Due to the discrepancy between the informal practice and the formal law, such elections seem incompatible with authoritarian regimes. Nonetheless, it is in fact possible to hold elections in an authoritarian context in such a way as to make the regime more durable than would be the case without elections (Geddes 1999).

As is evident, these electoral channels established in authoritarian regimes are not in fact used genuinely to push the regime in a more liberal direction but mostly work to support the incumbents' hold on power, the durability of the authoritarian regime and the hegemony of the Party. The entire system operates, of course, in the service of authoritarianism (Gallagher 2017: 43). On this subject, Manion (2015: 5) argues that the electoral arrangements as structured by the CCP actually represent an institutionalized flow of local knowledge, and can moreover provide the CCP leadership, particularly those in Beijing, with information about the Party's governing capacity in China's changing and sometimes challenging sociopolitical context. Given the dominance of the single ruling party in electoral mechanisms, it is understandable that the Party plays a decisive role in selecting and screening nominees for the elections, in accordance with relevant electoral rules (Interview 55-17-JMGD01). Nonetheless, it is not an easy political task for local Party officials to screen and select politically submissive and representative nominees and manipulate the electoral process within the confines of the law. In this regard, due to the legalistic requirements prescribed by the law and constantly stressed by the CCP leadership in Beijing during each election, the exercise of elections – through which the electorate have the legal right to vote on the nominees, particularly in multicandidate elections – can to some extent serve as a test of the CCP leadership's governing capacity at local levels regarding whether local Party officials are able to select those who are politically supportive of the regime and, more importantly, to ensure that they are elected by the electorate; this may entail their efforts to mobilize the electorate through various tactics or campaigns as necessary. In fact, these electoral exercises under the CCP's political control are more suitable for use by the CCP to identify and resolve potential problems, challenges or even crises, as well as to smooth out and regularize internal and external conflicts through these formal institutions under their control. The expression of such conflicts through institutionalized channels under the political control of the single ruling party is much safer than alternatives (e.g. in the street) for illiberal regimes (Gandhi 2008: 11).

Of course, the practice of conducting elections is not unique to China but is also evidenced in other illiberal regimes, such as Vietnam. The experience of Vietnam has shown that the Communist Party of Vietnam (CPV) has attempted to incorporate some democratic elements into the regime, while the National Assembly or Local People's Councils can operate smoothly in accordance with the state Constitution (Sidel 2009: 131). For example, during the period of the 11th National Congress of the CPV, 175 members of the Central Committee of the CPV were elected from 218 candidates in 2011. In terms of elections for members of the Politburo, more than 70 per cent of these were multicandidate elections. Moreover, the interpellation system has also been adopted and practised in Vietnam (International Herald Leader 2011). Of course, the nature of illiberal elections often varies among non-democratic regimes, with incumbents allowing different degrees of autonomous organizing among candidates and parties (Gandhi and Lust-Okar 2009). Broadly speaking, at the institutional level, these politically controllable electoral mechanisms, as a channel for potential opposition forces to express themselves, can be better used by authoritarian regimes to maintain their capacity of political control compared to other potential avenues (e.g. the expression of such sentiments on the street or, at the extreme end, even some potential rebellion outside the formal channels). As long as these potential dissidents or challengers dissent through these formal "democratic" channels, they are less likely to become a substantial threat to the incumbents' hold on power; the latter can easily settle these disputes through strategies of either co-option or repression. This may be partially evidenced by the case of China, where independent candidate campaigns were actually forbidden by the Party through various tactics in practice, clearly demonstrating that the "democratic" channel is not genuinely used by incumbents for regime change.

Moreover, these electoral mechanisms may be used to associate the most "popular" elites with the regime and co-opt elite investment into the regime; in particular, they can be employed as an informative tool by national leaders to check the loyalty and overall competence of Party cadres as regards regime maintenance. In addition, the electoral mechanism enables the powers that be to identify their bases of support in society, particularly those intolerable forms of opposition that may undermine the durability of the regime and will accordingly be purged through either legal or extra-legal measures, thereby signalling to the public that any real opposition to their political dominance would be futile (Ames 1970; Brownlee 2007; Gandhi and Lust-Okar 2009; Miller 2013;

Magaloni 2006; Malesky and Schuler 2011; Simpser 2005). Admittedly, the form of democratic elections in authoritarian regimes varies between one regime and another. On the extreme end, single-candidate plebiscites may be widely adopted, often demonstrating the regime's dominant power and ability to tightly control the elections from the beginning to the end. Of course, in order to achieve the desired voting results, a variety of tactics, sometimes including extra-legal and/or even coercive measures, may be used by incumbents in practice, particularly when some politically undesirable dissidents or even confrontations arise in the election process. Of course, on the other end of the authoritarian election spectrum, opposition candidates may be permitted and afforded a certain degree of freedom to compete with the single ruling party through competitive multicandidate elections (Brown 2001; Lindberg 2006; Roessler and Howard 2009). Authoritarian leaders' motivations for allowing this to occur, in addition to the benefits of elections for authoritarian leaders discussed earlier, could be complicated. For example, elections may be used to avoid the authoritarian regime being violently overthrown, to avert the threat of revolution or to facilitate greater integration into developed democracies due to increasing geopolitical pressure from authoritarian regimes, offering an alternative route to these who may be likely launch a coup, etc. (Acemoglu and Robinson 2005; Cox 2009; Gandhi and Lust-Okar 2009). Of course, the nature of an authoritarian election is that it is used to favour the dominant power of the single ruling party, and the durability of the authoritarian regime will not change substantially, regardless of the form of election and degree of electoral freedom it may adopt and allow, unless it results in a victory for a democratic opposition through which democratization may be promoted (Gandhi and Lust-Okar 2009).

In the same way, it is also possible that a liberal democratic system may be converted into an illiberal democracy if the election is substantially and continuously manipulated by the same party through its overwhelming political control over the state authorities, including the parliamentary system and courts.

Having said this, it can be seen that the CCP's initiatives regarding the reform of intraparty democracy and other electoral systems (including the possible expansion of multicandidate competitive elections in the future) can in principle only be expected to occur in the sense that these electoral reforms are beneficial for supporting the CCP's leadership; in actuality, there is no desire to promote a genuine liberal democracy that may threaten the leadership of the CCP in itself. More importantly, aside from the benefits these democratic elections provide the incumbents in the sense of bequeathing a sense of mass legitimacy domestically (Gallagher 2017: 43), the practice of holding elections can be easily used rhetorically as a political tool – both domestically and in the international community – to defend the regime's idiosyncratic model of elections/democracy by resorting to cultural relativism, critiques of the drawbacks of Western liberal democracies, etc.

As is evident, the structure of dual congresses under the dual constitution does not hinder the CCP from being capable of action and judgment, capable of initiating its activities and having the machinery to hand for the expression of the wishes of the represented. The CCP may respond to these wishes unless there are good reasons not to, as is similarly required by a representative government (Pitkin 1967: 232). To some extent, the exercise of electoral mechanisms according to the Party Constitution has served as a political rehearsal prepared months in advance for subsequent electoral exercise under the state Constitution. Moreover, under the dual constitution, a two-layer preventive structure has developed to ensure the compatibility of these elections – either in single-candidate or multicandidate form – with the political dominance of the single ruling party. The first layer is the intraparty election through the Party Constitution, which is prior to the second layer, i.e. the state election through the state Constitution. By its very nature, the intraparty election is more disciplinary than the state election under the Party's leadership; this is because the Party, as a prerogative authority over the state, operates under strict Party discipline, as can be reflected in the Party's basic principle of "democratic centralism" (民主集中制 *minzhu jizhong zhi*), according to which individual Party members are subordinate to the organization, the minority to the majority, the lower level to the higher level and all organizations and members to the National Congress and the Central Committee of the Party, as prescribed in the Party Constitution (article 10). Therefore, if the desirable outcomes of the electoral exercise within the Party are achieved, this would practically reflect on the subsequent state election under the Party's control. To a significant extent, this kind of two-layer preventive structure can help incumbents to prevent, identify and remove potential challenges or threats to the regime arising from the electoral exercise in a way that maintains and underpins the Party's hold on power.

In this regard, it is understandable that due to the political importance of elections for authoritarian regimes, the Party takes the elections seriously in practice, ensuring that they operate according to the formal channels prescribed by the law. Otherwise, any dysfunction of the electoral exercise if perceived by the public – such as the involvement of corruption or "stolen elections" – may indicate the weak governing capacity of the Party; this may further erode the legitimacy of the regime, potentially leading to some revolutionary outcomes, or finally even causing it to break down, particularly if such strategies are used by opponents through actions outside of the electoral arena (Bunce and Wolchik 2010; Beissinger 2007; Gandhi and Lust-Okar 2009; Thompson and Kuntz 2004).

Dual Judiciaries

Similarly, in a broad sense, it is possible to grasp the dual structure of the judiciary under the dual constitution. On the one hand, according to the state Constitution, China has established a formal judicial system, including the courts and procuratorates, which operates in accordance with the law. On the other hand, based on the Party Constitution, the Party has its own quasi-judicial system, the Discipline Inspection Commission (DIC), which has been designated with a constitutional name at the same time through the constitutional amendment of 2018 – Supervision Commission (SC) (监察委员会 *jiancha weiyuanhui*) – as well as the Political-Legal Committee (PLC) of the Party, the leadership of which is exerted over all relevant judicial organs (including the police, procuratorates and courts) at the corresponding level. In some sense, the formal judicial system in the state Constitution constitutes a normative component of the dual constitution, while the Party's quasi-judicial institutions constitute a prerogative component of the dual constitution.

The dual constitution has in some ways demonstrated the practical possibility of the coexistence of the empowerment of courts/judges – despite the apparent lack of fit between this concept and the traditional understanding of authoritarianism – and political control over the courts. Of course, in authoritarian settings, such empowerment may enable judges to develop more professional attributes, regarding the adjudication of normal non-political cases. This is clearly politically beneficial for authoritarian regimes in many respects, including the maintenance of social control and bureaucratic discipline, handling criminal prosecutions, resolving various social disputes, holding state officials accountable, enhancing regime legitimacy, attracting foreign investment by using courts to establish credible property rights and furthering certain government economic policies (Moustafa 2007; Solomon 2007; Ginsburg and Moustafa 2008). It should be noted that this degree of empowerment may vary among different authoritarian regimes. Nonetheless, there is no doubt that in an authoritarian setting, the regime has little to no intention of empowering the courts to be the defenders of rights, as in the ideal of a judge standing up for the rights of the individual against the state that has historically emerged in the traditions of the West (Peerenboom 2002; Solomon 2007). Instead, judicial empowerment in an authoritarian setting is in principle premised on the operation of courts being politically controllable by the authoritarian rulers. While the mechanisms of the control exerted over the courts in authoritarian regimes may vary from one regime to another, it is possible that judicial empowerment, acting as a double-edged sword, may provide some space for judicial activism; for example, the Supreme Constitutional Court of Egypt once struck down a highly restrictive law regarding non-governmental organizations being forbidden from receiving foreign funds as unconstitutional (Solomon 2007: 134). Of course, activism of this kind is limited and only made possible by its insulation within a fundamentally illiberal system (Ginsburg and Moustafa 2008: 18).

The ways in which empowered judges are contained within authoritarian politics may also differ among different authoritarian states. The common element is a prerogative component in the court system, whether a fragmented or unified one. For the fragmented system, the prerogative component can be eventually channelled through a special auxiliary court or tribunal system – typically one that is tightly controlled by the executive in various ways, such as non-tenured political appointments – designed to handle these politically sensitive cases, while regular courts may still be extended a substantial degree of autonomy by authoritarian rulers in adjudicating disputes (Ginsburg and Moustafa 2008: 17). In this regard, what matters most for authoritarian regimes, given the benefits of judicial empowerment mentioned earlier, is the ways in which the prerogative component inherently entailed by authoritarian regimes – in whatever form this may take – is integrated into a court system empowered with substantial autonomy.

In the case of China, although there is a unified court system in place in the sense that the judicial system is not fragmented, there is also certainly a prerogative component in place that has been integrated into the regular court system. This prerogative component has been codified in both Party and state Constitutions.

First and foremost, under the Party's Constitution, at the macro level, the CCP's leadership is exerted over the courts through its authority over the personnel issues of judges according to the principle "Party manages cadres" (党管干部 *dangguan ganbu*). In addition, at the horizontal level, the courts are financially dependent on the CCP-led government, which has the authority to distribute various financial and social resources. Moreover, at the institutional level, Party Groups exist in all courts, such that the presidents of the courts at different levels are also secretaries of the Party group. In this regard, the president of the court (the title of which is of the state) has another face, which is of the Party. Undoubtedly, as the secretary of the Party group of the court, there is a political obligation for the president of the court to obey superior orders or directives from within the Party. The dual role of the court's president under the Party and state Constitutions respectively reveals the political-legal character of China's courts. Under the Party's Constitution, at the horizontal level, the Party's leadership over the court is exerted through the Party's PLC members, which are leaders of all legal enforcement authorities (including police forces and courts). To some extent, while China's judicial system is not formally fragmented, the PLC does in fact function as a supervising coordinator over all legal enforcement authorities at the horizontal level. In practice, the PLC may conduct supervision concerning the implementation of the Party's policy and general affairs in cases where the court has a designated position therein, or over the judicial outcome of some politically significant cases (in whatever sense in the eyes of the Party). Legalistically speaking, the PLC's supervision is in practice informal, not accessible and transparent to the public, and exercised outside the formal regular court system, usually through coordination, instruction or even investigation through the Party's intraparty rules (as distinct from formal statutory laws and mechanisms). The Party's supervision is in practice selective, while the court's adjudicative function in the sphere of judicial autonomy and empowerment is for the most part performed routinely with minimal interference from the outside, a state of affairs that is in fact politically required and desired by the Party (Li 2019). Institutionally speaking, as China has adopted a well-organized bureaucratic model for the judiciary, the entire judicial system is able to operate in compliance with the regime's interests through periodic evaluations of judges' behaviours, the criteria for which are set by a superior political authority in a top-down manner, as well as informal judicial documents of superior judicial authority, which can function as a means of translating Party directives into rules of adjudication that have a de facto binding force in practice if formal state laws are insufficient to meet these contingent sociopolitical needs (see Chapter 4).

Moreover, under the state Constitution, the state law has established a special authority inside each court, namely the Adjudication Committee (审判委员会 *shenpan weiyuanhui*). This Adjudication Committee, which operates under the leadership of the President of the courts, is in fact "the highest judicial organisation of a people's court, which plays an important role in summing up the judicial experiences and hearing hard, complicated and important cases" (Supreme People's Court 2010a). However, no specific statutory definition of "complicated and important cases" is given in practice. Therefore, due to the requirement for the Adjudication Committee to adhere to the Party's leadership on the work of People's Courts as prescribed by the SPC (2010a), this mechanism can be used to review and modify the opinions of the adjudicating judges (He 2012a). In the same vein, the Adjudication Committee also has a mixed political-legal character, as these senior judges (including the president, vice president and presiding judge of a trial division) who sit as members of the Adjudication Committee are all Party-managed cadre members in leadership positions. In this way, if the case in question gains regional or national importance, this committee can ensure that the collective decision[11] made by the court in its sphere of autonomy is compliant with the relevant principles of the Party-state (Supreme People's Court 2010a). In other words, the Adjudication Committee in fact has a prerogative authority to selectively determine the adjudication of these difficulty and significant cases, as distinct from the ordinary cases adjudicated regularly by ordinary judges.

These two mechanisms – the PLC outside of the court system and the Adjudication Committee within the system – have formed an intertwined framework of political control over the operation of the judiciary. The Party's informal practice of political control can on the one hand ensure that the court operates in compliance with the regime's interests and to support Party leadership. On the other hand, if any problem arises (such as a wrongful conviction case accidentally being exposed to the public), it can shift the responsibility to the court, and finally to the individual judge(s) involved, while the responsibility of the Party's informal practice can be shifted away contingently from the public sphere. It is even possible that the Party's post-monitoring behaviours – standing

[11] In China, all decisions made by the court are issued in a collective way: a judge's personal opinion does not appear in the decision. Instead, only the names of the adjudicating judges appear on the decision.

on the side of justice – may even further strengthen the Party's leadership in the public sphere.

Of course, the function of criminal law is the central mechanism of social control in authoritarian regimes (Ginsburg and Moustafa 2008: 4). In addition to the already mentioned dual character of legal institutions under the Party and state Constitution respectively, the maintenance of social control through the function of criminal law in China has been underpinned through the so-called "iron triangle" (铁三角 *tian sanjiao*), comprising the public security bureau (police), procuratorate and court. Although the court is the final adjudicator of all criminal cases under the formal state law, the actual political practice is that the public security bureau is more politically important than the other two institutions in the "iron triangle"; this may be reflected in the fact that the minister of public security occupies a higher rank within the CCP's administrative structure, as the deputy secretary of the Party's Central Political-Legal Affairs Commission (CPLC), than the presidents of the SPC and SPP, as members of the CPLC only.

It is true that China's criminal law and criminal procedural law have been both developed: tangibly, with the codification of both Criminal Law (刑法 *xingfa*) and Criminal Procedural Law (刑事诉讼法 *xingshi susong fa*), which were first adopted on 1 July 1979, and followed by progressive and comprehensive revisions thereafter (Chen 2013; Standing Committee of the National People's Congress 2018a).[12] Undoubtedly, the basic established principle of legality in criminal justice has evolved in many ways towards an international standard, even accompanied with the development of a Chinese criminal jurisprudence (X. Chen 2010; Chen 2013). These laws are certainly capable of better enabling the public security bureau, procuratorate and court – which are becoming increasingly professional – to routinely deal with regular crime-related issues within a legal framework. Of course, in an illiberal context, this is not to say that the prerogative component inherently required by authoritarian rulers to maintain social control or other political contingencies would disappear. Rather, under the scheme of legality, the authoritarian core has been largely maintained through the "iron triangle" with its political ordering: specifically, the public security

[12] Since the first comprehensive revision of the Criminal Law in 1997, there have been eleven amendments made by the NPCSC, with the latest one made on 26 December 2020. The Criminal Procedural Law, since its adoption in 1979, has been amended three times, in 1996, 2012 and 2018 respectively.

bureau has been placed in a politically dominant position within the criminal justice system and granted a wide range of discretion in the context of law enforcement. More importantly, there is an emphasis on the "mutual coordination" (互相配合 *huxiang peihe*) among law enforcement authorities under the PLC's leadership; while these are designated with different functions under the law, there are few (although not zero) substantial checks and balances among them like those present in liberal separation-of-power systems. Therefore, in practice, the law enforcement of the public security bureau often prevails regarding both the legal and factual issues concerned; in practice, it is very difficult to challenge, check and examine them in the subsequent legal proceedings by the procuratorate and court at a substantial level, provided they meet the basic formal requirements within the legality scheme (Wang and Liu 2019). Moreover, the SPC's rule has explicitly excluded from the scope of judicial review all acts performed by public security organs, state security organs and other organs according to the explicit authorization granted by the Criminal Procedural Law (Supreme People's Court 2018). This provides a practical legalistic underpinning for the prerogative of the public security bureau and procuratorate in handling crime-related issues, owing to its immunity from judicial review.

In practice, under the PLC's supervising coordination, the "iron triangle" has enabled politics to penetrate into the legal framework of criminal justice, enabling issues that arise from political contingencies to be addressed selectively and separately from normal criminal cases. Moreover, the campaign-style law enforcement often employed by the Party-state during political campaigns can be activated and systematically employed to swiftly handle any crime-related problems involved (Wang 2019). To a certain extent, the relationship involved in China's criminal process – despite its surface appearance of being norm-bound – may be reflected in a widely known joke: "Police officers cook the dishes, procurators bring the dishes, and judges eat the dishes" (Wang and Liu 2019: 8).

Furthermore, the authoritarian core of the criminal justice system has been further underpinned through the prerogative extra-legal institution under the Party Constitution, namely the DIC, which operates outside the formal judicial system. Undoubtedly, the DIC has been an effective channel for use by the CCP in monitoring and disciplining Party members, particularly those assuming leadership positions in the government. More importantly, it has played a crucial role in filing and investigating cases in which a Party official is suspected of violating Party discipline (often simultaneously committing occupation-related illegal and criminal activities), including any non-Party members involved as accomplices for example. After the DIC investigation is completed, cases involving criminal activities are transferred into the formal judicial process for handling first by the procuratorate and finally by the court. Nonetheless, as noted earlier, due to the prevailing political status of the DIC within the Party, DIC investigations are difficult for the procuratorate and the court to challenge under the formal judicial process regarding both legal and factual issues presented by the DIC. This clearly shows the dominant role of the DIC as a political prerogative in China's criminal justice system. Nonetheless, it is true that extra-legal de facto detention (双规 *shuanggui*) as employed by the DIC according to Party rules – such as Party's Regulation on the Work of Case Investigation by the DIC (中国共产党纪律检查机关案件检查工作条例 *zhongguo gongchandang jilv jiancha jiguan anjian jiancha gongzuo tiaoli*) (article 28) – was often criticized for being unconstitutional, as the Legislation Law (articles 8, 9), enacted by the NPC, stipulates that: "[T]he following matters can be regulated by laws only: . . . (4) Crime and its punishment; (5) Sanctions resulting in citizens being deprived of their political rights, and coercive measures resulting in a limitation of the freedom of their person." Indeed, in practice, the Party has attempted to take relevant self-restraint measures to regulate its extra-legal activities within the Party and reduce the potential negative impacts of using the DIC, which may undermine the Party's authority. For instance, it was perceived that "*shuanggui* can be used only by organs at the district level. Supervision and review mechanisms have also been introduced. Moreover, *shuanggui* can be sanctioned only by a plenary session of a commission's standing committee" (Sapio 2008). To ensure that the DIC's prerogative could be more formally integrated into the state, a fundamental constitutional reform was undertaken with the aim of establishing a more unified model of national supervision mechanism (i.e. supervision commission) on the basis of the DIC system, which was finally institutionalized by the NPC as the Supervision Law (监察法 *jiancha fa*). The new SC has the statutory supervisory power, covering all public functionaries and those performing statutory duties, to file a case that investigates cases of occupation-related illegal and criminal activities undertaken by an official of the Party-state (National People's Congress 2018b). The procuratorate may only exercise the power to file an investigation of any crime detected by the procuratorate during its legal supervision of litigation activities, while the scope of filing such a case for investigation has been restricted to a limited number of crimes committed by "judicial officers" (司法工作人员 *sifa gongzuo renyuan*) (including persons who exercise the statutory functions of investigation, prosecution, adjudication and supervision as prescribed in article 94 of Criminal Law).[13] Of course, due to the principle of "Party manages cadres", in practice, if a judicial officer (e.g. judges, procurators) above a certain rank is involved, prior approval from the Party leadership is a prerequisite for the procuratorate to file a case for formal investigation.

Although the SC is a new constitutional authority in the legal form, it is in fact staffed with the same DIC personnel. The arrangement of "one body with two names" has in reality caused the DIC/SC to become both a Party organ when operating in the name of the DIC and a constitutional authority when in the name of the SC. In practice, the function of the DIC has been legalized through such reforms. In particular, the SC – literally referred to as a "supervisory organ" under the law – has been defined as a "political organ" (政治机关 *zhengzhi jiguan*) as distinguished from "judicial organs" (司法机关 *sifa jiguan*) and "administrative organs" (行政机关 *xingzheng jiguan*). This means the SC is immune from the specific laws applicable to judicial and administrative organs and their public functionaries. As a result, the SC has an absolute prerogative *within* the law, and its power can only be self-checked by the Party itself (China Discipline Inspection and State Supervision Newspaper 2018). Furthermore, the CCP has created a procedural

[13] Article 19 of Criminal Procedural Law (Standing Committee of the National People's Congress 2018a) states that,

> A people's procuratorate may put on file for investigation any crime detected by the people's procuratorate during legal supervision of litigation activities that infringes upon the rights of citizens and undermines judicial impartiality, such as illegal detention, extorting confession by torture, illegal search, etc., and is committed by a judicial officer by virtue of his/her powers. Where any major crime committed by a staff member of a state organ by virtue of his/her powers that is under the jurisdiction of public security organs needs to be directly accepted by a people's procuratorate, the people's procuratorate may put the case on file for investigation upon decision by the relevant people's procuratorate at or above the provincial level.

In addition, the SPP (2018) has issued specific rules on these matters concerning the procuratorate's filing a case for investigating the occupation-related crimes committed by judicial officers.

self-monitoring framework through its intraparty regulations for investigating and examining these cases (General Office of the Central Committee of the Chinese Communist Party 2019a; Central Discipline Inspection Commission of the Chinese Communist Party 1994).

Undoubtedly, from an external perspective, SC is a sword of Damocles for all officials of the Party-state due to its prevailing power to file cases for investigation with compulsory measures; these include "holding the parties under investigation" (留置 *liuzhi*), a kind of detention, as well as other investigative measures such as interrogation, inquiry, search, retrieval, sealing-up, inquisition and inspection, as prescribed in the Supervision Law (article 41) of the NPC (2018b). Moreover, due to the SC being defined as a "political organ", parties under investigation by the SC have no right to counsel or a hearing as otherwise prescribed and protected under the Criminal Procedural Law (Standing Committee of the National People's Congress 2018a). Furthermore, although the DIC/SC adopts the dual leadership system commonly applied in China's regime, this dual leadership is in reality more highly centralized than normal; this is because the Party's rules – specifically, CCP Rules on the Work of Monitoring DIC's Enforcement of Disciplines (中国共产党纪律检查机关监督执纪工作规则 *zhongguo gongchandang jilv jiancha jiguan jiandu zhiji gongzuo guize*) (article 3) – state clearly that the superior DIC/SC (rather than the local Party committee at the horizontal level) takes primary leadership over the inferior DIC/SC, notwithstanding that the DIC/SC reports to and also falls under the leadership of the horizontal Party committee (General Office of the Central Committee of the Chinese Communist Party 2019b).

A fundamental impact of the SC on the criminal justice system is that the investigation and collection of evidence by the SC becomes a legal process, such that the evidence collected is directly taken as a factual basis considered by the procuratorate for initiating prosecution; this differs from the previous practice, under which the investigations of DIC – purely as a Party organ – were not legal processes, while evidence gathered by the DIC was not adoptable in a legal sense and required a transferring process to be undertaken by the procuratorate according to the law to become legally adoptable for initiating prosecution. More importantly, due to the prevailing authority of DIC/SC in the Party-state, both legal and factual issues as determined by the SC are difficult to check in a substantial sense by the procuratorate and court in practice, although a formal review of legality is conducted legalistically on the surface.

Truthfully, it has been difficult in practice to distinguish between the DIC and the SC, despite the fact that the former is in theory a Party organ while the SC is ostensibly a state organ. The form of "one body with two names" has enabled the Party's prerogative in the judicial arena to be covered with a cloak of law.

Dual Executive and Military Systems

As for the executive system, Party leadership has penetrated into the entire system of government. Of course, under Party leadership, there have been tremendous efforts to develop a law-based governance since 1978 in an attempt to advance the government's capacity to govern the whole of society. For example, the Regulation on the Disclosure of Government Information (政府信息公开条例 *zhengfu xinxi gongkai tiaoli*) encouraged the government to become more transparent, as it granted citizens a legal right to apply for the disclosure of relevant government information (State Council 2019).[14] To some extent, this reveals the normative facets of the Party-state. In parallel, the Party is also endeavouring to operate based on its increasingly improved intra-party regulations. Functionally, in practice, there has been no substantial difference between Party officials and government civil servants, as they are all treated as public functionaries under Chinese law and moreover sometimes overlap in the form of one person with two positions in the Party and state respectively. Meanwhile, their homogeneous nature can also be glimpsed through the common practice of general offices of the CCP and state administration jointly issuing national directives.[15] Given that each state organ has a Party organization, with the former under the political leadership of the latter, it is very easy for the departments of the Party and the state to operate in practice either separately or jointly, according to their own functions. Of course, normatively speaking, the Party insists on the "rule-of-law" principle in its political rhetoric. Nonetheless, in every practical sense, the Party controls all state organs, including the legislature, and is in essence above the law. Moreover, Party

[14] In order to implement the Regulation on the Disclosure of Government Information, the Supreme People's Court (2010c) has issued specific provisions on the trial of administrative cases concerning open government information.

[15] For example, the Provisions on Party Organ and Government Personnel's Personal Investment in Securities were circulated jointly by the General Office of the CCP Central Committee and the General Office of the State Council in 2001.

affairs are specifically regulated by its own intra-regulations in a highly centralized model, rather than the statutes produced by lawmakers. In this regard, given the Party's political hegemony over the entire state (including the legislature, government and courts), it is in fact impractical – and, of course, politically disallowed – to challenge intraparty regulation according to the statutes made by the legislature.

Regarding the military system, the state Constitution has provided a normative constitutional framework under which the chairman of the CMC of the state, elected by the NPC, can exercise military power and is responsible to the NPC and NPCSC (article 94). It is the NPC that decides on questions of war and peace, or otherwise the NPCSC that decides (when the NPC is not in session) on the proclamation of a state of war in the event of an armed attack on the country or in fulfilment of international treaty obligations concerning common defence against aggression (articles 62, 67). Furthermore, the president of the state has the power to declare a state of war and issue a mobilization order (article 80).

In practice, as mentioned, two CMCs actually coexist in the form of "one body with two names" (i.e. with the same staff); this guarantees that military power is exercised smoothly and integrally without any split. Comparatively, such an institutional arrangement is similar to that of the DIC and SC, taking the form of "one body with two names".

However, due to the timing of the Party Congress (held several months earlier than the NPC under the state Constitution), a potential window of time does exist during the handover period; that is, the military power of the Party and the state (two chairmanships) may be exercised by two persons separately at the same time. In practice, for example, in September 2004, CMC Party Chairman Hu Jintao granted military ranks to military personnel, while Jiang Zemin was the chairman of the state CMC. Likewise, during a similar time interval in 2013, it was the CMC Party Chairman Xi Jinping who was entitled to bestow military ranks upon military personnel rather than the state CMC Chairman Hu Jintao. This largely illustrates the Party's insistence on the principle of the "Party commands the gun", while the CMC of the state merely serves as a form to legalize the CMC of the Party under the state Constitution. In this regard, it could be said that the People's Liberation Army has not yet in fact been nationalized.[16] Of course, practically speaking, if both the

[16] In fact, it has been perceived that, in China, the People's Liberation Army has always been a branch of the CCP. Recently, more people have advocated for shifting the army's allegiance from the Party to the state (Carter 2012).

army's allegiance to the Party and the Party's hegemony over the state can be politically guaranteed, the likelihood of a military coup such as those that have occurred in other illiberal states might be reduced due to the Party's dominant leadership. There is, however, no doubt that, since 1949, China has not undergone the succession of power at the top in as peaceful and orderly a manner as tends to be found in modern democracies (Y. Wang 2018). Although the succession of power is largely unpredictable after Xi, the control of military power is almost a political prerequisite for China's top leader to be hegemonic in Chinese politics, regardless of their capacity to govern the whole country. The crucial importance of the control of military power for the Chinese leader may be indicated by the case of Deng Xiaoping, treated as the second generation of Chinese leader after Mao Zedong, who was the leader of the army (i.e. chairman of the Party CMC), but not the leader of the Party (i.e. general secretary of the CCP) nor the leader of the state (i.e. president under the Constitution).

Conclusion

Since the end of the Cold War, post-communist countries have embarked down different roads towards a liberal or illiberal democracy. At the same time, over the past decades, some remaining socialist countries, particularly China and Vietnam, have undergone in-depth reforms in many fields. After more than four decades of development, the rise of China has taken a different form through the creation of a dual constitution comprising the Party and the state; this cannot easily be explained by the traditional Party-state theory under which the law tended to be disregarded, as occurred – to an extreme – in the era of Mao Zedong. The dual constitution has evolved into a more norm-bound system for both the Party, based on its intraparty regulations under the Party's Constitution, and the state, based on statutory laws under the state Constitution. In the framework of legality as utilized instrumentally by the Party, some informal prerogative institutions may even be formally legalized, as evidenced by the SC, apart from these informal prerogative practices. In an illiberal context, the prerogative institutions – whether formal or informal – are definitely significant for maintaining the authoritarian core of the regime (e.g. the CCP's leadership in China's context). In the meantime, these relatively stable normative institutions are pragmatically valuable for authoritarian rulers in many ways as regards economic development, enhancing government capacity, etc., provided that these

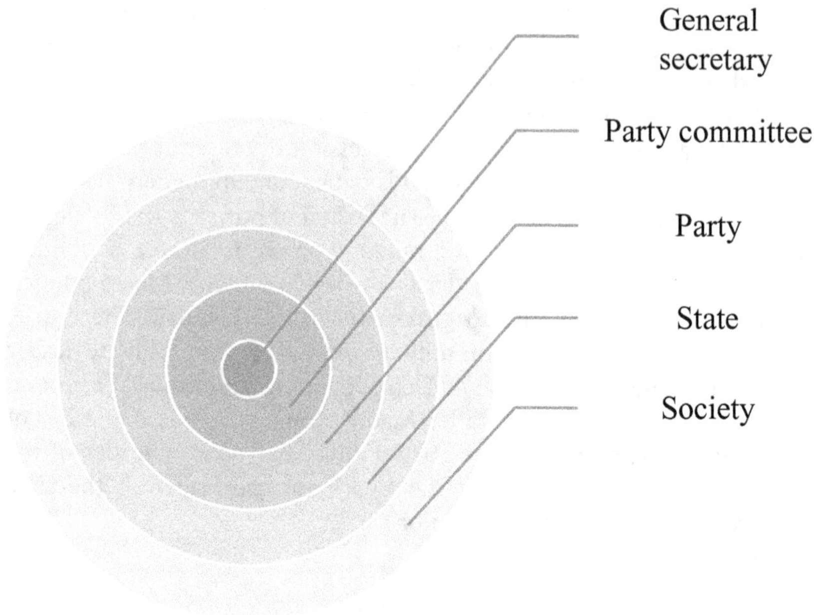

Figure 2.1 Prerogative chain of the dual constitution.

practices do not pose a challenge or threat to the fundamental illiberal principles embraced by authoritarian rulers. The normative and prerogative components of the Party-state are often intertwined with each other. In terms of the key distinction, normative institutions are typically more visible than prerogative ones in the public sphere; it is even possible for people to fabricate a seamless imagined vision of a normative system that is highly similar to those in liberal democracies, although this is only possible if the eyes focus only on the normative expressions made rhetorically by authoritarian rulers. Of course, for authoritarian states, the more important prerogative layers are usually progressively embedded into the normative institutions in a centralized way, usually from the society to the state to the Party (culminating in the Party Centre and the top leader), as illustrated to some extent by the case of China (see Figure 2.1).

In most situations, the greater the proximity to the centre of power, the more prerogative is expected, while the more closed the practice is, the stronger the social image of justice and authority (at least as upheld by the regime) it desires politically. Following this logic, it would be no surprise that in the populist opinion, the root cause of existing problems (if any) in society – as sometimes publicly condemned by people – is usually not the Centre in Beijing, but elsewhere. In the same vein, if the ruling Party, and in particular its Centre (including the top leader), is condemned for any reason, speech of this kind would be far less tolerated by the government than otherwise, although it is possible that some individual Party leaders (often those involved in factional politics) may be condemned and jailed, usually for committing crime(s) relating to corruption, and often as a warning example for Party officials of "what not to do".

The dynamic interaction between the normative and prerogative institutions may vary from one authoritarian regime to another. By way of comparison, the dual constitution form is also employed in other authoritarian states, although the degree and form of the prerogative may vary from one state to another. More broadly, considering the phenomenon of democratic decline, the prerogative practice as illustrated in the dual constitution may emerge in these (even long-standing) democracies. As Scheppele (2018: 545–547) points out, charismatic leaders elected by democratic publics may use "democratic mandates to launch legal reforms in order to remove the checks on executive, limit the challenges to their rule, and undermine the crucial accountability institutions of a democratic state", consolidate power and finally remain in office indefinitely.

3

Judicial Interpretation as a de facto Primary Statute for Adjudication

Law is fundamentally a matter of interpretation, since the meaning of law is largely determined through such interpretation. In the Anglo-American legal tradition, after a law is passed, courts are the primary interpreters of the meaning of law in adjudicating concrete cases. By contrast, in a socialist legal tradition, after a law is passed, it is in principle exclusively interpreted by the lawmaker, i.e. the state legislature. This was the practice of the former Soviet Union, where it was the role of the Soviet legislature to interpret the law (Smith 1988: 95–99). Moreover, judicial interpretation was once argued as being limited in terms of its scope and status under China's positive law system; its application was unstable in both theory and practice, and it was not taken seriously by the Party and the Congress it controlled (Li 1997: 88; Kong 1991: 498). However, there is no doubt that judicial interpretation has come to play an increasingly vital role in lawmaking under China's legislative system (Finder 1993; Ip 2010). As a matter of practice, the SPC has gradually become a primary authority for interpreting statutes passed by the legislature. Furthermore, the SPC's interpretations have been legally categorized as "judicial interpretation"(司法解释 *sifa jieshi*) in China's positive law system, according to the Legislation Law. In this regard, it has been argued that judicial interpretation functions as "secondary law" in trial practice (Keith and Lin 2009). However, as discussed in this chapter, the SPC's formal judicial interpretation has in reality become a de facto primary – rather than secondary – source of law for use by judges in adjudicating cases. This clearly further indicates that, given the lack of case law in China's legal system, the legislative power, involving lawmaking activities, has been formally shared by the state legislature with the SPC; this represents a substantial difference from both the traditional judicial explanation of Chinese criminal law in history (Wang 1995) and the general understanding of the separation of powers, such that "[t]he legislature prescribed general rules, the executive implemented those rules and the judiciary resolved conflicts between private parties, or between the state and private parties, about the rule's application" (Tushnet 2014: 94). Therefore, this chapter aims to explore the rationale behind the SPC's legislative function as performed through its judicial interpretation mechanism under China's authoritarian system, which is in turn difficult to understand – albeit easy to criticize – outside of its sociopolitical context.

Emergence of the SPC's Judicial Interpretation

Historically, after the CCP took power in mainland China, the SPC as a political subordinate of the CCP did in fact produce various documents for use by the courts in adjudicating cases. The form of these documents varied from specific directives or replies to interpretations of relevant laws or regulations. For example, in order to implement the CCP Central Committee's directive, issued on March 1950, on suppressing counterrevolutionary activities (Central Committee of the Chinese Communist Party 1950), the Government Administration Council of the Central People's Government (中央人民政府政务院 *zhongyang renmin zhengfu zhengwuyuan*), as the chief administrative authority, jointly issued a specific directive with the SPC on suppressing counterrevolutionary activities in July 1950 (Government Administrative Council of Central People's Government and Supreme People's Court 1950). Of course, the SPC's practice of producing relevant documents to specify the CCP's top-down instruction was significant at that time. Notably, the CCP abolished all laws made by the previous government of the Republic of China (although these are still applicable in Taiwan), and China's legislative system had not yet been established at the time; therefore, the SPC's documents became an expedient means of providing specific rules to the courts for implementing top-down instructions in their adjudication. Moreover, due to the lack of a comprehensive positive law system, judges relied heavily on specific instructions from superior courts – particularly the SPC – to adjudicate relevant cases in order to ensure that their adjudication was in line with CCP policies and directives. In political reality, if judges encountered a difficult and complicated case that the court was incapable of handling for whatever reason (i.e. legal and/or political), it was common practice – as well as a form of self-protection under an authoritarian political system – for judges to make a request to the superior court for clarification. Thus, until its abolishment, the formal reply of the superior court to the request of the inferior court became another form of judicial document that was both of a legislative nature and applicable to courts in adjudicating subsequent relevant cases in practice. For instance, in May 1952, the SPC issued a formal reply to the Hunan High People's Court regarding its request for clarification of the application of a suspended sentence and the probationary sentencing period for offenders found guilty of corruption (Supreme People's Court 1952).

More importantly, although the CCP did not adopt a form of separation of powers, it clearly practised a separation of functions in the Party-state, where the courts were responsible for and had relevant experience – along with professional skills – in adjudicating cases. The courts thus differed from the CCP's other political subordinates due to their professional adjudicative skills. In particular, the SPC, possessing substantial legal expertise, has been largely staffed since its inception with legal professionals who routinely interpret statutes (Li 1997: 104–105). In this regard, it has in fact proven quite essential for the SPC, when implementing the CCP's policies or directives, to translate the CCP's political instructions into the language of courts through producing corresponding judicial documents suitable for use by judges in adjudicating relevant cases, thereby ensuring the effective implementation of the CCP's policies or directives in adjudication.

The early practice of statutory interpretation by the SPC under the Party-state system shows that, first and foremost, the SPC as the CCP's political subordinate had political responsibility for translating the CCP's top-down instructions into the language of the courts by producing corresponding judicial documents that functioned as a basis for adjudication in the court system. Moreover, given the superior court's political authority over inferior courts, superior courts (in particular the SPC) were in reality required to respond to any significant issues – in either a legal or political sense – arising from trial practice, as requested and due to the inferior courts' inability to handle such issues within their political capacity. To a certain extent, this mechanism represented a combination of a top-down and bottom-up approach to adjudication in China's authoritarian regime.

The SPC's Judicial Interpretation in the People's Congress System

Accompanying the CCP's state-building efforts, in 1954, a new written Constitution for the PRC was enacted that provided a basic constitutional framework for the state, adopting the Soviet model of the People's Congress system as its foundation (National People's Congress 1954).

According to the People's Congress system, as stipulated in the Constitution of 1954, the NPC is the highest organ of state authority in the PRC (article 21) and is also the only legislative authority in the country (article 22). The NPCSC is a permanent body of the NPC (article 30) with the functions and powers to interpret laws and adopt decrees (article 31). In this regard, given the practical need for the SPC to interpret laws and decrees in trial practice at that time, in 1955, the NPCSC formally delegated the task of interpreting national laws pertaining to the application of laws and decrees in court trials to the Adjudicative Committee of the SPC in its Resolution on Matter of Legal Interpretation (关于解释法律问题的决议 *guanyu jieshi falü wenti de jueyi*). It states that:

> 1. In cases where the limits of articles of laws and decrees need to be further defined or additional stipulations need to be made, the Standing Committee of the National People's Congress shall provide interpretations or make stipulations by means of decrees.
> 2. Interpretation of questions involving the specific application of laws and decrees in court trials shall be provided by the Adjudicative Committee of Supreme People's Court.
>
> (Standing Committee of the National People's Congress 1955)

At this time, there were no other specific legal rules governing such judicial interpretations, which largely did not differ substantially from the SPC's other documents (see Chapter 4). In practice, however, the SPC made judicial interpretations on very few occasions and only when significant issues arose at trial. Most of these judicial interpretations were in fact requested by lower-level courts (Ji 2007: 12). To a large extent, the NPCSC's resolution indicated recognition of the necessity of the SPC's interpretation of laws and decrees in China's trial practice. Of course, historically, since 1957, China had witnessed the prevalence of various political movements within the CCP's political agenda; in an extreme example of this, during the Cultural Revolution that took place from 1966 until 1976, legal institutions were mostly paralysed by the "smash the Police, Procuratorate, and Court" (砸烂公检法 *zalan gong jian fa*) movements. Under such prevalent legal nihilism, the courts were taken over by the Military Control Committee (军事管制委员会 *junshi guanzhi weiyuanhui*), and the SPC existed in name only (Zhou 1994). The courts during this period functioned as a tool of the CCP to fight counterrevolutionaries and class enemies. Consequently, "judicial interpretation became nothing more than an explanation of the CCP's policies that superseded the law" (Li 1997: 90). However, following the death of Mao Zedong and the end of the Cultural Revolution, the Chinese leader

Deng Xiaoping learned a lesson from the past and decided to adopt the "opening-up" policy to promote China's economic development, which – if achieved – would successfully strengthen the CCP's performance-based legitimacy. Of course, the building up of a comprehensive legal system was a key element of the CCP's opening-up agenda. Moreover, the People's Congress system resumed its regular function of procedural endorsement, and the SPC's practice of interpretation of laws and decrees during trial was revived. In particular, in 1979, the right of the SPC to issue judicial interpretations was formally stipulated in a national law of the NPC (1979), the Organic Law of the People's Courts (人民法院组织法 *Renmin fayuan zuzhi fa*), article 33 of which stated that the SPC was to interpret questions concerning the specific application of laws and decrees in judicial proceedings (National People's Congress 1979).

The legal status of the SPC's judicial interpretations of national laws was reiterated in an NPCSC resolution of 1981. This resolution aimed to establish a legal framework of legislative interpretation under the NPCSC's constitutional authority to interpret the limits and definitions of national statutes; this involved not only the SPC's power of statutory interpretation but also the legal interpretations of other authorities, including the State Council and the SPP. In addition to reconfirming the NPCSC's and SPC's interpretation of laws and decrees as stipulated in the Resolution of NPCSC (1955), it further states that:

> 2. . . . Interpretation of questions involving the specific application of laws and decrees in the procuratorial work of the procuratorates shall be provided by the Supreme People's Procuratorate. If the interpretations provided by the Supreme People's Court and the Supreme People's Procuratorate are at variance with each other in principle, they shall be submitted to the Standing Committee of the National People's Congress for interpretation or decision.
> 3. Interpretation of questions involving the specific application of laws and decrees in areas unrelated to judicial and procuratorial work shall be provided by the State Council and the competent departments.
> 4. In cases where the limits of locally enacted rules and regulations need to be further defined or additional stipulations need to be made, the standing committees of the people's congresses of the provinces, autonomous regions, and municipalities directly under the Central Government which have formulated these rules and regulations shall provide the interpretations or make the stipulations. Interpretation of questions involving the specific application of local rules and regulations shall be provided by the competent departments under the people's governments of the provinces, autonomous regions, and municipalities directly under the Central Government.
>
> (Standing Committee of the National People's Congress 1981)

It is clear that the NPCSC-delegated interpretation mechanism has inherently enabled the SPC to act as a de facto lawmaking authority in trial practice, given the lack of case law in China. Unlike the case law system, the SPC's lawmaking authority has no substantive difference from that of the national legislature in terms of its effectiveness in trial practice, as it is of a definitively legislative nature and not performed through the development of a rule of law in the adjudication of specific cases.

Throughout China's rapid economic development since 1978, the SPC has played an indispensable legislative role in providing relevant statutory rules for the country's economic development through the NPCSC-delegated interpretation mechanism, which has flexibly responded to the rapid changes in China's society in the reform era. This legislative task in the reform era would have been difficult to achieve flexibly in a short period of time through the China's People's Congress system, the primary function of which (as distinct from democratically elected deliberative parliamentary systems) is procedural endorsement for political purposes. Over the past decades, moreover, China has witnessed the overwhelming development and increasing legislative significance of the SPC's judicial interpretations in its legal system. For example, based on these judicial interpretations included in volumes 1, 2 and 3 of the Collection of SPC Judicial Interpretations (司法解释全集 *sifa jieshi quanji*), the SPC published over 1,500 judicial interpretations between 1981 and 1996, in addition to the over 1,000 pieces issued between 1949 and 1980 (Research Office of the Supreme People's Court 1994; 1997; 2002). Moreover, the SPC's judicial interpretation not only covered criminal law issues – which was a primary practice before the reform era – but also expanded to all other areas of law, including constitutional law, administrative law, civil and commercial law, procedural law and international law. Furthermore, in terms of the requests from inferior courts for clarification on how to adjudicate a particular case, the SPC adopted China's administrative practice of a superior Party organ or government agency using an official reply to exert its supervisory authority over the inferior one (Li 1997: 97). Of course, in trial practice, the court's formal reply is largely of a legislative nature – beyond the adjudication of the individual case – in that it can function like a statutory rule that is applicable to all relevant cases. In particular, since 1984, the SPC further expanded its legislative practice through its judicial interpretation mechanism by creating a complete package of interpretation involving all major questions pertaining to the application of the newly promulgated statute (Li 1997: 97–98). For example, after the Civil Procedural Law [Interim] (民事诉讼法(试行) *minshi susong fa [shixing]*) was promulgated by the NPCSC (1982), the SPC provided a comprehensive and systematic interpretation of all major articles involved in this law (Adjudication Committee of the Supreme People's Court 1984). This type of judicial interpretation in fact takes a plainly legislative form, comprising specific numbered provisions that largely correspond to provisions in the statute as interpreted. In other words, the SPC's judicial interpretation of this kind acts in reality as another detailed version of the entire statute. This practice definitively indicates that the SPC in effect performs a de facto legislative function that goes beyond so-called "interpretation" as usually understood in the specific application of laws and decrees in court trials.

Institutionalization of the SPC's Judicial Interpretation

Owing to the importance of the SPC's judicial interpretation in the development of China's legal system, the SPC made efforts to improve its judicial interpretation mechanism by establishing a special team in 1993 to research how the regulation of judicial interpretation activities might be improved (Zhao 2010). Subsequently, in 1997, the SPC (1997) formally produced a specific document on its judicial interpretations, entitled Rules on the Work of Judicial Interpretation (关于司法解释工作的若干规定 *guanyu sifa jieshi gongzuo de ruogan guiding*). Moreover, in 2007, the SPC (2007a) comprehensively improved the mechanism of producing judicial interpretations via the Provisions on the Work Concerning Judicial Interpretation (关于司法解释工作的规定 *guanyu sifa jieshi gongzuo de guiding*) (hereinafter "the Provisions 2007"), which contained details regarding procedures, legal titles, legal statuses, proposals, drafting, submissions, deliberation, promulgation, implementation and the filing of judicial interpretations. The Provisions 2007, while acting as a self-regulatory mechanism for the SPC, greatly institutionalized the judicial interpretation mechanism, enabling the SPC to regularly perform its legislative function in trial practice. In addition, the legal status of the SPC's judicial interpretations was later formally confirmed in article 104 of the Legislation Law by the NPC (2015).

The institutionalization of the SPC's judicial interpretation can be distinguished from the SPC's other forms of interpretation conducted through judicial documents. This is because judicial interpretation has been legally institutionalized as a type of formal statutory law that can be cited, like other statutory laws, by judges during judicial decision-making. The Provisions 2007, as revised in 2021, clearly stipulate that judicial interpretations can be classified into five types: "interpretations" (解释 *jieshi*), "provisions" (规定 *guiding*), "rules" (规则 *guize*), "replies" (批复 *pifu*) and "decisions" (决定 *jueding*) (Supreme People's Court 2021). When the issue at hand is that of how a particular law or judicial interpretation should be applied to a specific type of case or issue, the interpretation type shall be adopted. Regulations or opinions that need to be formulated based on legislative intention shall adopt the provisions format. With regard to judicial interpretations formulated to request the direction of the High People's Courts, or the military courts of the People's Liberation Army, regarding the specific application of laws in a trial, the reply format shall be adopted. Finally, with regard to the amendment or repeal of a judicial interpretation, the decision format shall be adopted (Supreme People's Court 2007a). In this regard, the SPC's judicial interpretations have become a type of statutory law, and, by their very nature, can be distinguished from other judicial documents that fall outside the scope of formal statutory laws. As a common practice since 1997, all formal judicial interpretations have been issued seriatim with a formal document number: "Fa Shi (法释) [Calendar Year] Number"; this is different to the format of judicial documents, which have a formal reference number, such as "Fa Fa (法发) [Calendar Year] Number", "Fa (法) [Calendar Year] Number" and "Fa Fu (法复) [Calendar Year] Number" (W. Wang 2010: 201). In practice, it is typically the SPC's responsibility to create the proposal and draft, in consultation with the SPC's Research Office, which is followed by a review conducted by the SPC's vice president in charge, and then the approval of the SPC's Adjudicative Committee and a public announcement. In the meantime, it is circulated to all inferior courts on a level-by-level basis for implementation.

Of course, in the People's Congress system, the legislative power wielded by the SPC through its judicial interpretation mechanism is premised on the NPCSC's delegation. Therefore, due to the development of the SPC's judicial interpretation, the NPCSC (2005) has accordingly established a record and review system that ensures its supervisory authority over the SPC's judicial interpretations, as first stipulated in its internal document entitled Working Procedures on the Record and Review of Judicial Interpretations (司法解释备案审查工作程序 *sifa jieshi bei'an shencha gongzuo chengxu*) in 2005, which requires that all of the SPC's judicial interpretations be submitted to the NPCSC for record and review. Subsequently, the record and review of SPC's judicial interpretations was legally endorsed in the NPCSC (2006) statute Law on the Supervision of Standing Committees of People's Congresses at Various Levels in 2006. Furthermore, the NPC (2015) further confirmed its supervisory authority over the SPC's legislative function through its judicial interpretation mechanism by specifying the scope of the SPC's judicial interpretation in the amendment of the Legislation Law 2015; in more detail, article 104 states that the interpretation issued by the SPC on the specific application of the law during adjudication work shall focus primarily on specific legal provisions and be consistent with legislative purposes, principles and intent. Moreover, the SPC's interpretation shall be submitted to the NPCSC for record-filing within thirty days of promulgation. Distinguished from the SPC's judicial interpretation of a law, as stated in article 45, the NPCSC shall interpret a law if (1) the specific meaning of one of its provisions needs to be further defined, or (2) after enactment of the law, new developments make it necessary to define the basis on which it should be applied.

Undoubtedly, the literal distinction between the SPC's and the NPCSC's interpretation of a law largely grants the NPCSC the final authority on legislation and its constitutional control – whenever necessary – over the SPC's legislative power, resulting inherently from its interpretation of a law. This is because, due to the lack of separation of powers in China's single-party state, there is in practice no effective review of the NPCSC on the SPC's interpretation of a law that may involve the definition of a provision's specific meaning or the basis on which the law is applied, particularly as regards the SPC's complete package of interpretation for a statute of the NPC/NPCSC. Of course, in the case that the NPCSC and SPC arrive at different opinions on the same legal issue, the matter is usually resolved through political channels, such as the SPC's internal communication with and reporting to the NPCSC during the drafting process; the SPC, as an inferior political authority, will doubtless follow the NPCSC's directives. Any effective system of checks and balances between the NPCSC and SPC, both of which are under the CCP's centralized leadership, would be in reality impossible to implement: any such system would suggest a split in, or even failure of, the CCP's highly centralized leadership over the NPCSC and SPC, which is politically disallowed by the CCP. In practice, due to the NPCSC's supervisory authority, the SPC consults and communicates with the NPCSC when drafting a judicial interpretation. In addition, the NPCSC, the State Council and its ministries or commissions also consult and communicate with the SPC to seek out its opinions when enacting relevant statutes (W. Wang 2010: 23). This kind of dialogic lawmaking practice can provide the authorities involved with information they might not have had access to at the outset, and is further able to address relevant political difficulties that arise under the CCP's centralized leadership. Of course, this dialogic form of lawmaking under CCP leadership also makes it almost impossible to challenge a statute once enacted, as the Party-state cannot be challenged under China's authoritarian system. In this regard, although it may be argued that many of the SPC's judicial interpretations have exceeded the authorization of the 1981 resolution in both form and substance (Keller 1989; Li 1997: 103), the NPCSC's political acquiescence has made this argument essentially meaningless.

China's Constitution is often criticized, even domestically, as being unenforceable in practice. Accordingly, in an effort to strengthen the legality of the authoritarian system, in the 19th National Congress of the CCP on 18 October 2017, Xi Jinping clearly stressed the importance of strengthening oversight to ensure compliance with the Constitution, advancing the work of constitutional review and safeguarding the Constitution's authority (Xi 2017). In order to implement Xi's report, the NPCSC (2019) has made attempts to enact a specific statute – i.e. the Working Measures, in 2019 – that provides more details of the relevant procedures involved in reviewing non-NPC/NPCSC statutes, including the SPC's judicial interpretations. This is conducted largely on the basis of its previous work handling relevant written requests and suggestions for examination of relevant problematic statutes according to article 99 of the Legislation Law, albeit with almost no details regarding the review procedure provided therein.[1] Although the Working Measures 2019 has

[1] Article 99 of the Legislation Law states that:

> When the State Council, the Central Military Commission, the Supreme People's Court, the Supreme People's Procuratorate and the standing committees of the people's congresses of the provinces, autonomous regions and municipalities directly under the Central Government consider that administrative regulations, local regulations, autonomous regulations or separate regulations contradict the Constitution or laws, they may submit to the Standing Committee of the National People's Congress written requests for examination, and the working offices of the Standing Committee shall refer the requests to the relevant special committees for examination and suggestions.
>
> When state organs other than the ones mentioned in the preceding paragraph, public organizations, enterprises and institutions or citizens consider that administrative regulations, local regulations, autonomous regulations or

legalized the NPCSC's internal working procedures at the general level, this makes no substantial difference regarding the NPCSC's actual work; this is because the law is general, providing the NPCSC with broad discretion, and the procedures are closed-door and non-judicial, which does not allow interested parties to engage in adversarial proceedings before the court. In particular, the grounds of review, as stipulated in the Working Measures, include both legal and political criteria. Article 37 of the Working Measures states that, when reviewing a regulation or a judicial interpretation, the NPCSC's working authorities shall offer official opinions to the competent authority involved for correction if any inconsistency is found with the CCP's major policies or the principles of the state reform agenda (Standing Committee of the National People's Congress 2019). This article is clearly defined as a political criterion by the Institute for Recording and Review (备案审查室 *beian shencha shi*) of the Legislative Affairs Commission of the NPCSC, stating that the CCP's leadership is the foundation of China's socialism, and that the CCP's policies shall be firmly implemented. If inconsistent with the CCP's policies, these normative documents shall be corrected through the recording and review system in a way that preserves the CCP's authority and centralized leadership (Institute for Recording and Review of the Law Committee of the National People's Congress Standing Committee 2020: 100–101). In this regard, the promulgation of the Working Measures is of political importance, as it clearly shows the NPCSC's efforts to firmly implement Xi's call to advance the work of constitutional review; moreover, the promulgation of the Working Measures has been widely propagandized as an important achievement in the development of the constitutional review process. From a legal perspective, the legalization of the NPCSC's working procedures further strengthens the NPCSC's supervisory authority over lower-level statutes, including the SPC's judicial interpretations.

separate regulations contradict the Constitution or laws, they may submit to the Standing Committee of the National People's Congress written suggestions for examination, and the working offices of the Standing Committee shall study the suggestions and shall, when necessary, refer them to the relevant special committees for examination and suggestions.

The relevant special committees and the working bodies of the Standing Committee may take the initiative to review the normative documents submitted for record-filing.

(National People's Congress 2015)

Why Does Judicial Interpretation Matter under China's Authoritarian Regime?

The historical evolution of the SPC's judicial interpretation indicates its profound entrenchment into China's authoritarian system over the past decades. There is no doubt that the SPC's legislative function differs substantially from that of a common law system, in which the lawmaking function is performed by the courts through case law on the basis of the courts' adjudication of particular cases. Of course, a further intellectual issue that must be addressed in China's context is as follows: given the existence of the SPC's legislative function through the judicial interpretation mechanism, why has such a legislative mechanism been able to be entrenched into and made suitable for China's authoritarian system while the SPC has necessarily exercised a shared legislative power with the NPCSC/NPC?

To a significant extent, the SPC's exercise of legislative power can be institutionally ascribed to the People's Congress system, the primary function of which is the procedural endorsement of (in particular) the policies articulated by the CCP leadership, a marked difference from the operation of democratically elected parliamentary systems with a politically deliberative function. Officials occupying leadership positions in the People's Congress system are usually those who have left similarly powerful posts within the CCP after approaching their retirement age. In other words, in terms of constitutional rhetoric, the People's Congress is strong in the sense that the Constitution defines it as the highest organ of state power but also politically weak in the sense that its primary function is procedural endorsements that translate the CCP's decisions into law, and that it effectively operates entirely under CCP leadership. In practice, the standing committee of the People's Congress has comparatively less political authority than other political subordinates of the CCP, such as the Education Bureau and Police Bureau, which generally have more substantial powers and amounts of resources to allocate.

This political arrangement in which the People's Congress system remains under the CCP's centralized leadership is suitable for China's authoritarian system. This is because, firstly, the routine operation of the People's Congress system according to the Constitution is able to strengthen the legitimacy of China's socialist system. Moreover, the CCP's unilateral leadership can be solidified through the People's Congress system, under which a democratically elected parliamentary system with a deliberative function is disallowed. Of course, deputies – both nominated by and supportive of the CCP – may make certain suggestions or proposals in order to (for instance) attract some attention or seek support from relevant authorities during the plenary session of the People's Congress.

Having said this, it can also be seen that the procedural endorsement function, while frequently criticized as a political "rubber stamp", determines the ways in which the People's Congress system operates in practice, given its relatively weak lawmaking capacity in terms of legal knowledge and experience when compared to the SPC's professional capacity. For example, the NPC has around 3,000 deputies, usually nominated by the CCP from all over the country, and holds only one plenary session every year in Beijing, lasting only about ten days. Notably, this session is by no means intended to actually deliberate on the items within the NPC's tight agenda – for instance, during the annual session of the NPC on 5–15 March 2017, such items included hearing and deliberating reports on the work of the NPCSC, the State Council, the SPC and the SPP respectively, examining and approving the plan for national economic and social development and the report on its implementation, examining and approving the state budget and the report on its implementation and reviewing various bills proposed by the NPCSC. In fact, the "deliberation" of these items is already carried out in various forms by relevant authorities before they are ever scheduled by the NPCSC to appear on the NPC agenda. Accordingly, when NPC deputies attend the annual NPC plenary session, it is to participate in a well-planned event where deputies come to Beijing from all over the country to carry out constitutional endorsement. Therefore, due to the fact that the function of the People's Congress system is primarily one of endorsement, it is politically unrealistic – in most situations – for them to make laws with any specificity and certainty. This may largely explain why "preferring the coarse to the fine" has become a general policy for the NPC's legislative activities, as well as the fact that the NPCSC's interpretation of statutes has been a far less regular practice when compared with interpretation conducted by the SPC (Li 1997: 103–104). It has been observed that these basic laws and statutes produced by the NPC are customarily written in an ambiguous fashion, in the form of principle-like pronouncements (Corne 2002: 374). Of course, apolitical provisions pertaining to civil and commercial laws may be relatively clear and specific, due to their being largely irrelevant to authoritarian politics; however, these are still ultimately subject to interpretation, in particular by the SPC, whenever an ambiguity arises in practice.

The vague quality and ambiguous nature of the basic statutes promulgated by the NPC has meant that they can remain stable while translating the often complicated circumstances of authoritarian politics into the domain of law, at least on the surface, while "creat[ing] an inevitable variance in levels of understanding" (Li 1997: 91). Of course, given that China's socialist system prohibits the establishment of any case law framework based on the Western style of judicial independence, this ambiguous quality of national laws enables the SPC – as the highest court – to specify the meaning of these laws so that the courts might apply them in the process of adjudication. Different from the lengthy lawmaking procedure engaged in by the NPC, the SPC's specification of law in trial practice through the judicial interpretation mechanism has served as a useful shortcut enabling urgently needed interpretations to be produced without the need to go through the normal legislative procedure (Li 1997: 104–105). This approach is both politically temporal and flexible, enabling it to respond deftly to the complicated circumstances and capricious needs of authoritarian politics. More importantly, compared with the NPC, the courts – acting as political subordinates of the CCP – are staffed with professional judges who have ample legal expertise and are involved directly with handling cases. The SPC is therefore typically more sensitive, owing in part to its practical skills and experience, to the temporal demands of legislation for authoritarian governance than the NPCSC in the context of Chinese politics. The legislature, for its part, is able to enjoy the benefits of the SPC's judicial interpretations, which can relieve it from the burden of reviewing and amending statutes for which it should rightly be responsible (Li 1997: 104). This has allowed the SPC to occupy a de facto significant position in the lawmaking enterprise in China's authoritarian context. It is possible that some of the SPC's temporal legislation, after being experimented with for a period of time, may eventually be transformed into laws by the NPCSC, provided that it is not bound over the space of authoritarian politics, as inherently desired in the policy of "preferring the coarse to the fine".

Of course, although the SPC has in practice been exercising a de facto legislative power through adjudication, this is not to say that the courts are outside the political control of – or even able to defy impositions from – political leaders. Two main channels have been established to ensure that the SPC's legislative authority is ultimately subject to the CCP's centralized leadership. The first of these is the constitutional channel, where the SPC's rulemaking activities through the judicial interpretation mechanism are always able to be reviewed by the

NPCSC, as already discussed. The constitutional framework was established by an NPCSC resolution in 1981, stipulating that the SPC may only interpret questions concerning the specific application of national statutes, rather than their constitutionality. For any questions raised concerning the definitions or limits of a national statute, or involving stipulations of matters beyond a specific statute, the SPC, along with the State Council and the SPP, shall be subject to and defer to the NPCSC's authority (Li 1997: 92). In practice, the NPCSC's review mechanism is largely politically preventive, in the sense that it ensures the SPC's legislative activities remain politically controllable, and is by no means intended to be a close supervision of SPC's legislative activities, as the SPC's relatively specialized legal knowledge inherently requires some insulation from other political authorities.[2] If this were not the case – if, in fact, its legislative activities were closely monitored by the NPCSC or other hierarchical political superiors – the legislative task of the SPC might not be performed very well. Moreover, this constitutional arrangement has been politically substantiated by the order of political power in which the chairman of the NPCSC, as a member of the standing committee of the CCP's Politburo (comprising seven members in total for the 19th CCP Central Committee) has a far higher political status than the president of the SPC, who is only a member of the CCP Central Committee (comprising 204 members in total for the 19th CCP Central Committee) and is never promoted to the next highest political level as a member of the CCP Politburo (25 members and 172 alternate members in total for the 19th CCP Politburo).

The second, more important channel is the political channel: that is, the CCP's personnel have control over judges and supervision over the work done by the courts. According to the CCP's policy of "Party manages cadres", personnel issues pertaining to judges, including promotion, are addressed by the CCP's organizational department, either inside the SPC for general positions or outside the SPC to the next higher level for senior leadership positions. In addition, the CCP's PLC, of which the court's president acts a core member as Party group secretary (党组书记 *dangzu shuji*) of the court, is in charge of supervising the work of all judicial organs (including courts, police bureaus and procuratorates) and is able to intervene in cases that are difficult or

[2] Under the premise of CCP's tight political control, it is possible, as observed by Ng and He (2017: 196), that in practice, at the micro-level, "slight non-conformities, deliberate leakages, veiled resistance to policies and offstage deviance from rules with respect to judicial decision-making are more subtle and difficult to detect".

complicated (for whatever reason), usually through providing instructions or directives to the court's leaders (who are PLC members) in PLC meetings. Given the all-encompassing leadership of the CCP over state organs, the implementation of CCP policies or directives is finally guaranteed by its top-down disciplinary inspection system. In the same vein, the order of power within the CCP also applies to the relationship between interpretations of the SPC and those made by other bodies. In practice, for instance, when it comes to legal interpretations made by prevailing authorities such as the State Council and its ministries, it is politically understandable that the SPC will tend to concur with them for the sake of maintaining conformity. In certain situations, in order to ensure that the interpretation or rule is implemented more effectively (particularly for those principles that are not purely designed for court trials), it has been good practice for the SPC to consult not only with the national legislature but also with the State Council and any ministry concerned, as well as to sometimes join with the State Council or relevant ministries in order to make a formal interpretation; this, ultimately, is half administrative and half judicial, but it is more effective politically speaking (Li 1997: 93, 109).

These constitutional and political channels, based on the CCP's control over the legislature and the SPC (Li 1997: 108), ensure that the SPC's exercise of legislative power cannot represent any substantial defiance or potential threat to the CCP-led People's Congress system in China's authoritarian context.

Given the SPC's legislative power to temporally specify the meaning of national laws through its judicial interpretation mechanism, the courts have relied heavily on the SPC's specific judicial interpretations to supply answers to judges making judicial decisions. Due to the SPC being the highest level of the court system, its judicial interpretation is pragmatically more authoritative than other kinds of legal interpretations in trial practice. In particular, as already noted, there is in practice no effective constitutional review system capable of challenging the SPC's judicial interpretations; moreover, the SPC's judicial interpretations, with their relative concreteness, matter much more in practice than national laws with their inherent ambiguities. In other words, the SPC's judicial interpretations have become de facto primary legislation for adjudication under China's positive law system.

Functions of the SPC's Judicial Interpretation

Owing to the institutionalization of the SPC's judicial interpretations, the court has come to play an important legal and political role in China's legal system.

First, from a legal point of view, judicial interpretations have evolved from being documents excluded from the scope of sources of law that shall be cited in the judgement to being consistently recognized as a formal legal basis that will be cited in the judgement, as illustrated in Table 3.1.

Given the basic legislative policy of "preferring the coarse to the fine", the SPC's judicial interpretation has come to play an indispensable legislative function in unifying the application of laws in trial practice, closing legal loopholes arising over time due to societal changes, etc. As already discussed, judicial interpretation has been formally recognized as a legal basis for adjudication and has been procedurally distinguished from the SPC's other informal judicial documents, as discussed in Chapter 4.

Moreover, due to the flexibility of the SPC's judicial interpretation, it has a significant political function, as reflected in the following two aspects.

First, it is able to incorporate politics into the process of applying the law in a way that achieves not only a "legal effect" but also a "political and social effect" in response to the political concerns of the changing society; this suggests that the Chinese approach to adjudication is more flexible and responsive to social concerns than (Western) legal formalism (Seppänen 2018: 35). This is particularly true when a social problem arises that may pose a threat to social stability and that is prioritized by the CCP agenda, such as a large number of migrant workers striving to be rewarded for their labour or a widespread scandal caused by some significant food safety incident. Due to the hysteretic effect of ordinary legislation, the SPC's judicial interpretation, as a political expedient, is able to temporally and flexibly respond to challenges posed by the changing society to the authoritarian regime. One relevant example occurred in 2008, when China's tainted milk scandal was exposed after sixteen babies in Gansu Province – who had been fed infant formula produced by one of China's leading infant formula producers – were diagnosed with kidney stones. This event quickly raised serious concerns about food safety and political corruption in the country, which were dire enough to pose a potential threat to the legitimacy of the Party-state due to the malfunction of food safety regulations across China (Ghazi-Tehrani and Pontell 2015). In response, the SPC produced a judicial interpretation of relevant provisions in China's Criminal Law that imposed severe penalties for all types of crimes relating to food safety, which achieved the effects of both punishment and deterrence in society (Regulation Editorial Center of People's Court Press 2014: 141).

Table 3.1 *Evolution of the status of Supreme People's Court's judicial interpretation in trial practice*

Time	Status and sources
1986	"The documents – produced by the SPC in order to implement various laws, such as Opinion, Reply, etc. – shall be implemented by courts, but prohibited from being directly quoted in legal instruments." Source: Reply on How Courts should Cite Statutes and Documents when Producing Formal Legal Instruments (关于人民法院制作的法律文书应如何引用法律规范性文件的批复 *guanyu renmin fayuan zhizuo de falü wenshu ying ruhe yingyong falü guifanxing wenjian de pifu*) (Supreme People's Court 1986).
1993	"The judicial interpretations of the SPC on [the] particular application of a law, shall be observed and implemented by all local people's courts and may be quoted in legal instruments." Source: Minutes of Meeting on National Trial Work of Economic Cases (全国经济审判工作座谈会纪要 *quanguo jingij shenpan gongzuo zuotanhui jiyao*) (Supreme People's Court 1993).
1997	"The judicial interpretation and relevant stipulations of law shall be quoted in the judicial instrument if used as the basis of the judgement or order of the people's court. When the judicial interpretation is quoted as the basis of the judgement or order, the applicable law shall be quoted first, and then the applicable judicial interpretation" (article 14). Source: Rules on the Work of Judicial Interpretation (Supreme People's Court 1997).
2000	"When a people's court applies the judicial interpretations of the SPC in adjudicating an administrative case, the people's court *shall* cite the judicial interpretation in the written judgement/ruling. When adjudicating an administrative case, a people's court *may* cite rules and other normative documents that are lawful and valid in the written judgement/ruling" (article 62). Source: Interpretations on Several Issues concerning the Application of the Administrative Procedure Law of the People's Republic of China (关于执行<中华人民共和国行政诉讼法>若干问题的解释 *guanyu zhixing zhonghua renmin gongheguo xingzheng susong fa ruogan wenti de jieshi*) (Supreme People's Court 2000).
2007	"Where the SPC approves or disapproves the death penalty of a case in accordance with these Provisions, the judgment documents *shall* quote the relevant articles of laws and judicial interpretations, and explain the reasons" (article 12).

Table 3.1 (*cont.*)

Time	Status and sources
	Source: Provisions on Certain Issues Concerning Review of Death Penalty Cases (关于复核死刑案件若干问题的规定 *guanyu fuhe sixing anjian ruogan wenti de guiding*) (Supreme People's Court 2007b).
2007	"After the implementation of the judicial interpretation, if the people's court deems it to be the basis of the judgement, the court shall cite it in the judicial documents. If the people's court simultaneously cites the law and the judicial interpretation as the basis of the judgement, the court shall cite the law first and then cite the judicial interpretation" (article 27).
	Source: Provisions on the Work Concerning Judicial Interpretation (Supreme People's Court 2007a).
2009	"If numerous regulatory documents are cited, the order of citation shall be as follows: laws and interpretation of laws, administrative regulations, local regulations, ordinances on autonomy or special ordinances, judicial interpretations" (article 2).
	Source: Provisions on Citation of Laws, Regulations and Other Normative Legal Documents in Adjudicative Documents (Supreme People's Court 2009).

Second, this approach is a flexible and efficient means of implementing top-down policies or directives from the central authorities. This political function is determined by China's dual Party-state structure, under which the SPC is responsible not only to the NPC, according to the Constitution, but also to the CCP, to which it is politically subordinate. The latter is more important than the former, as the former is also politically submissive to the leadership of the latter. It is thus clear that Chinese courts, unlike other state institutions, are never authorized to act as apolitical bodies (Liu 1997: 61). Therefore, in practice, the SPC under the CCP's leadership – usually through the CCP's PLC – may make judicial interpretations in order to implement policies or directives of the CCP. In some exceptional cases, relevant national laws of the NPC/NPCSC may be substantially changed – or, arguably, "violated" – in order to efficiently implement a CCP policy or directive. As already discussed, given that the Party-state, which incorporates the CCP and its subordinated SPC and NPC/NPCSC, is not separated but rather a dynamic political unity, the SPC's substantial change to or arguable "violation" of laws is in practice unable to be challenged. Accordingly, the CCP's absolute control makes it possible for the SPC's expansion of legislative power through the judicial interpretation mechanism to go beyond authorized limits, or arguably to serve the "law" by "breaking" a law (Li 1997: 111). In practice, moreover, these constitutionally suspicious or even arguably (from a purely legal perspective) ultra vires interpretations are tolerated and acquiesced to for the purpose of serving political ends (Li 1997: 105, 108). Before the promulgation of the SPC (1997) rule on judicial interpretations in 1997, the SPC did in fact make a large number of judicial interpretations of this kind. For instance, in 1999, the SPC interpreted numerous provisions of civil and commercial laws – including the General Rule of Civil Law and Contract Law – relevant to trials involving disputes over agricultural contract issues (Supreme People's Court 1999a); this, in reality, was done for the purpose of implementing the CCP's decisions on agriculture and rural work (W. Wang 2010: 52–53), which were passed in the third plenary session of the fifteenth CCP Central Committee (1998).

Of course, after the SPC passed a specific regulation on judicial interpretations in 1997, which could be distinguished procedurally from its informal judicial documents due to its formality, the political function of implementing the CCP's policies or directives has been largely performed through the SPC's informal judicial documents (see Chapter 4). For instance, after the CCP adopted the global development strategy referred to as One Belt and One Road (OBOR), the SPC (2015b) enacted a judicial document detailing its options for providing judicial services and safeguards supporting the implementation of OBOR.

Finally, apart from the legal and political function discussed earlier, the SPC's practice of lawmaking through the judicial interpretation mechanism has functioned as a legislative experiment for the lawmaking of the NPC/NPCSC. After the rules involved in the relevant judicial interpretations have been implemented in practice for a period of time and found to be suitable for China's sociopolitical conditions, they may be converted into NPC/NPCSC legislation, particularly for apolitical civil and commercial rules. For example, in the 2001 amendment to China's Marriage Law, the criteria of breakdown of marital relations stipulated in its article 34 was taken directly from the SPC's (1989) judicial interpretation of how the breakdown of marital relations should be defined when adjudicating divorce cases. As SPC Justice Hu Yunteng stated, judicial interpretation is an effective way of developing and experimenting with law in practice; it is not only an SPC achievement in terms of legislative application but also an important source of legislation itself. The development of Chinese law over the past decades has largely involved summarizing the experiences that emerged from the process of applying national laws by the courts, then making those local experiences that can be applied at the general level into a judicial interpretation of the SPC, which may subsequently be followed by the endorsement of the legislature (i.e. the NPC/NPCSC) and finally transformed into formal law by the national legislature (M. Li 2010: 73).

Of course, the extent to which rules first stipulated in SPC judicial interpretation can be transformed into national legislation depends largely on several factors: not only whether they can be applied at a general level across the country but also the extent to which they are apolitical and suitable for authoritarian politics. Given the capricious nature of authoritarianism, subject as it is to the decisions of political leaders, the more apolitical the rules in question, the more likely they are to be transformed into concrete national legislation. Otherwise, if legislated, a rule is usually open in nature, providing a thumbnail sketch of the parameters of regulation, and taking the form of principle-like pronouncements with wording permitting broad discretion (Corne 2002: 374) in order to cover all possible scenarios that may arise in the authoritarian context.

Conclusion

Generally speaking, there has been no substantial difference in terms of the legislature enacting general rules that "were often so general that it required specification with greater detail in order to implementing them, for it was unrealistic to describe what was occurring as the mere implementation of legislative rules" (Tushnet 2014: 95). It has even been argued that, realistically, the implementers were in fact making law. For example, in the three-branch model, it appears as though executive officials in the US context were exercising legislative power (Tushnet 2014: 95). This may be the general case in a liberal context in which there is a democratically accountable parliamentary system and an effective judicial review system implemented by courts with political independence. By contrast, however, as already discussed, under China's socialist legal system with its rejection of the separation of powers, the legislative power has been allocated in a unique way, such that courts with their relatively specialized legal knowledge have been an important means of implementing the Party-state's policies and directives. Constitutionally, the SPC's judicial interpretation, which enables it to exercise substantial legislative power, may be argued to be unconstitutional, since the Constitution does not plainly authorize the court to exercise any kind of legislative function (Hong 2017: 14–19; Li 1997: 92–93). Nonetheless, as already discussed, such a normative argument in fact makes very little sense in China's authoritarian context. Over its multiple decades of development, the SPC's judicial interpretation has indeed become a de facto source of primary legislation under China's positive law system. It has been pivotal in both China's lawmaking and trial practice, since it is able not only to meet political needs in reality but also to implement the top-down directives or policies of the hierarchical superior authorities by translating them into legal language for use in the courts. As a formal legal basis of Chinese law by which judges can make judicial decisions, the SPC's judicial interpretation has maintained a hybrid quality of political flexibility and legal formalism that is highly suited to China's authoritarian regime. Such a mechanism first and foremost adopts a legalistic approach to adjudication in a way that incorporates legal formalism into making the rules for such adjudication; while politically temporal, these rules are also relatively stable and predictable, particularly for apolitical cases. On the other hand, its political flexibility facilitates the effective involvement of increasingly professional courts in the implementation of the policies and directives of hierarchically superior political authorities. Unlike the legal nihilism once praised during the Cultural Revolution, the SPC's judicial interpretation – in line with China's political rhetoric stressing the role of law in society – is able to strengthen the legality of the authoritarian system, further solidifying the legitimacy of China's authoritarian regime by using law as an effective instrument for improving its governance.

4

The Judicial Document as Informal State Law

Modern courts in major jurisdictions around the world have increasingly engaged in lawmaking when deciding cases.[1] Distinctively, China's judicial interpretation has become a unique judicial lawmaking mechanism that does not involve a concrete case or controversy (in contrast to the more commonly encountered situation in which judges do not initiate the judicial lawmaking process until a case or controversy is brought before them). Moreover, apart from the SPC's formal judicial interpretations, courts may even engage in informal judicial lawmaking through judicial documents (S. Wang 2018; Lo 2016; He 2013; Xi 2013; Liebman 2007b; Peerenboom 2007). This chapter investigates such an informal judicial lawmaking enterprise, which has been largely underexplored particularly from a socio-legal perspective. It finds that due to China's instrumentalist legal system with its lack of case law, the courts, with no delegation from the legislature, have been exercising and attempting to expand judicial lawmaking authority by making informal state law through the issuance of judicial documents (司法文件 *sifa wenjian*). However, these judicial documents have no relation to concrete cases or controversies. This informal judicial lawmaking mechanism exists in a "twilight zone", discussed in this chapter, and through judicial documents the courts are able to make judicial decisions on the basis of statutory laws instead of non-statutory sources; as such, they are able to meet the legalistic requirement of adjudication in an authoritarian context. It also enables the courts to fill the gaps in the law, in order to respond to a changing society, subnational diversity and the capricious politics of CCP in a way that has embedded authoritarian political resilience in China's legal system.

Conceptually, official documents are the official paperwork produced by governing bodies, distinguished from personal papers, media

[1] The existing scholarship has focused on such judicial lawmaking enterprise in democracies (Stephan 2018; Zhang 2016; Steiner 2015; Ursin 2014; Lehavi 2011; Fyrnys 2011; Steinman 2004; Tomlinson 1997; Moens 1992; Cappelletti 1981; Devlin 1976; Friedland 1974).

publications and other kinds of non-governmental documents (Wu 1995: 25). In China, these documents are an essential instrument for all Party and state organs, including the courts, and play a critical role in the regime. To standardize, systemize and improve the management of official documents, the General Office of the Central Committee of the CCP and the State Council (2012) jointly issued the Regulations on the Work of Party and Government Organs on the Handling of Official Documents (党政机关公文处理工作条例 *dangzheng jiguan gongwen chuli gongzuo tiaoli*) in 2012. Chinese politics, as opposed to democratic politics, has been called "documentary politics", which refers to the "rule by documents" process within this oligarchic setting (Wu 1995; Jing 2016; Shi 2008; Xie 2006). Official documents, disseminated step by step through the ranks of the political hierarchy, work like a central nervous system, linking relevant political bodies and offering guidance and directives for political judgments and criteria for policy choices (Wu 1995: 26).

In the era of Mao Zedong, and up to 1978, when China had not yet devoted itself to constructing a new legal system and rules, the courts, like other subordinate political bodies of the CCP, were administered entirely via such documents (C. Wang 2010: 3). In producing documents in their respective area, the courts, as a state apparatus, were no different than other political authorities subordinate to the CCP. For example, in 1957, the SPC, together with the SPP and the Ministry of Public Security, produced the Joint Directive on the Implementation of the NPCSC's Resolution on Adjudicating Cases Concerning Anti-revolutionaries by the People's Courts (关于执行全国人民代表大会常务委员会<关于对反革命分子的管制一律由人民法院判决的决定>中若干具体问题的联合指示 *guanyu zhixing quanguo renmin daibiao dahui changwu weiyuanhui guanyu dui fan geming fenzi de guanzhi yilv you renmin fayuan panjue de jueding*) for the purpose of attacking the CCP's political rivals (Supreme People's Court, Supreme People's Procuratorate and Ministry of Public Security 1957). This is such a document with binding force on courts.

After 1978, Deng Xiaoping realized the importance of a relatively stable legal order for the survival of the CCP and the prosperity of the country (2008 [1978]: 141). Since then, China's legislature, the NPC/NPCSC, has built a comprehensive socialist legislative regime comprising thousands of statutory laws. Both the NPC, as the highest legislative body, and the SPC, as the highest adjudicative body, have created specific rules on the scope of statutory laws that can be directly cited as the basis on which judges make judicial decisions.[2] In this regard, it is a basic principle that judges are to apply, rather than interpret or make, the law, and that statutory laws rather than policies or political documents produced by non-legislative authorities are to be the legal basis of court judgments. Of course, this is by no means to say that the courts under the CCP's leadership have abandoned the practice of producing documents. Rather, in line with the regulation of central leadership (General Office of the Central Committee of the Chinese Communist Party and the State Council 2012), the SPC has provided a definition of official documents for the courts, as well as detailed methods of producing them, through the Measures for the Handling of People's Court's Documents (人民法院公文处理办法 *renmin fayuan gongwen chuli banfa*) (hereinafter "the Measures"), issued on 16 November 2012. Article 3 of the Measures states that:

> The official documents of the people's courts come into being in the course of adjudication and administration with legal effect and standard form. They are the important tools for carrying out the guidelines and policies of the Party, implementing national laws, issuing judicial interpretations, directing, arranging and discussing the work, requesting instructions and replying to requests, reporting information, and exchanging experiences.
>
> (Supreme People's Court 2012)

Interestingly, in practice, it has been common for the courts to engage in judicial lawmaking enterprise by producing judicial documents, many of which have been published in the SPC *Gazette* or by local courts. These judicial documents fall outside the scope of statutory laws, which means they should not be used as a legal basis for court judgments. However, because it is a political subordinate to the CCP, a superior court produces more than just judicial and administrative documents – it also produces political documents, with various titles,[3] as illustrated in Table 4.1.

[2] According to the Legislation Law, which was promulgated by the NPC (2015), and the PCLRAD, which was promulgated by the SPC (2009), a judge shall cite the following types of statutory laws for judicial decision-making: (1) national laws created by the NPC or its standing committee, or their interpretations; (2) judicial interpretations produced by the SPC; (3) administrative regulations enacted by the State Council, or their statutory interpretations; (4) local regulations enacted by the LPC or its standing committee of the prefecture-level city or at the provincial level; (5) ordinances on autonomy and special ordinances enacted by the LPCs of national autonomous areas; (6) the administrative rules of the departments under the State Council.

[3] The titles as listed in article 9 of the Measures include "order (writ)" (命令[令] *mingling [ling]*), "resolution" (议案 *yi'an*), "report" (报告 *baogao*), "decision" (决定 *jueding*), "regulation" (规定 *guiding*), "announcement and circular" (公告通告 *gonggao tonggao*),

Table 4.1 *Types of Chinese court documents*

	Purpose	Nature of norms	Influence over the adjudication
Judicial documents	Judicial lawmaking, offer concrete interpretation or new rules for adjudication	Justiciable, applicable rules and principles	Direct, de facto binding force on inferior courts
Administrative documents	Non-judicial lawmaking, guide the administration of courts, including personnel, finance and trial tasks	Administrative, non-justiciable rules, principles and guidelines	Indirect (normally at judge's discretion), no legal effect over the adjudication
Political documents	Ideological propaganda	Political and ideological guidelines	Almost none

The first is judicial documents, including the concrete interpretation of statutory laws and the creation of new rules for adjudication. The second is administrative documents, covering topics such as personnel, finance and office space. The third is political documents, created for an ideological purpose, such as documents transmitting important instructions or information from superior political authorities to the judges. Administrative and political documents are different from judicial documents, which have a lawmaking function, and cannot be applied directly by judges in practice.

The SPC often produces documents for the ideological purpose of asking the courts to study the speeches of the state leader or for briefing the courts on the CCP's important meetings, particularly after a plenary meeting of the CCP Central Committee. In practice, administrative or political documents usually are disregarded by legal professionals as they

"notice" (通知 *tongzhi*), "circulation" (通报 *tongbao*), "reply" (批复 *pifu*), "request" (请示 *qingshi*), "letter" (函 *han*) and "summary of minutes" (纪要 *jiyao*).

are not directly relevant to judicial decision-making and inapplicable to adjudication. As one senior judge says:

> We usually care almost nothing about these documents asking the judges to study, for example, a briefing of the CCP National Congress, or the speech of the CCP General Secretary, with no applicable rule for adjudication. These kinds of documents, though produced by the SPC, have almost nothing to do with our daily judicial work in the court, although the courts may organize some relevant learning activities as required, but merely for political formality.
>
> (Interview 50-17-NSSZ01)

Of course, the atmosphere created by these political or administrative documents may exert indirect influence over judges. If there is a need, for whatever reason, to implement these administrative or political documents in adjudicating disputes, a superior court may engage in judicial lawmaking by producing a judicial document.

Judicial documents, which involve lawmaking practice, have played an indispensable role in judicial decision-making and are used by judges to adjudicate relevant cases (Interviews 50-17-NSSZ01, 51-17-NSSZ02). Actually, it has been common practice for Chinese courts to produce judicial documents involving specific, substantive and procedural rules. The rules involved have become a robust, though informal and mostly inaccessible, basis for judicial decision-making. Due to China's instrumentalist legal system, the conditions, the extent and the manner in which the courts engage in judicial lawmaking by producing judicial documents have been examined in the following from a socio-legal perspective. In particular, it explains how judicial documents can be formed without a clear legal basis and even in contravention of an explicit prohibition from the legislature, how they function as a robust basis for judicial decision-making, why they usually exist in the twilight zone between legal and illegal and why such an informal mechanism is suitable for maintaining the political resilience of China's authoritarian regime.[4]

Judicial Lawmaking and Informal State Law

Traditionally, the separation of powers doctrine means the legislative, executive and judicial powers are vested in different branches of

[4] The existing literature has primarily focused on documentary politics in China and the non-judicial function of Chinese courts (Finder 2019).

government though with various forms in different regimes, and judges have not been allowed to usurp the lawmaking function of the legislature (Devlin 1976); however, there is no doubt that judges not only declare existing law but also make law.[5] In the process of adjudicating a case, interpretation of a statute on the part of the judge is almost unavoidable. As Lord Diplock states, "courts by the very nature of their function are compelled to act as legislator" (1978: 266). The judicial lawmaking process is different from the general legislative process in the parliament (Cappelletti 1981: 42), as judicial lawmaking activities are normally connected with particular cases and controversies. Of course, the judge, unlike other political actors, should be an impartial adjudicator and ensure a fair hearing for the parties concerned.

Case law, in various forms in different jurisdictions, has been the primary channel for judicial lawmaking activities. The US courts utilize a practice of prospective overruling, whereby a court has the authority to "announce in advance a new better rule or interpretation for future cases whenever it has reached a decision that an old rule established by precedent is unsound" (Steiner 2015: 2). As Posner states, appellate judges are occasional de facto legislators and "judges may have as many degrees of legislative freedom, albeit only in the subset of legalistically indeterminate cases, as formal legislators do" (2008: 81–82). In France, a civil law jurisdiction, judges must not usurp legislative lawmaking; however, judges do develop the vast majority of jurisprudence, the equivalent to case law in France (Bell 2006: 70–72). Case law increasingly plays a significant role in both common law and civil law jurisdictions (Steiner 2015: 14). Of course, higher courts may go beyond case law and demonstrate lawmaking power – primarily focused on procedural issues – by providing practice directions or issuing advisory opinions; as practised by certain courts in Canada, India, Sweden, Finland and some states of the USA (Cappelletti 1981: 45).

A growing scholarly literature indicates that the traditional dichotomy between common law and civil law is being challenged, for example, in Europe mostly with a civil law tradition and the USA with a common law tradition (Xi 2013: 40). Comparatively, in former socialist countries, due to the lack of case law, the supreme courts provide general guidelines for legal interpretation that have binding force over lower courts (Cappelletti 1981: 46).

[5] The term "judiciary law" was used by Jeremy Bentham to indicate that the judge truly makes a law (Barwick 1980).

In China, the SPC's judicial interpretations of statutory laws, made with congressional delegation, have formal legal force. Nonetheless, these informal judicial lawmaking activities of the courts are not undertaken in response to concrete cases or controversies and have no congressional delegation. Some scholars have noticed that, although the subnational courts are prohibited from lawmaking without an explicit congressional delegation, they have developed a survival strategy by which to make new legal rules to fill the gaps that result from the inadequate responsiveness of the law to local affairs (Xi 2013: 39). The legal rules created by the courts range from determining the applicable law for certain issues to filling the gaps in statutory laws and producing novel laws (Xi 2013: 56). However, this does not address the de facto legal force of these rules, nor the ways in which these kinds of legal rules are created and applied by the courts without the formal delegation of the legislature.

Socio-legal studies have shown that, contrary to the belief that the courts are passive under an authoritarian regime, Chinese courts have demonstrated considerable innovation in their application of statutory laws and issuance of judicial suggestions. The courts may strategically seek support from the Party to enhance their authority and undertake innovative measures that are not stipulated by formal statutory laws (He 2013: 20). The courts may even expand their own jurisdictions, strike down regulations that are not compatible with national laws or create legal requirements, all with little legislative basis (Kellogg 2007: 141). As Xin He observes, although the power of the courts is ostensibly limited, there is room for them to manoeuvre in China's current political structure; as such, "under the seemingly peaceful surface of iron control exists dynamic turbulences of conflict, repression, resistance, competition, compromise, and cooperation" (2007: 203–205). Likewise, given the wide discretion of Chinese judges, some courts have issued decisions "that appear directly to challenge existing legal norms or consciously to break new legal ground" (Liebman 2007a: 632).

The judicial document involves judicial lawmaking enterprise. Given that the courts have demonstrated significant innovation in lawmaking enterprise, it is important, from both practical and theoretical viewpoints, to understand the practice of judicial documents as distinguished from formal statutory laws and in particular their nuances. Judicial documents can involve the concrete interpretation of statutes or the creation of new legal rules; but they take an informal form, as the courts normally do not make them accessible to the public, as they do with other formal laws, primarily because of the lack of congressional delegation. In this regard, judicial documents cannot be easily categorized as formal statutory laws. Since judicial documents take various forms – they may be written or unwritten, governmental or non-governmental, and transparent or non-transparent – they more readily meet the standards of informal laws (Friedman 1998: 37).[6] Judicial documents are also informal in the sense that they cannot be officially used as a legal basis for adjudication. However, the judicial document is produced in a top-down approach, often through consultation with senior judges with rich trial experience in respective areas. To a large extent, the judicial document is a type of informal state law with binding force, distinguished from informal customs with no binding force. Hence, it is intellectually desirable to understand how judicial documents have become symbiotic with existing statutory laws, how they have been mixed with statutory laws in the process of judicial decision-making, the forms in which they exist in practice, the extent to which their existence has been politically embedded in China's legal system, the ways in which they have enabled the courts to translate politics into adjudication and how they have covertly influenced judicial decision-making. Understanding these issues could be also helpful to enrich the theoretical understanding of related concepts, such as authoritarian political resilience, informal law, political embeddedness, judicial lawmaking and information asymmetry in an authoritarian context.

The SPC's Judicial Documents: Formal and Informal State Laws

The Provisions afford the SPC the right to perform judicial lawmaking through the formal mechanism of judicial interpretations. In contrast, while judicial documents do not possesses a similar legal basis for adjudication, they are still an essential tool for the adjudicative and administrative work of the courts. Despite the SPC's judicial interpretations becoming formal law, the SPC still retains its lawmaking practice of interpreting laws in the form of judicial documents, which have a similar lawmaking function to the SPC's formal judicial interpretations.[7] In fact,

6 Friedman (1998: 46) believes it is impossible for a legal system to be purely formal or informal; invariably, it is a mixture of both.

7 "Judicial documents", which may sometimes be used interchangeably with "judicial interpretation documents" (司法解释性质文件 *sifa jieshi xingzhi wenjian*), refer to those documents involving judicial lawmaking functions, rather than the political or administrative documents of the SPC without judicial lawmaking functions.

after decades of the SPC interpreting laws on the basis of the NPCSC's delegation, in 2011, the NPCSC made wholesale changes to the legislation work plan to safeguard the uniformity of the legislative regime. This forced the SPC to conduct a systematic clean-up of all its formal judicial interpretations and informal judicial documents. In particular, the local courts, which had not been delegated any judicial lawmaking authority by the NPCSC, have been explicitly prohibited from creating documents that involve judicial lawmaking activities, such as interpreting statutory laws (Supreme People's Court and Supreme People's Procuratorate 2012). Apart from judicial interpretations that had been put into practice, the SPC also retained a large number of informal judicial documents. These were finalized and officially published by the SPC in the Compilation of the SPC's Judicial Interpretations (1949–2013) (Zhou 2015). This retention of previous judicial documents was tacitly agreed to by the NPCSC, which indicates that at that time it endorsed the SPC's judicial lawmaking practice through the mechanism of judicial documents.

It is easy to argue that the SPC's judicial lawmaking practice through informal judicial documents has no constitutional basis, as the Constitution of the PRC does not permit the SPC to exercise judicial lawmaking power of this kind. This is a power that is meant to be exclusively exercised by the legislative authority, the NPCSC, instead of the SPC, a judicial authority.[8] However, because China adopts the People's Congress system, the NPCSC acts as the executive body of the NPC and actually has a higher constitutional status than other NPC-created state organs, including the SPC. At the same time, the NPC is subject to the CCP's leadership in practice and the NPCSC is a political subordinate of the CCP. In this regard, the NPCSC has the final constitutional authority over determining whether an issue or practice is constitutional. If a matter is unconstitutional according to the NPCSC, it can prohibit it. Therefore, the delegation of the NPCSC, mentioned earlier, is the basis for the SPC's judicial lawmaking function via judicial documents, and against which no constitutional or political barriers can be erected. Due to this, it is common practice for judicial documents produced by the SPC to be effectively enforced by lower-level courts.

Given that the SPC's formal judicial interpretations are a type of statutory law, courts are constitutionally required to enforce them.

[8] Relevant articles are articles 62 and 67 of the Constitution of the PRC and articles 45 and 104 of the Legislation Law.

In contrast, the SPC's judicial documents fall outside the scope of statutory laws, so their enforcement is largely based on the political hierarchy of China's courts. In practice, the SPC's judicial documents are normally issued and circulated to lower-level courts through an "official notice" (通知 *tongzhi*), according to articles 9 and 16 of the Measures (Supreme People's Court 2012). These courts will further disseminate the notice to the next level of the courts within their respective jurisdictions in sequence. Implementing an official notice from a higher-level court is a political requirement for all lower-level courts. This is normally indicated at the end of the notice in the following format: "[The courts] are required to act in accordance with the above notice and report in a timely manner the information on implementation and problems encountered to the SPC" (Supreme People's Court 2006).

The SPC's informal judicial documents function as a bridge between law and politics. On the one hand, given that a judicial document is non-statutory, the SPC, as the CCP's political subordinate, is able to implement the will of higher political authorities through the flexible mechanism of judicial documents. On the other hand, given the higher adjudicative status of the SPC, it is understandable that the SPC's judicial documents will be observed by the lower courts when adjudicating relevant cases. However, judicial documents, though effectively implemented in trial, inhabit a twilight zone due to their lack of an explicit constitutional status.

Political Resilience of Judicial Documents

In comparison with the SPC's judicial interpretations, judicial documents have a crucial function in China due to the flexibility and adaptability afforded by the absence of lengthy statutory procedures by which to abide. This allows a court to respond to the will of a higher authority by swiftly and efficiently translating its directive into a rule of adjudication. This is clearly compatible with a crucial feature of a single-party authoritarian state, which is that there must be an effective channel for all political subordinates, including the courts, to swiftly and efficiently respond to and implement the will of the higher and ultimate political authority. For instance, if the CCP launches a special nationwide political movement to address a particular problem (Schoenhals 1999), all state organs will make efforts to enforce it cooperatively as a political task. In this vein, the SPC will immediately produce relevant judicial documents to respond to a directive or policy from the central authority, ensuring that it can be carried out effectively inside the court system.

It is common practice for the SPC to be notified, asked or negotiated with to enforce a decision or policy of a political authority inside the Party, such as the Central Committee of the CCP, the State Council or the NPCSC. The heads of these organizations are members of the CCP Politburo Standing Committee (seven members in total), with a higher political status than the president of the SPC, who is merely a member of the CCP Central Committee (more than 200 members in total). For example, after the General Office of the CCP Central Committee and the General Office of the State Council jointly produced the Opinions on Carrying out the Special Work for Combating Commercial Bribery (关于开展治理商业贿赂专项工作的意见 *guanyu kaizhan shangye huilu zhuanxiang gongzuo de yijian*) (hereinafter "the Opinions") on 8 February 2006, the SPC immediately issued the Notice on Bringing into Full Play the Functional Role of Adjudication and Properly Handling the Special Work for Combating Commercial Bribery (关于充分发挥审判职能作用切实做好治理商业贿赂专项工作的通知 *zuigao renmin fayuan guanyu congfen fahui shenpan zhineng zuoyong qieshi zuohao zhili shangye huilu zhuanxiang gongzuo de tongzhi*) on 5 April 2006. This judicial document provided detailed guidance and principles on how the courts were to perform their judicial function for the purpose of implementing the Opinions (Supreme People's Court 2006). After the NPCSC released the Decision of the NPCSC on the Ban on Evil Organizations, and Prevention and Suppression of Evil Religious Activity (全国人民代表大会常务委员会关于取缔邪教组织防范和惩治邪教活动的决定 *quanguo renmin daibiao dahui changwu weiyuanhui guanyu quid xiejiao zuzhi fangfan he chengzhi xiejiao huodong de jueding*) to combat the threat of Falun Gong on 30 October 1999, the SPC immediately issued a judicial document to all lower-level courts, providing concrete rules for adjudication as well as guidelines and principles for judicial decision-making concerning the relevant issues involved (Supreme People's Court 1999b).

Because the SPC's judicial documents are not formal statutory laws, it is common for the SPC, as the CCP's political subordinate, to jointly produce a document with other CCP-led political authorities to cooperatively and efficiently implement an inter-agency policy or decision nationwide. For example, in 2014 the SPC, the SPP, the Ministry of Public Security, the Ministry of Justice and the National Health and Family Planning Commission (2014) jointly produced a document providing concrete rules and principles on how to punish doctor-related illegal and criminal activities.

To enhance its judicial credibility with the public and ultimately strengthen its authoritarian governance, China has undertaken fundamental judicial reforms to create a more professional and transparent judicial system. In principle, the SPC's judicial documents are published in the SPC *Gazette* and other publications. Of course, in certain circumstances, a document may be officially identified as confidential with a confidentiality period. Article 10 of the Measures provides for three types of confidentiality: "strictly confidential" (绝密 *juemi*), "confidential" (机密 *jimi*), and "secret" (秘密 *mimi*) (Supreme People's Court 2012). Given the sensitivity – or, perhaps, political sensitivity – of some matters, judicial documents involving concrete interpretations of statutory laws and specific rules for adjudication may be sent to a limited number of judges at a certain level of administrative leadership and above, such as the presidents of all local courts. For example, in September 2017, when the annual BRICS (Brazil, Russia, India, China and South Africa) summit was held in Xiamen, to make a good impression for all overseas participants a judicial document was produced for only senior judges (the leaders of relevant courts or tribunals having jurisdiction over cases related to the Xiamen jurisdiction). This stipulated that court rulings for the jurisdiction were to be suspended during the period of the summit. Regarding the accessibility of judicial documents, some are categorized as only to be read by the judges being asked to implement the document in a designated office, and only when the officer in charge is present, and no notes are to be taken when reading it (Interview 59-18-HZ04). It is a common practice for some confidential judicial documents to be circulated, in a top-down, level-by-level fashion, to a select number of responsible cadres of a certain administrative rank at internal meetings. And these cadres are only allowed to read the document at the meeting; they are not allowed to retain a copy for their later use.

Thus, the SPC's judicial interpretations and judicial documents play different roles in China's adjudication. Constitutionally, the courts must apply statutory laws, including the SPC's judicial interpretations, as they are legally formalized for judicial decision-making. However, to maintain the political resilience of the authoritarian regime, judicial documents, which can be produced flexibly and expediently to respond to the will of the higher political authority or changing social needs, are indispensable when static statutory laws are insufficient to accomplish a social or political task deemed necessary by the state. Given the CCP's complete political dominance, the courts can easily be mobilized to join a nationwide campaign in whatever form this task may require. The SPC's informal judicial documents, involving specific interpretations of statutory laws and the creation of new rules for adjudication, play a crucial role in adjudicating cases. It is possible that some judicial documents, after being used as an expedient for a particular situation, may later be approved as suitable for wider social needs and translated into a statutory law by the legislative authority.

Judicial Documents as Informal State Laws in Local Courts

The NPCSC has not delegated any judicial lawmaking power to local courts and the SPC has tried to prohibit local courts from producing judicial documents, since they have a judicial lawmaking nature (Supreme People's Court and Supreme People's Procuratorate 2012). However, it is still common for local courts to perform a judicial lawmaking function by producing various judicial documents that, for instance, interpret statutory laws and make new rules for adjudication within their respective jurisdictions. In practice, these judicial documents also have de facto binding force on the judges in adjudication. Interestingly, local courts have circumvented the prohibition on producing judicial documents by producing them under different names (see discussion later in this section). Some local courts, such as the Shanghai High People's Court (2006) and the Jiangsu High People's Court (2011), have stipulated specific details of the conditions under which and how the court shall produce judicial documents. Given the lack of an explicit legal basis, the judicial documents of local courts also exist in a twilight zone, although they are tolerated by the SPC and relevant legislative authorities. Of course, such acceptance may indicate the embeddedness of judicial documents in China's legal system.

Prohibiting the Judicial Documents of Local Courts?

In principle, in China's legal system, the courts are merely the executors of the legislature and exercise their judicial power to adjudicate cases in accordance with the statutory laws provided by the legislative authority. It is understandable that the practice of producing judicial documents by local courts is controversial regarding its legality, due to its lack of an explicit legal basis or delegation by the NPCSC. Indeed, it has been criticized for encroaching on the NPCSC's legislative authority, which is its exclusive remit (Interviews 50-17-NSSZ01, 52-17-NSSZ03). Although the judges, as adjudicators, may have their own understanding of statutory laws, this does not mean that the courts are allowed to exercise judicial lawmaking power by producing a judicial document to interpret or make a law, given the lack of an explicit statutory basis or permission from the NPCSC. In 1987 and 2012, the SPC produced two formal documents that prohibited local courts from formulating judicial documents like those of the SPC, which had been given the exclusive remit to do so for trial practice. The Notice on Prohibiting Local People's Courts and People's Procuratorates from Formulating Judicial Documents (关于地方人民法院、人民检察院不得制定司法解释性质文件的通知 *guanyu defang renmin fayuan renmin jianchayuan bude zhiding sifa jieshi xingzhi wenjian de tongzhi*) states that:

> In accordance with the relevant provisions of the Resolution of the Standing Committee of the National People's Congress on Strengthening Legal Interpretations, issues concerning legal applications in trials by people's courts shall be interpreted by the SPC; and issues concerning law applications in prosecutorial affairs by people's procuratorates shall be interpreted by the SPP. From the date of issuance of this Notice, local people's courts and people's procuratorates shall not formulate judicial documents that are universally applicable within their respective jurisdiction or involve legal applications such as "guiding opinions" (指导意见 *zhidao yijian*) and "regulations" (规定 *guiding*), and shall not quote other normative documents formulated in legal instruments.
>
> (Supreme People's Court and Supreme People's Procuratorate 2012)

This prohibition does not forbid local courts from producing all types of documents. Rather, it reiterates the NPCSC's exclusive delegation to the SPC to formally interpret laws in trial practice. According to the Measures (Supreme People's Court 2012), the superior courts are permitted to produce other relevant documents that can be implemented by lower courts. In practice, the local courts have retained their practice of producing judicial documents. It is inevitable and necessary for local courts to exercise judicial lawmaking authority through documents in light of their local situations because, in practice, judges strongly desire concrete legal rules or instructions from superior courts where the relevant statutory laws are ambiguous or insufficient for judicial decision-making (Interviews 50-17-NSSZ01, 60-18-YJJL01).

Comparatively, in a jurisdiction with judicial independence, such as the USA, if the formal sources of the law fail the judge or if there are cases for which the formal legal system has no answers, a judge may seek the answer to a case based on considerations of social utility or "any other" considerations (Bodenheimer 1974: 349). As a matter of practice, it is proper for the judge to resort to notions of "natural justice and reason", sometimes blended with supporting arguments resting on other informal sources of law (such as public policies, social trends, customs and accepted moral standards), without any special authorization from positive law if the positive sources do not provide an answer to the point of law to be adjudicated, or where its provisions are vague or susceptible to different interpretations (Bodenheimer 1974: 350–351, 356).

The situation is different in China, where the courts have no political independence and, in practice, the NPCSC still insists that judges merely apply statutory laws (S. Wang 2018: 1085–1086). Given the lack of a doctrine of precedent, judicial documents play a crucial role in adapting static statutory laws and guiding judges to make appropriate judicial decisions according to changing social and political conditions. Judges state that if the relevant statute is insufficient or there is a legal lacuna they have difficulty making judicial decisions. In this situation, the court may make a request to the next higher-level court for specific instructions, either through informal consultation with judges from the superior court or the formal internal request system (Minzner 2009). Judges will feel safer making a judicial decision if the legal loophole involved in the case is closed by a higher-level court in the form of judicial documents (Interview 60-18-YJJL01). Judges' dependence on judicial documents indicates their indispensability for adjudication in practice.

Circumvention of the Prohibition on Judicial Lawmaking Documents by Local Courts

According to Article 127 of the Constitution of the PRC, courts at higher levels supervise the administration of justice by those at lower levels. In particular, the SPC has issued the Certain Opinions on Regulating Trial Relations Between Courts in a Vertical Relationship (关于规范上下级人民法院审判业务关系的若干意见 *zuigao renmin fayuan guanyu guifan shangxia ji renmin fayuan shenpan yewu guanxi de ruogan yijian*), which state:

> The high people's court shall provide guidance on the trial of cases to the local people's courts at various levels and the special people's courts under its jurisdiction through trying cases, formulating documents in respect of

> trial, issuing typical cases, convening trial work meetings, organizing judge training, etc. The documents in respect to trial work formulated by the high people's court shall be adopted through discussion at the judicial committee. If the SPC finds documents in respect of trial formulated by the high people's court are in conflict with the existing laws and judicial interpretation, it shall order them to make corrections ... The intermediate people's court shall guide the trial of the people's courts at the basic level through trying cases, summarizing trial experience, and organizing judge training.
>
> (Supreme People's Court 2010d)

Interestingly, the superior courts are constitutionally permitted to produce relevant judicial documents for the purpose of guiding the trial work of lower courts. In other words, while there is an explicit prohibition on local courts producing judicial documents, they may produce judicial documents in the name of guidance. Local courts have circumvented the prohibition by producing judicial documents with different titles, to distinguish them from those explicitly prohibited. These include "summaries of minutes" (会议纪要 *huiyi jiyao*), "adjudicative guidances" (裁判指引 *caipan zhiyin*), "implementation opinions" (实施意见 *shishi yijian*), "implementation rules" (实施细则 *shishi xize*) and "guiding opinions". In practice, these documents have substantially enabled local courts to perform a judicial lawmaking function if the statutory laws are ambiguous or insufficient on certain matters.

Normally, before issuing this kind of judicial document, the court holds a conference or meeting at which representative judges from inferior courts are usually asked to attend. Afterwards, a formal "summary of minutes" is collectively issued by the Adjudication Committee (or its subcommittee) or a subdivision of the superior court (He 2012a). The judge explained that, given the higher authority of the superior courts, it is appropriate for the committee or a subdivision, comprising experienced senior judges, to produce the summary of minutes, which includes clarification of relevant statutory laws and new legal rules for adjudication based on the trial experience of the members of the judicial committee. In this way, the summary of minutes can largely meet the practical needs of localities (Interview 50-17-NSSZ01). Procedurally, the committee or division deliberates relevant issues and makes a decision in a collective manner.[9] However, given the decisive authority of the

[9] A major symbol of collective approval is the formulation of a document. Such a form of decision-making is rooted in the CCP's tradition of producing documents (Wu 1995: 26).

president of the court, it is possible that the president may strategically infiltrate his or her personal preference into the collective decision, regardless of the methods that may be used (Interviews 56-18-HZ01, 57-18-HZ02).

From a legal point of view, this "summary of minutes" falls outside the scope of statutory laws and, to a certain extent, can be criticized as encroaching upon the legislative authority of the People's Congress, because it involves a judicial lawmaking exercise. One senior judge said that, to avoid public criticism, "the courts are extremely cautious in producing this kind of document. Strategically, the courts normally choose not to actively publish these documents if they are produced, and they are often circulated internally to relevant judges from the inferior courts handling the cases in the relevant area, for fear of being criticized for encroaching upon the lawmaking authority [of the People's Congress]" (Interview 50-17-NSSZ01). For instance, the normal practice of the Intermediate People's Court of B (a pseudonym) was that the court would hold internal meetings or conferences for the lower-court judges under its supervision for the purpose of guiding their trial work, exchanging trial experiences or delivering relevant new policies from higher authorities. Normally, lower-level courts will send representative judges in relevant trial areas to the meeting, during which the new judicial documents will be made available. Afterwards, the participating judges will distribute these documents to the relevant parts of the courts to which they belong (Interviews 50-17-NSSZ01, 52-17-NSSZ03, 53-17-NSSZ04). It is possible that, in some developed areas, the superior court may disseminate some judicial documents to lower courts directly through the internet, such as the court's internal network system.

As the dissemination of these judicial documents is normally not officially publicized, it is no surprise that, in practice, some junior judges with very limited experience may not even be aware of them. As a result, these junior judges sometimes need to seek advice from experienced senior judges in their relevant trial areas. The newly established Professional Judges Committee (专业法官会议 *zhuanye faguan huiyi*) in China's courts, comprising senior judges from various trial areas, offers professional advice and expertise to junior judges when they encounter difficult or complicated cases (Interviews 50-17-NSSZ01, 61-19-FS01, 63-19-FSSD01).

As the summary of minutes involves judicial lawmaking enterprise and is produced by superior courts, it has a de facto binding force on judges from lower-level courts when they are adjudicating relevant cases. If the judicial decision does not follow the concrete legal rules set out in the summary of minutes produced by superior courts, it can be easily reversed on appeal, which is disadvantageous for the annual assessment of the court's performance.[10] It's admitted that in comparison with formal judicial interpretation this is merely a change in form but not in content (Interview 54-17-CQ01). In practice, it is understandable that judges are normally very alert to updates from superior courts' judicial lawmaking exercises, including interpretations or new rules included in the summary of minutes.

It can be seen that not all judicial decision-making rules are statutorily promulgated to the public by legislative authorities. Because of the inaccessibility of local courts' judicial documents to the public, there is information asymmetry among legal practitioners. In practice, experienced lawyers need to search for and access these unpublished but extremely important judicial documents, like a summary of minutes produced by a local court, sometimes even through their connections with the judges, in order to equip themselves with the living law applied by the judges, as a way to increase the likelihood of success in the litigation (Interviews 70-17-GZ01, 50-17-NSSZ01, 53-17-NSSZ04). This was confirmed by a senior judge, who said that, "in practice, the defence counsel will be in an extremely advantageous position if they can find a channel to access relevant unpublished judicial documents through personal connections with the judges, or in other ways" (Interview 50-17-NSSZ01).

As a legal practitioner, it is almost a professional requirement to master the applicable legal rules set out in these unpublished judicial documents, in order to have a comprehensive understanding of the living law as applied by the judges. It is normally difficult to access unpublished judicial documents. However, the degree of difficulty may vary from one place to another. For example, for courts in a developed area with relatively high credibility, such as Shenzhen, it may be relatively easy for the parties to access documents.

During nationwide political movements, such as "strike hard" (严打 *yanda*) campaigns and the "campaign against the black and evil forces" (扫黑除恶 *saohei chu'e*), relevant laws may give way to politics. As such, there are almost no constitutional challenges to the relevant judicial lawmaking, given the overwhelming political imperative of the Party at these times.[11] During such campaigns, all relevant state organs, including

[10] In China's courts, the annual performance evaluation normally includes the rate of judicial decisions reversed by the appeals court (Kinkel and Hurst 2015).

[11] During a "strike hard" campaign, judicial reasoning may give way to politics (Wang 2017: 807).

the courts, are politically obliged to carry out orders from superior authorities. In this situation, the courts may even actively announce exigent interim measures to the public, in the form of documents, to express their political commitment to the Party-led campaign.

Political Embeddedness of Judicial Documents

Institutionally, local courts are created by and responsible for the LPCs and are mostly financed by local governments at the corresponding level. Like other government agencies, the year-end assessment bonuses of judges, as allocated by the government, are often linked to the government's assessment of the court's performance. Financially, a given court has been somehow embedded with the government at the same level (Ng and He 2017: 25; Zhu, 2007). In addition, courts are clearly subject to the leadership of the CCP at the local level, with the organization department of the local Party committee at the corresponding level playing a crucial role in appointing candidates for the leadership positions of the courts. As set out by the Constitution, the superior court has a "professional guidance relationship" (业务指导关系 *yiwu zhidao guanxi*) with the subordinate courts at the next lower level and, accordingly, the leading Party group of a superior court normally has a say in filling the leadership positions of the next lower-level courts under its guidance, according to the CCP's fundamental principles of "Party manages cadres" and "managing one level down" (下管一级 *xiaguan yiji*).

Of course, the leaders of a local court are ultimately appointed by the LPC, which is governed by the local Party committee. In practice, it is possible that the nominee for president of a local court, as recommended by the leading Party group of the superior court, may be rejected by the local Party committee – the highest political authority at the local level (Interview 21-16-GX02). In particular, if the local economy is developed, the local Party committee normally carries, either explicitly or implicitly, a degree of political authority in the CCP. This means that the local Party committee may play a more decisive role in filling the leadership positions of the courts at the local level and, therefore, may be able to resist the recommendations from the leading Party group of the next higher-level court. For example, in F (a pseudonym) province, the economies of the cities in the south of the province are much stronger than those in the north. The local Party committees for the cities in the south have a higher political status than the ones in the north. A senior judge, who once worked in the organization department of the High People's Court of F Province, noted:

> With regard to the nomination of the president of the intermediate people's court of a city with an underdeveloped economy in F province, if the nominee is recommended by the leading Party group of the High People's Court of F Province (normally in consultation with the organization department of the provincial Party committee), the local Party committee of the city is normally submissive and accepts the recommendation. In contrast, in a developed economy in F province, given its huge contribution to the provincial GDP [gross domestic product], normally the secretary of the Party committee of the city is a member of the standing committee of the provincial Party committee at the same time, while the president of the High People's Court of F Province actually is not. Politically, in this situation, the leading Party group of the High People's Court of F Province needs to consult with the local Party committee of the city in order to ensure that the nominee recommended is acceptable to the former. In practice, the local Party committee of a developed economy normally can play a dominant role, if it thinks it is necessary, in filling the leadership positions of the local court, given the local Party committee has more political influence in the province.
>
> (Interview 69–16-JSJC01)

Under the dual leadership of both the superior court and the local Party committee the local courts are responsive to local politics. However, for the judges there may be an internal tension under this type of double consciousness. On the one hand, the judges see themselves as officials carrying out statutory law; on the other hand, like other bureaucrats, they are politically obliged to "maintain social stability and thereby sometimes refrain from carrying out the law" (Ng and He 2017: 20). The extent to which a local court is responsive to local politics largely depends on the extent to which the local political actor has greater political force and influence than other intertwined political actors, even from the higher level.

There is no doubt that economic performance is paramount in the political agenda of the local government and that the promotion prospects of local leaders are usually linked with regional economic growth, which further provides incentives for local judicial protectionism (Long and Wang 2015: 49; Li and Zhou 2005). Although the role of law may be limited regarding local economic development, this does not deny the crucial role that the law plays in facilitating and regulating economic activities (Ng and He 2017: 25). Given that firms are increasingly closely connected with their local government (or even the national government), the dual leadership of both the superior court and the local Party committee may result in the operation of courts being influenced by local government (Wang 2016: 319–341). Although local judicial protectionism has not yet impaired the function of the courts as adjudicators, it may take either passive or active forms. For example, a local court may be under pressure imposed, usually implicitly, by the local government to change the result of a case under its discretion. Judges usually act in favour of the interests of the local government (Shen and Shang 2020). Highly developed parts of the country, particularly sub-provincial divisions with wide discretion relating to economic policy, like Shenzhen and Shanghai, more frequently enact experimental and innovative measures to boost their economy compared to relatively underdeveloped areas; the courts, like other government agencies, can be an effective instrument of the local government in this regard.

Due to the relatively greater political authority of economically developed local economies like Shenzhen, Guangzhou and Nanjing, the local court is normally more submissive to the local Party committee and responds more to the demands of the locality by producing adaptable judicial documents when necessary. It is common for the local court in a developed local economy to engage in judicial lawmaking activity by producing adaptable judicial documents (including a summaries of minutes), normally called "interim provisions" (暂行规定 *zanxing guiding*),[12] that suit the social or political needs of the locality.

Pragmatically, given the dual leadership discussed earlier, the judicial document can become an effective tool to make the regulation of local economic activities more rule-based and transparent. Undoubtedly, the implementation of national laws in the localities is diverse. For example, specific instructions on adjudication of cases, as stipulated by various judicial documents in Shenzhen courts, may be different from those in other parts of China. In contrast, in a relatively underdeveloped local economy, there is less adaptation of national laws and policies and the courts usually produce fewer judicial documents. Instead, they may apply the relevant statutory law directly to the case, based on the judges' experience and understanding of the law (Interviews 21-16-GX02, 20-16-GX01). In this regard, local protectionism in these relatively underdeveloped areas is less rule-based. In practice, if a judge from an underdeveloped area encounters a difficulty in the application of

[12] The judicial documents, filed with the author, were collected during the visit to the E (a pseudonym) District Court, B city, Guangdong Province in 2017.

law, they may refer to the documents produced by courts in more developed areas for adjudication in the locality.

The SPC (2012) stipulates that a judicial document drafted in the name of the court is to be sent to the General Office for review, regarding the necessity of dissemination and the consistency of the content, type and format of the document. An important document handed down to a subordinate court shall be copied to the direct superior court (Supreme People's Court 2012). However, apart from this self-examination system, the SPC has not yet detailed an effective judicial review system of the judicial documents produced by the courts. In practice, the courts have wide discretion to engage in judicial lawmaking exercises by producing judicial documents in the "twilight zone". Of course, this is not to say that such judicial lawmaking exercises have no boundaries. In principle, judicial documents should not obviously contravene a statutory law. Otherwise, given their lack of legality and the media pressure if disclosed to the public, they may be labelled illegal.[13]

For example, the High People's Court of Zhejiang Province issued a judicial document in 2012 that stated that conducting gender determination of a foetus for non-medical purposes more than three times, and which leads to labour being induced, constituted a crime. However, such a situation did not constitute a crime according to the relevant statutory law – the Prohibition on Gender Determination for Non-medical Purposes and Selection of Termination of Pregnancy (禁止非医学需要的胎儿性别鉴定和选择性别人工终止妊娠的规定 *jinzhi fei yixue xuyao de taier xingbie jianding he xuanze xingbie rengong zhongzhi rencheng de guiding*) (National Health and Family Planning Commission, State Administration for Industry and Commerce and State Food and Drug Administration 2016). In this case, a judicial document contravened the statutory law. Nonetheless, the document was implemented, until it was disclosed to the media by a law professor who applied to the Institute for Recording and Review (IRR) of the NPCSC, asking for a review of the legality of the document. Given the disclosure of its manifest illegality to the public, the IRR consulted with the Standing Committee of the People's Congress of Zhejiang Province, which had constitutional authority to monitor the trial work of the High People's Court of Zhejiang Province. The IRR's reply to the applicant was that it would supervise and urge the High People's

[13] The media may exert an influence over China's legal system (Liebman 2007b).

Court of Zhejiang Province to modify its position as soon as possible. The non-confrontational coordination among these political actors meant that the court was given the opportunity to explain away the divergence as an oversight, stating that it would take action to reword the document according to the relevant statutory laws (Legal Daily 2018).

The above indicates that judicial documents have become a practical and effective way for local courts to engage in judicial lawmaking enterprise, to respond to dynamic local politics and to accommodate subnational diversity, as long as they do not obviously contravene statutory laws and are not subject to populist pressure (Liebman 2007a: 629). Judicial documents produced by local courts occur in the interstices, caused by changing local conditions, of the SPC's governing of subordinate courts.

Justiciability of Judicial Documents

Given the embeddedness of judicial documents in China's legal system, relevant channels to ensure that they can be enforced appropriately by judges in adjudication are required. The precondition for this is that the courts meet the formalistic and legalistic requirement that judges shall adjudicate cases in accordance with statutory laws. This is mostly compatible with China's ongoing project to build an instrumentalist legal regime with Chinese characteristics since 1978.

To clarify the status of various statutory laws and the informal judicial documents in adjudication, in 2009 the SPC issued a judicial interpretation, i.e. the PCLRAD. This provides details on how judges should cite various statutory laws in judicial decision-making. The PCLRAD state that, depending on the needs of the trial, "regulatory documents" (规范性文件 *guifanxing wenjian*), other than those statutory laws stipulated in the PCLRAD, may be used as a basis of the *reasoning* of a judgment if they can be confirmed as legal and effective upon examination (Supreme People's Court 2009). Regulatory documents include all documents issued by political authorities, which includes judicial documents, such as the summaries of minutes discussed earlier. Although, legally speaking, these documents should not be treated as statutory law, they can be cited by the judges as a *reason* for judicial decision-making, which is included in the grounds part of the judgment, rather than the legal basis for the adjudication part of the judgment. In 2016, the SPC restated this in its internal working document Specifications for Preparing Civil Judgments by the

People's Courts and the Style of Civil Litigation Documents (人民法院民事裁判文书制作规范 *renmin fayuan minshi caipan wenshu zhizuo guifan*):

> (3) Where there is any conflict between regulatory documents that are necessary to be cited, and the alternative application fails to be determined in accordance with the Legislation Law of the People's Republic of China and other relevant statutory provisions, the court shall request the authority and the decision-making power to make a decision, and it shall not independently determine the validity of relevant regulatory documents in the judgment.
>
> (4) In a judgment, the Constitution, the guiding documents, and the minutes of meetings of the courts at various levels, the reply opinions of all tribunals, as well as the documents jointly issued by the courts and other government authorities may not be cited as the basis for rendering a judgment; however, the principles and spirit embodied in the aforesaid documents may be elaborated in the reasoning.
>
> (Supreme People's Court 2016)

In terms of the relationship between statutory laws and regulatory documents, this appears to indicate that the former is the judicial basis for rendering a judgment, while the latter is auxiliary. However, as illustrated earlier, the latter has actually played a significant role in adjudication, given the more specific and manoeuvrable rules for documents than those for the corresponding statutory laws. As one judge confessed, in many cases, if there are no corresponding specific and manoeuvrable rules provided by relevant judicial interpretation and informal documents from superior courts, the judge may be in trouble when handling the case (Interview 50-17-NSSZ01).

The scope of which regulatory documents may be used as a *reason* for rendering a judgment is completely open; it may even include the documents produced by the Party. For example, in administrative law cases, the CCP's relevant rules, though they by no means fall within the scope of statutory laws, may sometimes be cited by litigants in their defence (Yang 2019). Regarding local-level judicial documents, the judges normally have wide discretion to determine whether the document is relevant to the case and compatible with relevant statutory laws before citing it as a supporting authority for the final judgement (Interviews 50-17-NSSZ01, 60-18-YJJL01). In practice, if a presiding judge thinks it inappropriate, for whatever reason, to cite the document as a ground, they normally choose to omit the reasons for ignoring it from the judgment, even if the document is referred to in defence by the litigants.

Table 4.2 *Categories of judicial lawmaking exercises by Chinese courts*

Category	Status	Accessibility	Citation form	Basis
SPC's judicial interpretations	Statutory, legalized	Public	Legal basis	Statutory law
SPC's judicial documents	Non-statutory, informal	Public	Reason	NPCSC's delegation
Local courts' judicial documents	Non-statutory, informal	Limited	Reason	Guide the trial work of lower courts

In this situation, the presiding judges will merely refer to relevant statutory laws to make a judicial decision (Heilongjiang High People's Court 2016).

This channel has enabled the courts to adapt to China's authoritarian legal regime. It largely meets the minimum formalistic requirement that only statutory laws, not non-statutory sources, are the basis for the courts to render a judgment. At the same time, in practice, it provides a channel for the politics from higher authorities to infiltrate into adjudication. In particular, if documents that involve judicial lawmaking exercises, such as the interpretation of statutory laws or new rules for adjudication, are produced by superior courts, the lower-level courts, in principle, will rely on them for judicial decision-making. To do otherwise would risk their decisions being reversed on appeal. Based on the analysis in this chapter, the categories of judicial lawmaking enterprise are set out in Table 4.2.

Conclusion

All major legal systems recognize the authority of judges to engage in judicial lawmaking, primarily in connection with a concrete case or controversy. Case law, in various forms, has played a major role in both common law and civil law countries. However, the case of China shows that, given the lack of case law and the existence of an instrumentalist legislative system comprising thousands of statutory laws covering almost all aspects of society, the judicial lawmaking function has been performed without cases and without congressional delegation. In this authoritarian society, given the political dominance of the ruling Party, the courts, as both an adjudicator and Party subordinate, must be able to meet the overarching legalistic requirements to adjudicate in accordance with statutory laws and efficiently and flexibly respond to authoritarian politics. Due to the lack of case law, judicial documents have become informal state laws, which exist in a twilight zone with no congressional delegation. This has become the primary form of judicial lawmaking by the courts, apart from the SPC's formal judicial lawmaking in the form of judicial interpretations.

Due to the exclusive congressional delegation to the SPC to produce judicial interpretations, local courts are prohibited by the SPC from creating judicial lawmaking documents. However, politically, the courts, as the Party's political subordinates, may produce relevant non-statutory internal documents for subordinate courts. It is a constitutional requirement that superior courts shall guide the trial work of their subordinate courts. As such, it is not surprising that local superior courts produce relevant non-statutory documents to guide the trial work of lower courts, performing a judicial lawmaking function in disguise. To distinguish these documents from those that are prohibited, local courts normally circumvent the rules and use different titles and forms, including the summaries of minutes produced by court judicial committees (or subcommittees) or tribunals, often after a professional meeting attended by representative senior judges and professionals. Functionally, the judicial documents fill legal loopholes and reflect the practical social needs of localities where the relevant uniform statutory law is ambiguous or insufficient.

Given the flexibility of judicial documents, such a judicial lawmaking practice has enabled the local courts to meet a basic political requirement in an authoritarian regime – as the Party's political subordinate, it must be able to positively, efficiently and effectively respond to differences in local politics. In this regard, the judicial document mechanism has been politically embedded in the dynamics of authoritarian politics and has become symbiotic with China's instrumentalist legal system. However, given that judicial documents lack a clear legal status, they usually exist in a twilight zone and, in principle, are not accessible to the public for fear of being criticized for encroaching unconstitutionally upon legislative authority. This has resulted in information asymmetry, with those who are able to access the updates having more advantages in legal proceedings than those who are not. According to the SPC's rules, the enforcement of these documents by inferior courts is mainly based on the political hierarchy of China's courts, which is different from statutory laws, which are constitutionally required to be enforced. Due to the embeddedness of this kind of judicial document in China's legal system, the court has strategically established a channel for judges to refer to them. That is, the judge may refer to the document if relevant to the case at hand, as a *reason*, instead of a legal *basis*, to render a judgment. Such a channel conforms to the legalistic requirement that only statutory laws shall be the legal basis for judicial decision-making, and has enabled local courts to apply relevant judicial documents to cases in unique ways.

This "twilight theory" of judicial documents as informal state laws shows that the judicial document, with no explicit congressional delegation, has become a crucial mechanism for the courts to flexibly engage in the judicial lawmaking practice and to respond swiftly and efficiently to subnational diversity and the various social needs of localities while addressing local political differences under the Party's governance. As an informal state law, it has strengthened China's version of the socialist rule of law, with an emphasis on building a resilient, rule-based legal system under the CCP leadership, distinguished from a Western-style system with judicial independence (Liebman 2007a: 628). To a certain extent, this has been derived from the legalistic approach to formal laws and the central definition of law with an effort to systematically apply rules and standards. Instead, it has made the living law more authoritarian because it enables the Party to institutionally impose ideological and bureaucratic controls on the court system (Minzner 2011: 938–939). This robust mechanism has been able to covertly bridge the courts' adjudication with authoritarian politics and is well suited to maintaining the political resilience of China's authoritarian regime.

5

Guiding Cases as a Form of Statutory Interpretation

In terms of legal systems, China, as a socialist state, generally falls within the domain of the civil law tradition, albeit with some distinctive features. Even though case law has played an indispensable role in both common law and civil law jurisdictions for hundreds of years, China did not adopt it formally until the SPC (2010b) promulgated the Provisions Concerning Work on Guiding Cases (PWGC) (关于案例指导工作的规定 *guanyu zhidao anlie gongzuo de guiding*) in order to establish a system of guiding cases in 2010. According to the PWGC, which comprise ten articles, the SPC will determine and uniformly release those cases as guiding cases that have the effect of guiding adjudication and enforcement work in courts throughout the country (article 1). This is the first time that China has attempted to adopt a new form of case law in practice. Furthermore, such a system was further specified in the Detailed Rules for the Implementation of the Provisions of the SPC on Case Guidance (<最高人民法院关于案例指导工作的规定>的实施细则 *zuigao renmin fayuan guanyu anlie zhidao gongzuo de guiding de shishi xize*) (hereinafter "Detailed Rules") in 2015.

The Guiding Case as Case Law?

Due to such developments, more attention has been paid to it in the scholarship, in particular by analogy with case law in other rule-of-law countries (Jia 2016; Deng 2015; Yang 2016; Xie 2016). Interestingly, both the Chinese and English literatures have focused on the importance and potential of the guiding case system for the future development of China's judicial system (Liu 2011: 56). For instance, in the Chinese literature, it is contended and expected that the newly created system can fill the gaps of statutory law, restrain the discretionary power of judges, enhance the efficiency of the judiciary, strengthen the determinacy of laws, unify the standards of legal application, improve judicial impartiality and authority and enrich the socialist judicial system (Z. Zhang 2012: 65–66). Similarly, in the English literature, some scholars, although they admit there is a difference between the guiding case system and the common law system, argue that the guiding case system has equivalent functions to the common law in adapting law to social needs, strengthening judicial autonomy and supplementing existing statutory law (Deng 2016: 48).

The guiding case system has a number of other advantages. As a tool of the SPC, guiding cases are easy to issue and are generally applicable. They can "fill scattered gaps in existing legislation, clarify the meanings of scattered existing articles, and incrementally reform outdated or inconsistent existing laws. Additionally, guiding cases may also help establish the rules of statutory interpretations" (Deng 2016: 69; see also Ahl 2014: 136). In addition, Ahl (2014: 121) argues that:

> [G]iven the complexity of cases, compared to law set out in statute, non-lawyers may have tremendous difficulty in understanding and assessing the effects of guiding cases; this in turn acts as a protective mechanism against extra-legal interference. The reform is an example of the SPC's delicate maneuvering in order to retain judicial professionalism in a hostile yet politically conservative environment. It reflects an attempt by the SPC to strengthen its position *vis-à-vis* other actors of the party-state and to consolidate the judiciary's function as an adjudicative institution that works on the basis of formal legal mechanisms.

It is further argued that in comparison with judicial interpretations which are enacted in a lengthy procedure that normally includes consultation with other state organs:

> [T]he procedure for selecting guiding cases is far more flexible. The SPC does not need to draft legal texts from scratch and take into account – similar to a legislator – the interests of all concerned parties. The court can simply select from the rich material of decided cases and promote any court decision to the rank of a guiding case. This puts the SPC in a position to react promptly to legal developments with a formal instrument that is more suitable for solving complex legal problems than judicial interpretations. Moreover, guiding cases allow the SPC to promote discretely legal developments that follow its own long-term institutional interests rather than the frequently changing policies of the Party.
>
> (Ahl 2014: 136)

Clearly, such arguments are made in the expectation that the guiding case system will function like case law in liberal democracies. The courts could use it as a tool to become more professional and independent, given the legislature and other actors of the Party-state have less formal control over the guiding case system. However, the argument that China's courts can somehow become less politicized and more independent seems fairly weak because, particularly during the era of Xi Jinping, the CCP has been attempting to strengthen its authoritarian regime and within that the courts are principally political subordinates of the Party-state in spite of their professionalization in some areas such as commercial law. These supposed merits, as already discussed, are mainly expressed from the perspective of common law in which case law is often regarded as its most distinctive feature, or from the perspective of liberal democracies of the civil law tradition with judicial independence where cases also play an increasingly indispensable role in trial practice (Montrose 1968: 9). This largely ignores the conditions under which the guiding case system emerged and developed in China.

Admittedly, the literature has provided much normative analysis on guiding cases, their scope of authority and their adoption and form, all of which have been covered by the PWGC to a large extent (Z. Zhang 2012). In order to have a deeper understanding and better explanation of the guiding case system in the context, it needs to move beyond the method of treating a guiding case in analogy with the case law of liberal democracies from a normative perspective, and pay more attention to the conditions under which guiding cases emerged and evolved under China's authoritarian regime.

Emergence of Guiding Cases

Historically, "case law" or "common law" reasoning was employed in China, for example, in the Han dynasty, long before the Qing dynasty (Ho 2010: 154). In practice, previous cases represented a rather mature source of law upon which judges could rely when written law was absent or ambiguous, even though, according to the Code, invocation of case law was prohibited unless a previous case was circulated or enacted as a sub-statute (Wang 2005: 341, 344). However, immediately after the establishment of the People's Republic of China, all laws of the previous government led by Kuomintang were abolished. The new government led by the CCP mainly used policies to rule the country (Huang 2011: 17), and legal nihilism prevailed in the era of Mao Zedong. Thus, no guiding cases with binding force existed in practice.[1] However, since 1978, China has been constructing its legal system at an unprecedented pace. In China, legally speaking, the courts, albeit in their role as the adjudicative

[1] The SPC once attempted to take some cases as guidance for judicial work in the 1950s but stopped such a practice due to political reasons (Jiang and Shao 2013: 110).

organ of the state according to the Constitution, are mainly executants of the legislature, i.e., people's congresses. However, politically speaking, the courts, under the leadership of the CCP, do not have the judicial independence of courts in liberal democracies. Previously, the SPC only issued a number of typical criminal cases inside the court system through internal documents, but then in 1985 the SPC issued its first *Gazette* to the public and started to publish typical cases that could be used as guidance.[2] Of course, all these kinds of cases, selected and even published in the *Gazette*, have no binding force in any sense and, in practice, are merely a sort of reference material which can be easily disregarded by judges. Although the SPC played its part by publishing guiding cases, strictly speaking, the initial form of the guiding case system began at a grassroots level, in a court in Zhengzhou city, Henan Province, in 2002.

Initial Experiment with a Guiding Case System

Undoubtedly, case law was first developed in a common law jurisdiction. It can first be identified at the end of the sixteenth century when English courts started to adhere to previous custom in matters of procedure and pleading. Previous practice was that if the precedents were reaffirmed by a sequence of consistent decisions over time, then they became more authoritative (Berman and Reid 1996: 446–448). Thereafter, due to the influence of legal positivism, the doctrine of *stare decisis* gradually became a principle in practice, thus giving rise to the common law notion of binding authority of precedent. This became formally established by the end of the nineteenth century (Evans 1987).

In contrast, the historical evolution of the civil law tradition shows that case law did not originally hold a prominent position because it was assumed that the judge had no inherent lawmaking power. In nineteenth-century Europe, the doctrine of the separation of powers was understood to imply that "[t]he role of the courts is to solve disputes that are brought before them, not to make laws or regulations" (David 1972: 180–181). Before the French Revolution, the orthodox principle of separation of powers was strictly insisted upon due to the general distrust of courts which were manipulated by the king. At the end of the Revolution, the ideological concerns over the judiciary's role were assuaged, and civil law jurisdictions gradually began to adhere to an

[2] The first issue of the Gazette published 15 judicial precedents.

informal system of precedent in practice where a sequence of analogous cases acquired persuasive force (Fon and Parisi 2006: 522). Thereafter, the difference in the case law between the two systems was no longer as marked as before, and it gained its increasing significance in practice because judges in both systems were sufficiently impressed by the authority of the prior court, were persuaded by its reasoning, were too lazy to think through the problem themselves or did not want to risk the decision being reversed on appeal, to name but a few reasons (Merryman 1985: 36, 47; Troper and Grzegorczyk 1997: 115–119).

In contrast, in China, the main reason why local courts began to experiment with case law was because of the increasingly perceived notion that similar cases were treated differently in practice. The famous example of this occurred in 1998 when the plaintiff Ge Rui sued three pharmacies in three different jurisdictions separately according to the rules of civil procedure but received three different decisions (Wang 2009: 23). This situation motivated the courts to pay more attention to establishing a suitable case law system in order to solve such issues in practice. As a result, the trial court in Zhongyuan District, Zhengzhou city, issued a specific regulation in 2002, stipulating that, after the cases are selected and decided by the Adjudication Committee, the highest decision-making body inside China's courts, and released by the court as precedent cases, they will be followed by judges as a point of *reference*, if not as the basis, to decide subsequent similar cases. If the precedent is ignored without legitimate reason, the judge who makes the incorrect decision will be sanctioned (Liu et al. 2004).

This pilot experiment at Zhongyuan District Court has had good results. First, it can offer guidance to judges in terms of applying laws in trials and can reduce the rate of misjudged cases. Precedents in themselves are legally effective judgments and are summaries of trial experience. Referring to these precedents can reduce the possibility of reversing or overruling judgments.

Second, it has saved judicial resources as well as enhanced judicial efficiency. As precedents are representative cases that have been deliberated by judges and the Adjudication Committee, it is no longer necessary to submit similar cases to the Adjudication Committee for deliberation. Rather, the judges or collegiate bench can decide similar hard cases by referring to precedents. As a consequence, the meetings of the Adjudication Committee have been reduced by 50 per cent and the cases deliberated by it reduced by 80 per cent. The rate of appeal has also been reduced by 12 per cent in Zhongyuan District Court (Liu et al. 2004).

Such an achievement is largely ascribed to the fact that the previous trial experience can be made use of by the judges in practice with no need to appeal to the Adjudication Committee any more as was considered normal when encountering controversial cases. At the same time, the judges are able to decide the case by referring to previous similar cases directly unless the issues have never been encountered by the court – this is extremely rare for a basic-level court in practice.

It appears that such practices provide a benchmark for judges to treat like cases alike and so maintain the consistency of judicial decisions. At the same time, it denotes that the judge, in particular when handling a difficult case, has a discretionary power to discern whether the case to be treated is similar to a previous case. Of course, once the case is decided by the Adjudication Committee, it will have binding force on the judges when they decide similar cases subsequently. It can be seen that this is a kind of centralized model of case law in the sense that the Adjudication Committee is the exclusive authority. In comparison, in the common law tradition, the central distinction is the rule of *stare decisis* according to which judges are supposed to be bound by previous decisions. This is not because the judges have the exclusive authority but because they must abide by the accumulated experience of legal customs, so that the law will be no respecter of persons, and so that people may be able "to act in the certitude that the law does not alter capriciously" (Kirk 2003: 185). In the civil law tradition, even though there is no formal rule of *stare decisis*, the courts do use precedents in a persuasive role in practice. Judicial decisions are regularly published in most civil law jurisdictions, and judges are influenced by and often refer to prior decisions. It has been observed that the practice of the courts does not become a source of law until it is definitively fixed by the repetition of precedents which are in agreement on a single point (Lamber and Wasserman 1929: 14). The higher the level of uniformity in past precedents, the greater is the persuasive force of case law (Fon and Parisi 2006: 15). It can be seen that, theoretically, the force of cases in both civil law and common law traditions is not actually from any exclusive authority in a centralized way but from accumulated experience of legal custom in a decentralized way.

Of course, Zhongyuan District Court was not taking a gamble by experimenting in this way as the idea of a case system had already been mooted by the SPC. Earlier, in 1999, the SPC (1999c) had issued its first Five-Year Reform Outline for the People's Courts (人民法院五年改革纲要 *renmin fayuan wunian gaige gangyao*) (1999–2003) in which it stated that, from 2000, the judicial precedents, if deliberated and published by the

Adjudication Committee of the SPC, could be referred to by the lower courts for adjudicating similar cases. Nevertheless, the experiment led to a fierce controversy over whether the court, in particular its Adjudication Committee, had the authority to create this kind of case law under China's authoritarian regime where the duty of the court was not to pronounce new laws but only to maintain and expound old ones. The function of a court, after all, was declaratory and merely to apply the law created by the legislature (Friedmann 1966).

Expansion of Guiding Case System

During this time, having realized the significance of guiding cases in unifying standards for judicial decision-making, the SPC promulgated the Second Five-Year Reform Outline for People's Courts (人民法院第二个五年改革纲要 *renmin fayuan di er ge wunian gaige gangyao*) (2004–2008) (hereinafter "Second Reform Outline") on 26 October 2005. The aim of the reform was mainly to ensure the unified application of laws and the use of a system of guiding cases to promote the coherence of judicial decision-making. It stated in paragraph 2 of the Second Reform Outline that:

> The courts shall establish and improve a system of guiding cases, recognize the important role of guiding cases in unifying the application of laws, directing the operation of lower courts, enriching and developing their jurisprudence, etc. The SPC shall lay down legal provisions on the system of guiding cases to specify the standards and procedures for selecting and compiling guiding cases, the way to release guiding cases and relevant rules, etc.
>
> (Supreme People's Court 2005)

Needless to say, the Second Reform Outline provided a policy basis for local courts to develop a guiding case system. As a result, many courts at the local level, like the Intermediate People's Courts of Kunming (2002), Zhengzhou (2003) and Chengdu (2003), and the High People's Courts of Jiangsu (2003), Tianjin (2002), Sichuan (2004), Henan (2005), Heilongjiang (2005), Shandong (2006), Shaanxi (2007), Xinjiang (2006) and Zhejiang (2006), adopted a similar guiding case system with which to select and publish guiding cases to guide the lower courts to decide like cases alike (Wang 2009: 23–24).

However, the guiding case system of High People's Courts was substantially different from the initial one by Zhongyuan District Court.

First, not all cases decided by the Adjudication Committee became guiding cases automatically. Only the cases selected and determined by the Adjudication Committee of High People's Courts were guiding cases which could be referred to by the lower courts in adjudicating similar cases. Obviously, owing to the fact that the courts in theory do not have any lawmaking power in China, this kind of guiding case system practised by High People's Courts had no binding force and could definitely be disregarded by the lower courts. To put it another way, the guiding case system at this stage had no formal legal basis. Second, there was a selection process, i.e. the original case made by the trial court was recommended and submitted to the Research Office of the High People's Court which was in charge of selecting guiding cases for consideration. If it passed the review of the Research Office, it would be submitted to the Adjudication Committee of the High People's Courts for the final decision. These determined guiding cases would be published in the *Gazette*.

Given that there was no legal basis for the guiding case system during this time and the guiding cases had no binding force at all, it is understandable that the High People's Courts adopted a variety of performance appraisal mechanisms to incentivize lower courts to submit more high-quality cases to High People's Courts for guiding case selection. For instance, in Sichuan jurisdiction, if a case submitted by a lower court was selected and decided as a guiding one by the High People's Court of Sichuan, the court would be awarded RMB 300, and the submission courts might reward the trial judges accordingly or take other incentive measures as appropriate. This clearly shows that the courts at the provincial level attempted to promote such a mechanism even though the local experiment of guiding cases at the provincial level was not as effective as expected in practice and some problems did arise. For instance, the experiment in Sichuan illustrates that it is extraordinarily difficult to select enough guiding cases to cover all areas, and the number of guiding cases is very small or even decreasing yearly. At the same time, difficulties in implementing the guiding cases have arisen, including that (1) the trial judges in lower courts rarely refer to these guiding cases in their decision-making; (2) the guiding cases are not coherent and are difficult to search for because the task of compiling them is still underdeveloped; and (3) the judges are overloaded with cases and they have no time to study and refer to these guiding cases (Sichuan High People's Court and Sichuan University Collective Project 2013).

It can be seen that, once the guiding case system was adopted by the High People's Courts at the provincial level, it in fact largely deviated from the original practice of guiding cases trialled in Zhongyuan District Court in the sense that only a few cases, after being selected and determined by the High People's Courts, were treated as guiding cases. As illustrated, such a limited number of guiding cases is unable to maintain consistency for the majority of cases in practice. This contrasts with the original practice in which a large number of cases at the basic level of the same court could be summarized and applied similarly under the case guidance system. Nonetheless, it is clear that such a bureaucratic model of guiding cases has expanded the authority of the High People's Courts over lower courts in the sense that, given that the number of guiding cases has become an evaluation index in the courts' performance appraisal system, lower courts are actually required to select and submit their decided cases of "high quality" to the High People's Courts periodically for the final selection of guiding cases. Moreover, the High People's Courts have the final authority in selecting and determining a case as a guiding case. In addition, although guiding cases have no binding force, it is more likely that the guiding case is used by the High People's Court that has the appellate jurisdiction for policy reasons beyond the normal practice of adjudication. For example, during the "strike hard" period, the High People's Courts may select some relevant guiding cases intentionally in order that the relevant policy can be better implemented. Sometimes, the High People's Court may use guiding cases to draw judges' attention to new policy or legal issues in practice (Interviews 01-16-JS01, 03-16-JS03).

Formalization of Guiding Case System by the SPC

Although the local experiment did not fully achieve the desired effect, after years of local experiments, the SPC still moved forward to establish a formal national mechanism of guiding cases based on the previous local practice. In 2010, the SPC promulgated the PWGC to carry out the work on guiding cases, thus providing a clear framework for a guiding case system. However, it further deviated from the trajectory of local experiments in that the SPC became the exclusive authority on deciding guiding cases.

According to the PWGC, the purpose of the guiding cases is to sum up trial experience, unify the application of law, enhance the quality of trials and maintain judicial justice. The SPC shall select and uniformly publish guiding cases that have a guiding function for trial and enforcement by people's courts throughout the country (article 1). The PWGC also provide a definition of guiding cases. These are cases whose judgments have come into force and satisfy one of the following conditions: (1) attract wide attention from society; (2) the legal provisions concern principles of law; (3) are representative in nature; (4) are difficult, complicated or novel; or (5) have a guiding function in some other way (article 2). The SPC shall establish a Case Guidance Office to be in charge of the selection, examination and reporting for approval of guiding cases (article 3). Any trial division of the SPC, a High People's Court at the provincial level, or the Military Court of the People's Liberation Army may recommend a judgment to the Case Guidance Office while an intermediate people's court or a basic people's court shall report to the High People's Court level and suggest to the High People's Court to recommend the judgment to the Case Guidance Office. In addition, any other person, if they deem that a valid judgment complies with article 2 of the PWGC, may recommend it to the original people's court that rendered the valid judgment (article 4). After receiving the recommended judgments, the Case Guidance Office shall put forward examination opinions of them in a timely manner. Where cases comply with article 2 of the PWGC, the Case Guidance Office shall request that the president, or the vice president in charge, submit the cases to the Adjudication Committee of the SPC for deliberation and decision-making. The guiding cases determined upon deliberation of the Adjudication Committee shall be uniformly published in the *Gazette* of the SPC, the website of the SPC and the *People's Court Daily* in the form of announcements (article 6). The PWGC further state that, when trying similar cases, people's courts at all levels shall use the guiding cases issued by the SPC as a reference (article 7).

It is clear that the PWGC have provided a general framework for the guiding case system. However, it is not clear how the courts will use the guiding cases as a reference in trial practice. The Detailed Rules address this as they provide more details on how to ensure the effective implementation of the PWGC and, in particular, the ways in which the guiding cases can be used in practice (Supreme People's Court 2015a). They state that, where a case under adjudication by a people's court at any level is similar to a guiding case published by the SPC in terms of basic facts and the application of law, the people's court shall render a judgment or ruling by reference to the headnotes of the judgment or ruling on the guiding case, according to article 9 of the Detailed Rules of the SPC (2015a).

When a people's court at any level refers to a guiding case in the adjudication of a similar case, it shall quote the guiding case as part of the *reasons* for judgment or ruling but shall not quote the same as a basis for judgment or ruling (article 10 of the Detailed Rules). During the process of case handling, case-handling officers shall search relevant guiding cases. When relevant guiding cases are quoted in written judgments or rulings, the serial numbers of the guiding cases and the headnotes of their judgments or rulings shall be quoted as part of the reasons for the judgment or ruling (article 11 of the Detailed Rules).

Here, it can be seen that the SPC has strategically distinguished the reason from the basis for the judgment in terms of applying guiding cases. On the one hand, the SPC clearly shows that the establishment of the guiding case system was not done to give the courts any lawmaking power so it is compatible with the orthodoxy that the courts are only the executants of the legislature. On the other hand, the SPC has attempted to make the guiding cases binding on the lower courts in a flexible way and, in theory, this does not encroach upon the power of the legislature as discussed earlier but allows it to exercise its own adjudicative power according to the Constitution because only professional judges in the courts, rather than these politicians in the legislature, are able to adjudicate cases. On this basis, it is a matter of course for the SPC to establish the guiding case system in order to solve the issue of inconsistency of application of laws within its own domain of adjudicative power, as well as with a legitimate purpose, that is, "like cases should be treated alike".

Of course, the subsequent issue is how to define these select conditions, such as "representative in nature" and "wide attention". Undoubtedly, the recommendation bodies may have their own understanding about these conditions but they are ultimately subject to the SPC's decision. In other words, the function of the guiding case system is not just confined to "treating like cases alike" but also gives the SPC a broadened and exclusive authority to define the terms "wide attention", "principles of law", "representative", "guiding function" and the like.

It is clear that under the SPC's regulation of guiding cases the system has evolved into a different vision from previous local experiments. The local experiments have been formally stopped by the PWGC, and the SPC has become the sole authority to determine the guiding cases. Comparatively, the evolution of such a guiding case system dominated by the SPC has been substantially different to that of the civil law system as it has followed the general rule that no single decision binds a court and no relevance is given to split case law (Fon and Parisi 2006; Parisi and Depoorter 2003: 667–671).

Binding Force of Guiding Cases

Under the current guiding case system, only a case decided by the SPC has a binding force on lower courts, i.e., other non-guiding cases have no equivalent express force.

The Detailed Rules of the SPC (2015a) specified the distinctive ways that the guiding case shall be referred to in the adjudication. In principle, article 10 of the Detailed Rules stipulates that, "[w]hen a people's court at any level refers to a guiding case in the adjudication of a similar case, it shall quote the guiding case as part of the reasons for the judgment or ruling, but shall not quote the same as a legal basis for the judgment or ruling". This shows that the guiding case does not have the same legislative effect as other statutory laws. Rather, it can only be treated as a reference for adjudicating similar cases. In addition, article 11 of the Detailed Rules further states that: "Where relevant guiding cases are quoted in written judgments or rulings, the serial numbers of the guiding cases, and the MPA shall be quoted as part of the reasons for the judgment or ruling."

From this we can see the distinctiveness of the binding force of guiding cases, which is based on the unique structure of the guiding cases with a separate part, namely, the MPA. As for the structure of the guiding cases, the SPC has consistently used the format of dividing each guiding case into seven parts: (1) "Case number" (for example, Guiding Case No 1) and "Name" (for example, *Shanghai Centaline Property Consultants Limited* v *Dehua Tao*); (2) "Keywords" (to list keywords that indicate the nature of the dispute etc.); (3) "Main Points of Adjudication" (to include general principles prepared by the SPC that it expects other courts to refer to); (4) "Related Legal Rule(s)" (to list the legal rule(s) considered in the guiding case); (5) "Basic Facts of the Case" (to summarize the most important facts of the guiding case); (6) "Results of the Adjudication" (to report the outcomes of legal proceedings); and (7) "Reasons for the Adjudication" (to summarize the reasons for the final ruling/judgment).

In terms of the structure of the guiding case, Yang argues for the necessity of dual binding effects in Chinese guiding cases that involve concise rules and decisive judgmental reasoning, which can be compared with the headnotes or digests of precedents in Japan (Yang 2016: 312). Yang (2016: 318) further states that:

> [G]uiding cases are supposed to have full argumentation and necessary justification, especially to strengthen the analysis and affirmation of the controversial evidence during the process of cross-examination, to include references to replies in support of, or to retort to the requirements of the parties concerned on the basis of full argumentation, that is, in response to the requirement of the parties, explicitly and specifically stating what is reasonable, what is unreasonable, why it is reasonable or why it is unreasonable.

However, given that Chinese courts follows an inquisitorial system where the court is actively involved in investigating the facts of the case, as opposed to an adversarial system where the judges focus on the issue of law and procedure and act as referees in the contest between the defence and the prosecutor, in practice the full argumentation and necessary justification for a decision are not normally illustrated thoroughly in China's judgments. Moreover, as the SPC insists that no case law system is followed in China, the usual brief argumentation and reasoning of guiding cases can hardly be expected to function as case law does. In this regard, the assertion that the guiding case system represents a new trend in China's legal development – a merger of civil tradition and common law practice, or a combination of civil and common law systems as illustrated in the dual vehicles involving of concise rules and decisive judgmental reasoning – can be treated with a fair degree of suspicion in the context of China (Zhang 2017: 305; Yang 2016: 333). Comparatively speaking, for example, in Japan, because headnotes or digests of the precedents do not state the rules, their main use for adjudicators is to provide examples of argumentation and conclusions. Normally, judges are less likely to cite them in pending cases than they are to cite statutory law (Yang 2016: 317). However, as far as the guiding case is concerned, it is distinctive because, apart from the original judgment, the court will add a part – the MPA – to the guiding case, which is to be finalized by the SPC. For example, in Guiding Case No 3, a bribe-accepting case, as illustrated in Table 5.1, the SPC interprets article 385 of the Criminal Law by adding the MPA to the gazetted guiding case.

In this regard, the guiding case is not the original decision of the original trial court but rather a modified one with an added part by the court. Furthermore, the MPA's binding force was clarified by the judge of the SPC, Hu Yuteng, who was in charge of guiding case affairs. He stated that any case which contradicts the MPA of the guiding case is incorrect

Table 5.1 *Main Points of Adjudication of the Guiding Case to interpret the related legal rule(s) [an example]*

Related legal rule	Article 385, state functionaries who take advantage of their office to demand money and property from other people or illegally accept money and property from other people and give favours to the latter are guilty of the crime of bribery
Main Points of Adjudication	1. A state functionary who exploits the advantages of office to seek benefits for an entrusting person and, together with the entrusting person, obtains "profits" in the name of "jointly organising" a company but does not actually contribute capital or participate in the operation and management shall be punished for accepting bribes. 2. A state functionary who knows that a person has an entrusted matter and yet accepts his property shall be regarded as having promised to "seek benefits for others". The determination of "accepting bribes" is not affected by whether benefits were actually sought for the other person or whether benefits were actually obtained. 3. A state functionary who exploits the advantages of office to seek benefits for an entrusting person and purchases goods like houses from the entrusting person at obviously below-market prices shall be punished for accepting bribes. The amount of bribes accepted is calculated in accordance with the difference between the local market price at the time of the transaction and the price actually paid. 4. The determination of the crime of accepting bribes is not affected by the fact that after a state functionary has accepted property then returns it to conceal the crime due to the investigation of individuals and matters connected to her acceptance of bribes.

Source: Guiding Case No 3, SPC of China.

and subject to reversal or change by the appellate court. This has also been confirmed by the Detailed Rules of the SPC (2015a). Article 9 of the Detailed Rules states that: "[w]here a case under adjudication by a people's court at any level is similar to a guiding case published by the

SPC in terms of basic facts and the application of law, the people's court shall render a judgment/ruling by reference to the MPA on the guiding case". It is apparent that the MPA is used by the SPC as a form of statutory interpretation to clarify the ambiguities involved in the statutes. As illustrated in Table 5.1, the MPA is clear and specific and could be easily referred to by the trial courts in deciding similar cases in practice. For instance, in *Mei Min* v. *Zhang Dexiu et al.* (梅敏诉张德修等机动车交通事故责任纠纷案 *mei min su zhang dexiu deng jidongche jiaotong shigu zeren jiufen an*), the court referred to the MPA of Guiding Case No 24 *Baoying Rong* v *Yang Wang and Alltrust Insurance Co Ltd Jiangyin Branch* (荣宝英诉王阳、永诚财产保险股份有限公司江阴支公司机动车交通事故责任纠纷案 *rong bao ying su wang yang yong cheng caichan baoxian gufen youxian gongsi jiangyin zhigongsi jidongche jiaotong shigu zeren jiufen an*) to decide the case, as the MPA had confirmed the disputed points of article 26 of the Tort Liability Law (侵权责任法 *qinquan zeren fa*) and article 76 para 1, Item (2) of the Road Traffic Safety Law (道路交通安全法 *daolu jiaotong anquan fa*), by stipulating in the guiding case clearly that "if a victim of a traffic accident is not at fault, the effect of his [pre-existing] physical condition on the ramifications of the harm [he suffered] is not a type of legal circumstance that can mitigate a tortfeasor's liability" (Jiangyan District Court of Taizhou City of Jiangsu Province 2014).

However, as to the binding force of other parts of the guiding case, in particular, "Basic Facts of the Case", "Results of the Adjudication" and "Reasons for the Adjudication", it is observed that out of a hundred random judgments involving a guiding case,[3] the judges did not cite, compare or analyse the facts and reasons of the guiding cases involved. Interestingly, the Detailed Rules of the SPC (2015a) also do not provide further details on how other parts of the guiding case shall be referred to by the courts. Having said this, it does not prevent judges from understanding the MPA through facts and reasons involved in the guiding case.

In practice, judges are inclined to refer to a guiding case when statutory laws are not sufficient to decide the case at hand (Interviews 12-16-JSYHT01, 10-16-JSNJ01). Judges in other jurisdictions also have such an inclination because, as noted already, they do not want to risk reversal on appeal as well as other reasons (Merryman 1985: 36). If the judge should but does not refer to the guiding case when the case is similar, a cause of

[3] The 100 judgments that mention guiding case were randomly collected from the database Beidafabao, available at www.pkulaw.cn (visited June 7, 2018).

action may occur and the party involved may institute an appeal against the first-instance judgment based on the fact that the guiding case is not referred to by the trial court. For instance, in the Xi'an X Property Co Ltd and Lu XX Appealing Case (西安某房产信息咨询有限公司与卢某某居间合同纠纷上诉案 *xi'an mou fangchan xinxi zixun youxian gongsi yu lu mou jujian hetong jiufen shangsu an*), the plaintiff instituted an appeal claiming that there was an error in the application of the law as the court's judgment was inconsistent with the Guiding Case No 1(Xi'an Intermediate People's Court of Shaanxi Province 2014). In addition, the court of second instance may overrule the decision of the court of first instance based on the understanding of a guiding case. This happened in *Ningbo Pujie Taxi Co Ltd* v *Zhou Xiuqing Taxi Co Ltd* (宁波普捷出租车有限公司与周秀琴出租汽车运输合同纠纷上诉案 *ningbo pujie chuzuche youxian gongsi yu zhou xiuqing chuzu qiche yunshu hetong jiufen shangsu an*) where the court decided that the court of first instance confused the legal relationship involved in the case and applied different laws to the same fact repeatedly when referring to the Guiding Case No 24 directly in the judgment (Ningbo Intermediate People's Court of Zhejiang Province 2014). Therefore, the court was asked to correct it accordingly. As such, article 11 of the Detailed Rules of the SPC (2015a) stipulates that "[w]here the public prosecution organ of a case, or the parties to a case and the defense counsel or the agent *ad litem* thereof cite a guiding case as part of the reasons for prosecution (defense or litigation), the handling officers of the case shall respond in the reasons for judgment/ruling whether the guiding case has been referred to, and explain the reasons therefor".

It can be seen that the guiding case system does provide a channel for the parties to defend before the court and a benchmark for the judges to make a judicial decision, provided that there is ambiguity of law and the MPA of a guiding case is specific and applicable to the case concerned.

Therefore, with regard to the binding force of the guiding case, the MPA of the guiding case, supplemented formally by the SPC, has a de facto binding force according to the Detailed Rules of the SPC (2015a), i.e., it must be considered as a reason for the judicial decision-making. Yet, for other parts of the guiding case the courts are reluctant to refer to the details of the facts and reasoning involved, even though these might contribute to the understanding of the MPA in practice. Put another way, the guiding case system is not greatly concerned with the issue of "like cases treated alike". Rather, it is more concerned with the MPA of the guiding case through which the SPC is able to interpret the law formally. In essence, it is a form of statutory interpretation with binding force on lower courts in adjudicating all type of cases where the MPA of a guiding case is relevant.

However, as mentioned earlier, the implementation of the guiding case system has not been as effective as expected, and very few guiding cases have been referred to by judges for judicial decision-making.[4] First and foremost, this can be easily ascribed to the limited number of guiding cases selected by the SPC. Given the bureaucratic process of selecting guiding cases, only ninety-two had been selected by the SPC as of November 2017. It is clear that the overall effect of the very few guiding cases, such as in unifying legal application, will be extremely limited in the legal system, particularly in comparison with statutory laws and the SPC's judicial interpretations. Furthermore, legally speaking, given that China does not follow case law and the courts have no power to construe the law expressly in the adjudication, the judges in practice are normally reluctant to make an express statement of the rule of law out of the judgment for fear of being criticized for encroaching on legislative power or even threatening the People's Congress system (Interview 50-17-NSSZ01). As a consequence, the judgments are normally concise, setting out brief facts and application of laws but with no details on reasoning and argumentation. Moreover, politically speaking, as China is a communist state, the courts are definitely political subordinates of the CCP. In this regard, besides the statutory laws enacted by the legislative authorities as prescribed in the Legislation Law, the courts are politically responsible for implementing the directives issued by higher political authorities, normally in the form of a policy or internal document which might have more weight than a guiding case in the adjudication. More importantly, given the rapid rise of social disputes in recent decades, the average caseload of judges, in particular at the grassroots level, is extremely heavy. It is common for the annual caseload at the average level for each judge at the grassroots level to be more than 300 cases.[5] It is therefore the primary goal of the courts to settle cases and disputes. Practically speaking, it is generally unrealistic for judges to render a lengthy

[4] One scholar only ascribes the primary reason why judges lack enthusiasm in the application of guiding cases to the uncertainty of the legal status of guiding cases. This is definitely unconvincing as the Detailed Rules produced by the SPC (2015a) clearly set out the legal status of the guiding cases (Zhang 2017: 302).

[5] This is largely based on my interviews with judges from China's courts, including those in Guangdong Province, Guangxi Zhuang Autonomous Region and Jiangsu Province, from 2016 to 2018.

judgment with details of reasoning and argumentation. A presiding judge from Guangdong, who once rendered a celebrated judgment on a controversial issue with details of reasoning and argumentation, said: "If I render most judgments in this way, I will be incompetent with the position and incapable of settling the cases and disputes before me" (Interview 59-18-HZ04). It can be seen that, given the existence of social, political and legal factors as mentioned, it is understandable that the guiding cases can hardly function like the precedents do in both civil and common law jurisdictions with judicial independence, and they are normally disregarded by the judges in China unless the MPA – a form of statutory interpretation of relevant laws – is obviously pertinent to the case at hand.

Expansion of the SPC's Judicial Lawmaking Authority

The classical doctrine of *stare decisis* – i.e. the power and obligation of courts to base decisions on prior decisions – is obviously inconsistent with the separation of powers as formulated in civil law countries and is therefore rejected by the civil law tradition (Merryman 1985: 22). It can be concluded from the doctrine of separation of powers that courts should be denied any interpretive function and should be required to refer problems of statutory interpretation to the legislature itself for resolution. The legislature would then provide an authoritative interpretation to guide the judge. In this way, defects in the law would be cured, courts would be prevented from making law and the state would be safe from the threat of judicial tyranny. To the civil law fundamentalists, authoritative interpretation by the lawmaker was the only permissible kind of interpretation (Merryman 1985: 39). China follows this traditional formula which states that the court in itself does not have any legislative power. However, having realized the difficulties encountered in applying codified legal rules to an ever-changing pattern of factual circumstances and the fact that the ideals of certainty and completeness in the codified law are often elusive in practice, the case law system in civil law countries was gradually developed in order to maintain the consistency of judicial decisions. The situation in China is different because China's legal system was largely paralysed during the Cultural Revolution (1966–1976), and it has been impossible for the NPCSC to meet the social demand for law in such a short period of time thereafter. As an alternative, the NPCSC has taken a pragmatic attitude and delegated part of the legislative power to the SPC to make abstract judicial interpretations with legally binding force nationwide. However, upon the establishment of the guiding case system, the SPC actually changed from merely exercising the delegated legislative power from the NPCSC to creating its own judicial lawmaking power through particular guiding cases within its own constitutional domain.

Delegation of Legislative Power by the NPCSC

According to the Constitution of the PRC, the NPC is the highest organ of state power and its permanent body is the NPCSC. The NPC and NPCSC exercise the legislative power of the state (articles 57 and 58). In accordance with the law, the people's courts exercise judicial power independently (article 126). In parallel with the civil law tradition, case law is not permitted as only statutes enacted by the legislative power can be law (Merryman 1985: 22). Nonetheless, as mentioned earlier, due to the fact that the NPC and the NPCSC are incapable of providing a comprehensive legal framework by themselves immediately, after decades of legal nihilism, the NPCSC (1981) enacted the resolution concerning the interpretation of law. It provides in para 2 that "interpretation of questions involving the specific application of laws and decrees in court trials shall be provided by the Supreme People's Court". In such a way, the SPC, with exceptional centralized quasi-legislative power, is able to regulate the judicial activities of lower courts and assure uniform interpretation and application of laws in that all lower courts are subject to such abstract judicial interpretations.

By comparison, with regard to the development of a civil law tradition, although the dogmatic formula of separation of power has persisted, it gradually adopted a centralized judicial model by the delegation of legislative power. For instance, in France, as Merryman (1985: 40) states:

> They knew that the legislature would find itself flooded with difficult, often seemingly trivial, requests for interpretation, and that it would find the work of responding to such requests tiresome. The legislature was faced, however, with a theoretical dilemma: it might wish to avoid having to decide a constant stream of questions from the courts, but it could not allow the courts themselves to do the interpreting without undermining the doctrine of the separation of powers.

Under such circumstances, the French Tribunal of Cassation was created by the legislature and given the power to quash incorrect interpretations by the courts.[6] To a certain extent, it is a non-judicial tribunal that provides authoritative answers to questions of interpretation of statutes referred to it by the ordinary judges and it has become the highest court in the ordinary judiciary. In addition, in Italy, for example, the Supreme Court of Cassation hears only questions of "interpretation and application of the law". In Germany, the Supreme Court was also created and empowered to review the decisions of lower courts for legal correctness and to indicate the correct answer accordingly. The historical development of these civil law countries shows that the Supreme Court has incorporated a certain degree of legislative power while the dogma of separation of powers has been substantially blurred. Yet, the highest court in the jurisdiction – one that is manned by judges and that has primary responsibility for assuring the correct and uniform interpretation and application of the statutes by the lower civil and criminal courts – is the direct descendant of a legislative tribunal, and it was originally created to keep the power of interpretation out of the hands of ordinary judges (Merryman 1985: 41, 86–87).

By analogy, in China, the SPC has a certain degree of legislative power delegated by the NPCSC. However, the power is exercised in a different way as the SPC does not interpret the application of the law to specific cases. Rather, it makes the abstract judicial interpretation legally binding on lower courts. Legally speaking, this kind of judicial legislation is subject to the review of the NPCSC. Whenever the SPC exercises its delegated legislative power to enact judicial interpretations, it must ultimately submit the judicial interpretation to the NPCSC for it to be recorded and examined, according to the Woking Methods 2019 (see Chapter 3).

In addition, given the lack of a case law system, a case decided by the SPC in principle has no formal binding force on lower courts. Moreover, the system followed by the courts is that the second instance in principle is the last instance. Judgments and orders of second instance of intermediate courts, High People's Courts and the SPC and judgments and orders of the first instance of the SPC are all judgments and orders of last instance, that is, legally effective judgments and orders. As a consequence, in practice, the SPC seldom adjudicates cases as the appellate

[6] The Tribunal of Cassation was not itself expected to provide authoritative interpretations of the statutes involved in the cases that came before it. On the contrary, its original function, consistent with its separate, non-judicial nature, was merely to quash judicial decisions based on incorrect interpretations of statutes (Merryman 1985: 40).

court because most cases are adjudicated by the grassroot-level courts and can only be appealed to the next higher-level court – Intermediate People's Courts, in accordance with the doctrine of "second instance being final". In this regard, judges normally do not need to consider the SPC's decided cases for they have no fear that their decisions may be reversed by the SPC on appeal.

However, due to the fact that the courts have the constitutional authority to adjudicate cases, they will inevitably construe the statutory laws in order to apply the laws concerned to the facts in specific cases. In this sense, normally, the courts are free to "construe" the meaning of the statutory laws in specific cases implicitly. It appears that such construction of statutory laws in the process of adjudication is different from the SPC's interpretation of a legislative nature. Rather, it is only for the purpose of applying the laws in specific cases and has no binding force at all (Shangguan 2010: 149). In this regard, due to the lack of case law, it is definitely possible for different courts, based on their different constructions, to make different decisions on cases with similar facts. Furthermore, under the People's Congress system, the personnel and finance of the courts are partially decided by the local government and CCP at the corresponding level. Thus, local-level courts, in part, are responsible to and report on their work to the local government. In this regard, it is understandable that the courts, according to their discretion, may take into account local factors when adjudicating cases, in particular when some policies from the prevailing local or higher authorities are pertinent to the case. The result is that, as illustrated earlier, there may be inconsistency of application of national laws among different local areas, although the cases may be arguably similar.

Therefore, the SPC, although it is the highest, actually has difficulty supervising the judicial activities of intermediate courts and basic courts, where the overwhelming majority of cases were handled, through the appeal system. In this regard, legally speaking, the prevailing judicial authority of the SPC over lower courts mainly relies on its judicial interpretation of a legislative nature which derives from its delegated power from the NPCSC. As a judge from Shenzhen city said, "we as judges have been used to rely on relevant specific judicial interpretations of the SPC for judicial decision-making in practice. If no relevant specific judicial interpretation is reliable when adjudicating a particular case, sometimes it may make us into trouble. Of course, this kind of hard case seldom arises in practice" (Interview 50-17-NSSZ01).

In this regard, China remains a traditional authoritarian model of civil law where case law is not allowed in practice as it is assumed that the function of the judge is only to interpret and to apply "the law" as it is technically defined in his jurisdiction. It is required that the judge should resort only to "the law" in deciding cases; whatever the problem that may come before him, the judge will be able to find some form of law to apply – whether a statute, a regulation or an applicable custom (Merryman 1985: 23–24).

Judicial Lawmaking under Guiding Case System

Indeed, since the establishment of the guiding case system, the exact structure of legislative power under China's People's Congress system has become the subject of debate. For instance, Zhang argues that, by adopting the guiding case system, the SPC has actually moved beyond the normal scope of judicial interpretation as empowered by the statutes and expanded its power to establishing a case-based lawmaking framework under which the adjudication of people's courts is directed (Zhang 2017: 274). Furthermore, Zhang (2017: 274) points out that, "[f]ortunately, the move does not seem to have met any objection from the NPC". However, legally speaking, such a move does contravene the principle that China's courts should have no lawmaking power because legislative power should be exclusively exercised by the People's Congress or its delegated authorities through the statutes. For example, the NPCSC allowed the SPC to make an interpretation of the specific application of law in the trial work of the courts, first through the Resolutions on Strengthening the Work of Interpretation of Law (关于加强法律解释工作的决议 *guanyu jiaqiang falü jieshi gongzuo de jueyi*) in 1981 and finally in the amendment of the Legislation Law (article 104). In this regard, the SPC is able to make statutory interpretations of law if they are of a legislative nature, when it deems it necessary. However, the guiding case system, through which the SPC is able to make statutory interpretations of law, has received no statutory delegation from the NPC or NPCSC. The reason why this has been possible has not been thoroughly addressed in the scholarship.

As discussed, the emergence of the guiding case system in China has enabled the SPC to exercise its *judicial* lawmaking power within its own constitutional domain and do so by selecting and deciding guiding cases submitted by recommendation bodies. Clearly, such institutional innovation can only progress if it does not challenge China's authoritarian regime and in particular its People's Congress system. This contrasts with the situation in liberal democracies where historically case law has developed with more freedom (Kirk 2003: 190).

With the development of the guiding case system, the SPC has been able to exercise interpretative power of a quasi-legislative nature which could arguably be grounded on its judicial power enshrined in the Constitution, namely article 26 which states that: "[t]he people's courts exercise judicial power independently, in accordance with the provisions of the law, and are not subject to interference by any administrative organ, public organization or individual". This means that the SPC does not interpret the law through the delegated legislative power it receives from the NPCSC but rather by the power inherent in it as the highest judicial power for deciding specific issues in the process of adjudicating specific cases. In other words, the SPC "interprets" the statutory law in the process of determining the guiding cases through the MPA part of the guiding case. Given that the guiding cases determined by the SPC do have a binding force over all courts according to the Detailed Rules of the SPC (2015a), the SPC can be said to have self-empowered itself as a "lawmaker".

Interestingly, it seems that the SPC found a moral justification for developing the guiding case system in China. With the rapid development of judicial professionalism and transparency of adjudication, in particular with judgments becoming accessible to the public in principle, the problem of "like case are treated differently" has been getting worse and has started to negatively affect the credibility of the courts. Given that this principle has been overwhelmingly accepted as a central notion of justice (Strauss 2002), it is definitely appropriate for the SPC to justify the need for a guiding case system on the ground of this notion. Furthermore, as the precedent-related issues fall into the specialist domain of the courts as opposed to the NPC or NPCSC, it seems that it is the SPC's responsibility to create and implement the system appropriately.

Apparently, this is not to say that there was no fear of "harm to legislative power" because, as far as the legislative nature of this kind is concerned, the guiding case system is actually not substantially different to the SPC's current mechanism of judicial interpretation as delegated by the NPCSC which allows the SPC to fill statutory lacunae through issuing judicial interpretations of a legislative nature. In practice, such legislative activities of the SPC have encountered no "barriers" at all, and the requirement of submitting the interpretations to the NPCSC for review afterwards is merely a formality (Jia 2016: 2220; Li 2009). However, as far as the legitimacy of the reform is concerned, in a single-party state the "legal instruments" including the Constitution may give way to the "political instruments", in particular if the reform is to be or has been endorsed by the CCP's Central Committee. In this regard, as far as the guiding case system is concerned, the issue in question is not whether the SPC has encroached on the power of the legislature unconstitutionally but whether the SPC's reform of guiding cases has been supported and endorsed by the CCP. It is clearly the case that once the reform is endorsed by the CCP's Central Committee, all relevant state organs will cooperate with it. In fact, it has been perceived that, although the courts are normally passive actors in politics and simply implement the directives from higher authorities, they can effectively enhance their authority and apply the laws innovatively if they can seek support from the Party and, if this is achieved, other agencies will adjust their behaviour accordingly (He 2013). As far as the guiding case system is concerned, it was endorsed by the Party in the CCP Central Committee Decision Concerning Several Major Issues in Comprehensively Advancing Governance according to Law (中共中央关于全面推进依法治国若干重大问题的决定 *zhonggong zhongyang guanyu quanmian tuijin yifa zhiguo ruogan zhongda wenti de jueding*) (hereinafter "Decision"), which was passed at the 4th Plenary Session of the 18th Central Committee of the CCP. The Decision states that in order to guarantee judicial fairness and raise judicial credibility, it shall take effective measures to strengthen and standardize judicial interpretation and case guidance and unify standards for application of the law. Organs within the Party and government at every level and leading cadres need to support the courts in exercising their functions and authorities independently and justly in accordance with the law (Central Committee of the Chinese Communist Party 2014). Against this background, the SPC was bold enough to develop the guiding case system and, as described, has not encountered obstacles from the legislature.

In order to reduce the public concern about the encroaching legislative power of the SPC, it has made it clear that the guiding case system is by no means a type of case law such as exists in other jurisdictions. Technically, according to the Detailed Rules of the SPC (2015a), this is correct as guiding cases cannot be treated by the courts as a legal basis for judicial decision-making even though the courts will refer to them in their judgments' reasoning if the case in hand is similar to a guiding case. To not do so would mean that the judgment would be overruled by the appellate court afterwards. To put it simply, its rhetoric on this seems paradoxical as on the one hand the SPC clarifies that guiding cases by no means make law so as to avoid potential constitutional challenges, while on the other hand it has done its best to make guiding cases binding by adding a specific part, the MPA, which has a legislative nature, in the name of achieving justice by "treating like cases alike" in its own domain of judicial decision-making (Hu 2014a).[7] It is of note that in order to differentiate it, the guiding case system has often been labelled "socialist case law" or "case law with Chinese characteristics" (Hu 2014b: 1).

Admittedly, in theory, the guiding case system has placed the court in a better position to resist certain forms of external pressure and make the court's work less politicized in the sense that the work on guiding cases can only be done by the professional courts rather than other political branches. In this sense, the guiding cases to some extent can shield the SPC's interpretative power over the guiding cases against extra-legal influence. In addition, the SPC no longer needs to submit the decided guiding cases routinely to the NPCSC for them to be recorded and examined. That is to say, under a guiding case system, the SPC is able to exercise some degree of judicial lawmaking power independently. Furthermore, guiding cases have also created a new way for the SPC to regulate lower-court adjudication. The SPC has the exclusive authority to select from the rich material of decided cases and promote any court decision to the rank of a guiding case (Ahl 2014: 135–136). Such an appraisal and promotion mechanism is clearly centred on the SPC as all non-guiding cases of the lower courts, to a certain degree, are subject to the guiding case. As illustrated, although the SPC may not be the original trial court, it has the ultimate and exclusive authority to decide the MPA from decisions of lower courts.

Moreover, to some extent, the SPC is able to standardize the application of laws by the lower courts through interpreting the law in the MPA of the guiding case. Different from the abstract judicial interpretation that does not relate to the specific case, the MPA, although abstract, is based on the submitted cases and is applicable to all courts subsequently.

Furthermore, the guiding case mechanism is flexible as it is observed that, "[w]hereas judicial interpretations are enacted in a lengthy

[7] This is reflected the Detailed Rules (articles 9 and 10) in which it is stated that: "Where a case being tried by a people's court at any level is similar to a guiding case issued by the Supreme People's Court in terms of basic facts and application of law, a judgment shall be rendered by reference to the key points of judgment in the relevant guiding case. Where a people's court at any level refers to a guiding case in the trial of a similar case, it shall quote the guiding case as the judgment's reasoning, instead of citing it as the basis for the judgment" (Supreme People's Court 2015a).

procedure that normally includes consultation with other state organs, the procedure for selecting guiding cases is far more flexible. The SPC does not need to draft legal texts from scratch and take into account – similar to a legislator – the interests of all concerned parties" (Ahl 2014: 136). To a certain extent, such a flexible mechanism enables the SPC's exclusive authority to develop further. In China, such a development is clearly conditional given that the courts are subject to the leadership of the CCP politically and the People's Congress system constitutionally. Institutionally speaking, two main instruments have been used by the CCP to maintain its authoritarian regime with a facade of Chinese rule of law. One is the "legal instrument", that is, according to the Constitution, the courts are created by and responsible to the People's Congress system, with the strictly defined role as mere executants of the legislature and independent adjudicative power that can be exercised according to the Constitution and laws. The other is the "political instrument" based on the principle "Party manages cadres", according to which the cadres of the courts, in particular the president and vice presidents, and the cadres of the People's Congress system, are managed by the CCP's organization departments. These two instruments are in fact intertwined and interdependent in practice. Furthermore, as China is a single-party regime, the People's Congress system has not yet been democratized like in liberal democracies and can be manipulated to a large extent by the CCP for political purposes. In practice, it is principally the CCP that decides and recommends the nominees to the People's Congress for appointment, and the practice of single-candidate elections is generally followed (Gasper 1982: 160–169). In addition, people's congresses at or above the county level establish standing committees which are actually bureaucratic organs but are able to exercise most functions of the People's Congress at the corresponding level when it is not in session. Of course, under such a system, the courts are created by and are responsible to the People's Congress or its standing committee under the leadership of the CCP. In addition, the court establishes the Party organization, and its operation is under the leadership of the leading Party group of which the president of the court is the secretary at the same time. Therefore, it can be seen that although the establishment of the guiding case system has empowered the SPC with some special authority to develop the law, its development will definitely be controlled with China's authoritarian governance. Although the guiding case system might be helpful to promote the professionalization of the courts and strengthen the conditional judicial independence, particularly in adjudicating non-political cases, it must be ensured that the People's Congress system with authoritarian features is maintained and the courts continue to be subject to the political leadership of the CCP.

Conclusion

Although the case law system has been evolving in both common law and civil law countries for hundreds of years, the distinctive case law system recently established in China cannot be explained simply by current case law theories used in both common law and civil law jurisdictions. When guiding cases were originally tested by local courts, their effectiveness resembled that of other jurisdictions in that they could significantly solve the problem of like cases being treated differently and maintain the consistency of judicial decisions. However, the system deviated from the original practice when it was adopted by many higher courts at the provincial level as only very limited numbers of cases selected and determined by the higher courts at the provincial level were able to play the guidance role in practice. However, with the performance appraisal system somehow being incorporated into the guiding case system, the higher courts have gained more authority over lower courts by routinely asking them to submit a number of cases for the selection of guiding cases.

Furthermore, the formal establishment of guiding cases by the SPC in 2010 shows that the SPC has become the sole authority on determining guiding cases and is able to interpret the law through the MPA part of the guiding case. Such a part, in essence, is a form of statutory interpretation but in the form of a guiding case. In order to reconcile this legislative function with the People's Congress system where the NPC and NPCSC have the exclusive authority on the interpretation of statutory laws, the SPC (2015a) issued the Detailed Rules. These state that: "When a people's court at any level refers to a guiding case in the adjudication of a similar case, it shall quote the guiding case as part of the reasons for judgment/ruling, but shall not quote the same as a basis for judgment/ruling." This shows the SPC's attempt to promote the guiding case system within its own constitutional authority in the field of adjudication.

Under the guiding case system, and in contrast to previous practice where the SPC performed the legislative function merely through having it delegated by the NPCSC, the SPC is now able to exercise such a type of judicial lawmaking power through the MPA of the guiding cases independently with no routine surveillance of the NPCSC. The SPC has also strengthened its authority over lower courts by making itself the sole authority on determining guiding cases with binding force. Of course, in the context of China, the emergence of such a guiding case law system is compatible with the SPC's ongoing ambition to expand its institutional self-interest as it can be less influenced by extra-legal factors or ideologies (T. Zhang 2012: 46–54). In addition, the system has also kept pace with the reform measures of China's authoritarian regime under which the CCP, in its fourth Plenum of the 18th Central Committee, took a series of measures to strengthen the status of the courts on adjudicating cases independently, in particular at the local level where most cases are handled in practice. As a Chinese law scholar commented on the subject of China's judicial reform, "rule of law and judicial professionalism are possible to the extent they may strengthen and legitimise the CCP's rule", and "even in the best case scenario, the courts will continue to be submissive to the CCP and compliant to its political demands" (Fu 2016: 167, 181). For the future of the guiding case system, to a large extent, this is also applicable. The guiding case system has been further supplemented to article 18 of the Organic Law of the People's Court (National People's Congress 2018c), the legislative intention of which is merely to delegate the SPC with the authority to interpret national laws, i.e. these questions concerning the specific application of laws in judicial proceedings

6

Bureaucratization of Judicial Precedents

There is no doubt that the SPC's guiding case has become a source of law with a binding force on the courts when adjudicating similar cases. Indeed, a large amount of attention has been paid to the normative function of the guiding case, sometimes optimistically (Ahl 2014; Chen 2014; Deng 2016; Finder 2017a; Jia 2016; Li 2016; Zhang 2017). In particular, analysis of the guiding case system is often made in relation to case law in either common law or civil law traditions.[1] However, over a decade of its practice has largely demonstrated that guiding cases have not been implemented as effectively as expected or imagined in contrast to the practice of case law in other jurisdictions. So too, empirically, it has been found that although the guiding cases do have a certain de jure effect on judges according to the Detailed Rules of the SPC (2015a), such an effect can be easily disregarded in practice (Xie 2016). Moreover, the use rate of guiding cases is extremely low, almost negligible, and more than half of them have never been referenced in trial practice. As of 25 November 2015, the total number of cases in which guiding cases were cited was only about 241,146, and out of the 56 guiding cases then published, only 25 had been cited (Chinalawinfo 2015). Cohen offers the following statistics which confirm this:

> If one compared the nationwide references to guiding cases using, as an example, the 561 opinions referencing a guiding case out of 8,723,182 cases on the China Judgments Online website for 2016 (using a simple keyword search to "guiding case"), the citation rate would be about 0.0006%.
>
> (Cohen 2017)

In addition, as to the way of citing guiding cases in the trial practice, judges are reluctant to cite them directly in the judgment's reasoning in

[1] Some scholars have likened guiding cases to common law cases, or even argued that the guiding case system may bring China's system into closer alignment with the common law tradition (Yu and Gurgel 2012; Limmer 2013; Deng 2016; Jia 2016).

accordance with the Detailed Rules of the SPC (2015a). Moreover, when quoting guiding cases, judges normally only refer to the MPA – a form of statutory interpretation – in the judgement (Pkulaw.com 2018). In fact, judges normally respond to the litigants' quotation of guiding cases and explain the reasons *outside* the judgments, although the final judicial decision may, in principle, be compatible with the rules of the guiding case, as provided and defended by the litigants (Zhao and Guo 2017).

To some extent, the inconsistent use of guiding cases contrasts with the routine mechanism of judicial precedents in both common law and civil law jurisdictions. The civil law doctrine of precedent, which seems more comparable with China's system, can be used as an example.[2] Normally, although civil law jurisdictions do not adopt the principle of *stare decisis* in adjudication, precedents do have a persuasive role. This is because "civil law courts are expected to take past decisions into account when there is a sufficient level of consistency in case law. Generally speaking, when uniform case law develops, courts treat precedents as a source of "soft" law, taking them into account when reaching a decision" (Fon and Parisi 2006). Due to the fear of appellate reversal, the doctrine of *jurisprudence constante* has arisen in civil law systems. This gives authority a series of cases that continuously and uniformly apply the same rule of law and crystallizes legal rules through autonomous judicial action (Oliveira et al. 2012: 555, 576–577). Regardless of the legal system, the principle "treat like cases alike" is central to the notion of justice and is often associated with the rule of law which is in turn seen as a central feature of a liberal state (Dworkin 1998: 219–224; Strauss 2002). Judges normally have a tendency to refer to prior cases for decision-making. As noted by Merryman, judges in both civil law and common law systems have some features in common, i.e. they may be sufficiently impressed by the authority of the higher court; they are more likely persuaded by the reasoning of precedents in particular if the rule of the precedents has been repeated with practical consensus; they are too lazy to think through the problem themselves and find a justification for the departure of the principle "treat like cases alike" by themselves; or they normally do not want to risk the decision being reversed on appeal, etc. (Merryman 1985: 47). Of course, these doctrines of precedent, either binding in a common law tradition or persuasive in a civil law tradition, are based on the

[2] As China follows a civil law tradition, it is argued that China's guiding case system has more comparators with civil law systems of this kind (Jia 2016).

experience of legal customs and formed in a decentralized way, mostly in a liberal context where there is judicial independence.

In contrast, institutionally speaking, there is no judicial independence in China's single-party system like that in liberal democracies. The courts, though created by and responsible to China's people's congresses at the corresponding levels and though they exercise adjudicative power independently in accordance with the Constitution of 1982 (article 126), are actually operating under the leadership of the CCP in practice. Specifically speaking, the appointment and removal of the "leading group members" (领导班子成员 *lingdao banzi chengyuan*) of the courts, normally including presidents and vice presidents, are virtually entirely determined by the CCP's organization department, followed by the "approval" of the People's Congress or its standing committee which is also under the leadership of the CCP politically, in accordance with the Constitution and relevant laws. As of 2017, all presidents of the courts at basic and prefecture levels are principally administered by the CCP's organization department at the provincial level directly. For other leading group members, some of them are administered by the CCP's organization departments at the provincial level while others are administered by the organization departments at the prefecture level as delegated by the provincial level (Zhou 2017). Moreover, personnel issues of judges who are not leading group members are normally determined by the leading group of the courts where the president, who normally serves as the Party secretary of the court at the same time, plays a leading role therein. Also, personnel issues, such as appointment, will be "approved" by the People's Congress or its standing committee at the corresponding level afterwards according to the Constitution. In addition, due to most judges holding Party membership, it is not difficult to understand that the judges must insist on the leadership of the CCP and may be influenced by it in reality. Also, it is understandable that the CCP's Political and Legal Committee at the corresponding level, where the presidents of the courts are members, may exert its influence over or even guide the work of the courts politically within the domain of law in practice. However, this is not to deny the fact that, having realized the significance of judicial credibility for strengthening the socialist legal system under the leadership of the CCP, most cases are and can be handled by judges independently in practice, which to some extent is a feature of a dual state. As far as the importance of independent adjudication is concerned, the CCP reiterates that:

> Party and government organs and leading cadre must all not allow judicial organs to do things in violation of their statutory duties or that

> impede judicial fairness; judicial organs must all not enforce requests to interfere in judicial activities from a party or government organ or leading cadre. Party or administrative disciplinary actions will be given for interference in judicial cases; and where it causes in an unjust, false, and wrongfully decided case, or other serious consequences, criminal responsibility will be pursued in accordance with the law.
>
> (Central Committee of the Chinese Communist Party 2014)

This suggests that, in an authoritarian state, even though politically sensitive cases are more likely to be judged in an arbitrary manner, private parties in conventional legal disputes, e.g. property and contract, may gain fair judicature, occasionally even against oppressive institutions (Tóth 2017).

Having said this, it can be seen that the case law theory of routine practice of precedents in a liberal democracy with judicial independence cannot thoroughly explain judges' inconsistent reference to guiding cases in China or be applied to it, as the guiding case, although it has a normative binding force, can easily be disregarded by Chinese judges in practice (Xie 2016). Undoubtedly, the function of the guiding case system or broadly the role of judicial precedents can only be explained thoroughly in China's specific context, notwithstanding the comparisons that can be made with other jurisdictions. Therefore, the following discussion focuses on relevant context-specific issues of the guiding case system that have not yet been completely addressed, such as, given the SPC's consistent commitment to developing the guiding case system, what is the practical effect that has been achieved, notwithstanding its dysfunction as a type of case law? Furthermore, besides the guiding case, what is the role of non-guiding cases in practice and is there any context-specific theory that can provide a holistic view and explain the function of China's judicial precedents?

Dysfunction of the Binding Force of Guiding Cases

Although, normatively, guiding cases have binding force, they are not effectively referred to by the judges as already mentioned. The crucial issue to be further addressed is why this is the case.

Identification of Similarities between Cases and Judicial Independence

Article 9 of the Detailed Rules states that, "where a case being tried by a people's court at any level is similar to a guiding case issued by the

Supreme People's Court in terms of basic facts and application of law, a judgment shall be rendered by reference to the MPA in the relevant guiding case" (Supreme People's Court 2015a). Levi notes that, as a method of reasoning necessary for law, there is a three-step process under the doctrine of precedent: "similarity is seen between cases; next the rule of law inherent in the first case is announced; then the rule of law is made applicable to the second case" (Levi 1948: 501–502).

The first points to the precondition for judges to implement the guiding case system. However, the identification of similarities between cases is largely based on judges' discretion because in the event of ambiguities between statutes, in the main the specific issues presented by the controversies are complex and difficult and usually there are a wide range of possible decisions. For example, as far as the sentencing of convicted criminals is concerned, there is no general agreement about "whether some factors should be taken into account, such as whether the offenders came from disadvantageous social or economic circumstances. And there was nothing approaching general agreement about what weight was to be given to the various factors that were relevant to a sentencing decision" (Strauss 2002). In this sense, it can be argued that the choice surrounding how to "treat like cases alike" is just a variation of the dilemma over rules and standards, i.e. whether decisions should be governed by relatively determinate rules or by standards that allow more discretion (Strauss 2002).

Of course, some rules may be so clear that judges have no room for interpretation in the process of applying it to a particular case. However, as far as legal reasoning is concerned, some legal rules are never clear in reality and, "if a rule had to be clear before it could be imposed, society would be impossible" (Levi 1948: 501). It is simply not true that the law is a system of known rules applied by a judge. In fact, "it is only folklore which holds that a statute if clearly written can be completely unambiguous and applied as intended to a specific case" (Levi 1948: 505).

Due to the inevitability of ambiguity in both the statute and Constitution, as well as the case law, it is often a primary task for a judge when making a decision to figure out the way of clarifying the ambiguities involved either explicitly or implicitly. Obviously, given the fact that contemporary jurists have increasingly recognized and articulated the lawmaking functions of the courts, as well as the independence of the judiciary as stipulated in the Constitution in particular in liberal democracies, the judges are able to articulate a dictum in the judgments in the domain of their discretion.

In this regard, even with the traditional notion that judges are merely in place to apply the law made by the legislature, to a limited extent, judges are able to change or even subvert the governing norm without breaching the rules that govern their institutional role (Strauss 2002). As far as case law is concerned, the dynamics of this are described as follows:

> These characteristics become evident if the legal process is approached as though it were a method of applying general rules of law to diverse facts – in short, as though the doctrine of precedent meant that general rules, once properly determined, remained unchanged, and then were applied, albeit imperfectly, in later cases. If this were the doctrine, it would be disturbing to find that the rules change from case to case and are remade with each case. Yet this change in the rules is the indispensable dynamic quality of law. It occurs because the scope of a rule of law, and therefore its meaning, depends upon a determination of what facts will be considered similar to those present when the rule was first announced. The finding of similarity or difference is the key step in the legal process (Levi 1948: 502).

In relation to the reasoning of case law, in the process of determining the controlling similarity or difference between the present and prior case, the rules have been discovered and the case to a large extent has been decided. This actually shows that the case law mechanism, to a large extent, is grounded on judicial independence where the judges are able to create a rule or a legal category out of the present case. By the same token, a judge in the present case may find the existence or absence of facts which a prior judge thought significant to be irrelevant. Therefore, the judge is not bound by the statement of the rule of law made by the prior judge even in the controlling case (Levi 1948: 502).

Historically, the emergence of case law in England largely occurred in parallel with judges' independence and representative government (Kirk 2003: 189). In addition, in modern civil law countries, the prior case became increasingly significant and took on a persuasive force over the courts in deciding similar cases subsequently. It is also largely ascribed to the judges' independence and the representative government in that the judges are able to make a statement of the rule of law out of a case independently in a liberal context.

In contrast, as China does not have a decentralized model of case law system like those in liberal democracies, the courts are principally executants of the legislature and cannot make an explicit statement of the rule of law out of a case. This was reflected in the SPC's statement that China has not adopted any kind of case law system. What is distinctive about the guiding case system is that it is not the trial judge but the SPC that makes a specific statement of rule of law out of the original judgment. In this sense, the guiding case system, by its nature, is not a type of case law through which the judges are able to make a specific statement of rule of law out of a present case but merely a form of statutory interpretation in that the SPC is able to interpret the law by adding an additional part, the MPA, to a selected guiding case. Obviously, this is a centralized model in the sense that the relevant "rule of law" out of a guiding case is exclusively issued by the SPC, as opposed to the decentralized model in a liberal context where normal judges are free to make a specific statement of rule of law out of a case in hand.

Against this background, it is not logical for judges to explicitly refer to a prior case in a judgment as, to some extent, it challenges the widely accepted principle that China has no case law system. In an authoritarian context, judges, as cadres of the state, will be primarily concerned about whether they have enforced the legal rules issued by the sovereign political authority faithfully.[3] As far as case law reasoning is concerned, according to the Detailed Rules, it seems that judges are able to "identify" the similarity between a present case and a guiding case so as to refer to the MPA issued by the SPC (2015a). However, it is not possible to apply case law reasoning to the guiding case system. On the one hand, it is a fact that "in case law, when a judge determines what the controlling similarity between the present and prior case is, the case is decided" (Levi 1948: 505). At the same time, the construction and application of law has been made either implicitly or explicitly. Also, "the rules are discovered in the process of determining similarity or difference" (Levi 1948: 502). In this regard, assuming that the controlling similarity has been determined by the judge, there is no longer a need to impose an additional rule in the form of the MPA from outside on the judge. On the other hand, as

[3] These include all sources of Chinese law as defined by the SPC in the Provisions on Citation of Such Normative Legal Documents as Laws and Regulations in the Judgments. Specifically speaking, Article 2 states that, "[i]f several normative legal documents are cited in parallel, the citation sequence shall be as follows: laws and legal interpretations, administrative regulations, local regulations, regulations on the exercise of autonomy or separate regulations, and judicial interpretations". In addition, article 6 states that, "[w]-here the normative documents other than those as prescribed by Articles 3, 4 and 5 of these Provisions are confirmed as legal and effective upon examination in accordance with the needs for case trial, such normative documents may be taken as a ruling and reasoning basis" (Supreme People's Court 2009).

the SPC has clearly made a specific rule of law – the MPA – out of a guiding case, and what the judges shall do afterwards is just apply the specific rule to the present case, the facts and legal reasoning involved in a guiding case would actually play only a supplementary role to facilitate judges' understanding of the MPA when applied by judges. In other words, this is merely a process of applying a specific rule of the SPC rather than a process of case law reasoning.

Therefore, due to the fact that China has not adopted any type of case law and judges are largely reluctant to make a specific and explicit statement of rule of law out of a case independently, any attempt to develop the centralized guiding case system into a decentralized type of case law is doomed to be ineffective in reality. In practice, when judges were asked or even challenged by the plaintiff or defendant that a similar prior case should be referred to in the judicial decision-making, they easily defended their disregard of a prior case by saying that "China is not a case law jurisdiction". From the judge's point of view, it is much safer for them not to refer to a prior case. To a certain extent, this has been demonstrated by the malfunction of the guiding case system over the past years.

Collective Model of Judicial Decision-Making and Public Discourse

Although judges in China are reluctant to make a specific and explicit statement of rule of law out of a case, this does not mean that they cannot make a judicial decision independently in most situations. Indeed, adjudicative independence has been increasingly emphasized by the CCP in recent judicial reforms in a way that further enhances the credibility of the judiciary and builds up a more professionalized court system (Central Committee of the Chinese Communist Party 2014: chapter IV). Moreover, the fact that judges are able to make a judicial decision independently does not mean they can do it arbitrarily without any limits.

Historically, in contrast to written statutes issued by a sovereign political authority, case law has never been a corpus of acts passed by the legislature or the like but has grown out of practical cases over centuries, which have been sanctioned by popular assent to their fairness. To put it another way, because case law has arisen out of centuries of judges' decisions and is based on what people believed to be just, it can be said to have grown organically on the basis of custom and precedent over a very long period of time. Thus, there is no need for parliament or some comparable political authority to ratify such a "people's law" (Kirk 2003: 184–185). Kirk argues that in a free society:

> For a body of law to be really enforceable, it must receive the willing assent of the mass of people, living under such a law. Stable government grows out of law, not law out of government. If the political power decrees positive laws without reference to general consent, those laws will be evaded or defied, and respect for law will diminish, so that force must be substituted for justice.
>
> (Kirk 2003: 189)

The mechanism of legal reasoning of case law has actually accepted different views on the ambiguities of words in the forum under the "adversary" model of legal proceedings. In this sense, a significant function of the forum is to protect the parties and communities and make sure that the different arguments can be presented before the court. Broadly speaking, for the mechanism of case law reasoning:

> The examples or analogies urged by the parties bring into the law the common ideas of the society. The ideas have their day in court, and they will have their day again. This is what makes the hearing fair, rather than any idea that the judge is completely impartial, for of course he cannot be completely so. Moreover, the hearing in a sense compels at least vicarious participation by all the citizens, for the rule which is made, even though ambiguous, will be law as to them.
>
> (Levi 1948: 504)

Therefore, although judges are able to reinterpret a prior case and in doing so reject the idea of a prior judge, or convert a legal category out of a prior case into something, such a reasoning process is one "in which the ideas of the community and of the social sciences, whether correct or not, as they win acceptance in the community, control legal decisions" (Levi 1948: 504). In this way, it can be seen that the judicial decision-making process, though judge-centred, is actually situated in the public discourse. In other words, in a liberal context, the courts are bound by the statutes and carry the burden of all participants in the forum, in a broad sense of the public in particular through the mechanism of judicial transparency, where judges have to respond to them in the public sphere when identifying the similarities between cases or justifying the differences if the judicial decision departs from a prior case.

Such a public discourse of legal enforcement can also be illustrated by the jury system in a free society in the following way:

> Guilt or innocence must be determined in open court, by free men whose determination the judge cannot reverse. Whatever the deficiencies of the jury method, serving on juries became a powerful instrument for instructing the public in the nature of law. Jury service, besides, is a form of popular representation in public affairs.
>
> (Kirk 2003: 185–186)

In this way, people can assert a share of public concern, and a state-appointed judge cannot enforce the policies of the political authority without the sanction of a jury which comprises independent citizens. Therefore, the fact-finding jury can fundamentally prevent the judges from making an arbitrary decision. Due to this burden from the public, the judges, although they have discretion, "will not be permitted to create laws or to decide cases arbitrarily, or to favor particular persons in particular circumstances. They must abide by the accumulated experience of legal custom, so that the law will be no respecter of persons, and so that people may be able to act in the certitude that the law does not alter capriciously" (Kirk 2003: 185–186).

In contrast, in an illiberal context, the primary concern of the courts is the enforcement of legal rules issued by a sovereign political authority, rather than the consensus of the people in the community. In this regard, when ambiguities of law arise, given the absence of judicial independence, the judges will normally report the case, if it is complicated and difficult enough, to a higher-level judicial authority for a solution, rather than relying on local customs or consensus of the community. For example, in China, if a case becomes so complicated that the judges feel that it is too risky to handle it directly based on their discretion, it is more likely that they will submit it to the highest decision-making body of the courts, the Adjudication Committee, or seek a solution from the next-level court. In this way, the judges may shift away their burden from the public or elsewhere (He 2012a: 712). Of course, judges may take into account the public concern, but in an authoritarian context this would be limited.

In addition, in an illiberal context, an "inquisitorial" model of legal proceedings is frequently adopted by which the judicial authority is often actively involved in investigating the facts of the case. In line with this, a collective model of judicial decision-making is used, and the judges do not normally provide a detailed reasoning in the judgment to the public. As a result of the lack of judicial independence and judges' reluctance to make a specific and explicit statement of the rule of law out of a case in the judgment, judicial decisions are normally very short, only giving basic information on the parties and authorized agents *ad litem*, procedural history, claims, facts, grounds, the legal basis for the judicial decision, the disposition of the judicial decision and finally the signature of trial judges and the official seal of the court. There is little detailed reasoning about how the factual and legal issues were determined by the judges. Also, the judgment does not include any dissenting opinions of individual judges but is rendered by the court in a collective way through the phrase "the Court holds . . ." (Supreme People's Court 2016). Such a concise model of judicial decision has clear advantages for judges in the sense that it prevents litigants raising further disputes that would ensue from written judgments (Ling 2015: 101). Therefore, although the Western style of judgments with detailed reasoning has been guided and encouraged by the SPC for over two decades, the concise style of Chinese judgments, as discussed, remains almost the same as before.[4] Judges in the same collegiate panel have the right to express dissenting opinions during the closed-door meetings of the panel, during which the majority rule for the final judicial decision-making would be taken, in case of different opinions among the judges.[5] However, under such a collective model, any dissenting or minority opinions of judges would not generally be included in the judgment and made known to the public. In this regard, in the event of ambiguities of laws, judges normally construe the law implicitly behind closed doors and will not disclose their detailed reasoning, if any, to the public in the judgment. On the surface, this shows that judges are merely to declare – rather than make – the law given by the legislature.

This is being played out against the reality of an ongoing tension between "more cases and fewer judges" (案多人少 *anduo renshao*) in practice (Finder 2017b; Interview 14-16-HZ02). For example, from January to October 2015, the courts in Jiangsu employed 10,000 judges but received over 1.6 million cases, meaning that each judge had to

[4] Since 1993, the SPC has issued the Models and Styles of Litigation Documents (法院诉讼文书样式 *Fayuan Susong Wenshu Yangshi*), in order to provide guidance on how to prepare and improve the quality of judgments. In 2016, the SPC (2016) issued new guidance on this.

[5] In 2015, the SPC (2015c) issued a judicial interpretation, stating that judges are free to express their dissenting opinion independently when determining the factual and legal issues. The judges shall enjoy the right not to be removed or demoted from the post or dismissed, and the right to not be given a sanction without a statutory basis and without going through statutory procedures.

handle 160 cases (Jin 2015). As a guide, at the grassroots level, it is common for a judge to handle hundreds of cases per year. In addition, given the simplified style of the judgments in common practice, it is extremely difficult to identify how the factual and legal issues are determined by the judges in a prior case. As the judges stated, "a prior case involves a variety of factors, which cannot be revealed fully in the judgment and presented before the judges in handling a present case. Actually, no cases are the same although there may exist some facts in common" (Yang 2017). Therefore, it is more realistic for a judge to follow the concise style of the judgment, as mentioned earlier, and unrealistic for him to refer to a prior case with detailed reasoning for judicial decision-making because searching for similarities and differences between cases may be an arduous and fruitless endeavour.

Therefore, referring to a guiding case in the judgment can hardly be accepted as routine practice in China. However, in terms of the occasional practice of referring to a guiding case or a prior case, the situation is different. As a means of supporting their decision, judges may search out prior cases only after they had decided the case in their mind but were still uncertain about it. Meanwhile, when handling controversial cases, judges may use a guiding case or a prior case as a kind of defence for their judicial opinion, in particular if they wanted the Adjudication Committee to accept their judicial opinion, even though a similar case submitted could easily be disregarded by the Adjudication Committee because of the absence of a case law system. In addition, some new judges, particularly at the grassroots-level courts of Guangxi, said they may use high-quality judgments of Guangdong to learn how to make judicial decisions and write judgments. In short, referring to a guiding case or a prior case is mostly an inconsistent practice and normally not included in the judgment in China.

It can be seen that the lack of judicial independence has been the main barrier for judges to make an explicit and specific statement of the rule of law out of a case at hand in a way that would develop case law in China. At the same time, given the collective model of judicial decision-making in the event of ambiguities of laws, the judges' primary concern is not about the public consensus in the community but the will of the higher authority. Consequently, the concise style of the judicial decision without very detailed reasoning has become an obvious way for judges to protect themselves in the sense that it can, to a certain extent, avoid potential legal disputes based on the judicial decision from litigants and the public, and avoid the political risks that may occur otherwise in an authoritarian context. It has been a common practice for judges to exclude details on determining factual and legal issues, including their construction of laws and the reasoning, from the judgment. This then makes it extremely difficult for the judges to identify the similarities between cases which is a precondition for the legal reasoning of case law. Following this logic, the guiding case can hardly function as case law, but its main legal function is in fact through the MPA, which is added by the SPC and is a form of statutory interpretation. It can be foreseen that, in such an authoritarian context, the case law function of the guiding case system is doomed to ineffectiveness and is used in an inconsistent way, if it is applied at all.

Guiding Cases and the SPC's Typical-Case-Selection Movement

To be true, since its inception, it is fair to say that the legitimacy of the guiding case system has not been contested in practice, and there seem to be no political or constitutional barriers to the SPC moving forward and continuing to build up a more comprehensive system of Chinese precedents centred on guiding cases. For example, using the current guiding case system, the SPC established the Research Base (Beijing) for Intellectual Property Case Guidance (知识产权案例指导研究[北京]基地 *zhishi chanquan anlie zhidao yanjiu Beijing jidi*) in 2015, based in the newly established Beijing Intellectual Property Court. It has also moved to establish a comprehensive intellectual property case guidance system, including guiding cases and reference cases (Tao 2015). According to the Outline of the Juridical Protection of Intellectual Property in China (2016–2020) (中国知识产权司法保护纲要 *zhongguo zhishi chanquan sifa baohu gangyao* (2016–2020)), the intellectual property case guidance system incorporates the following precedents: (1) the intellectual property guiding cases published by the SPC; (2) the prior cases published in the SPC's *Gazette*; (3) representative/typical cases published by the SPC's Intellectual Property Division;[6] (4) prior cases published by the SPC's Research Base (Beijing) for Intellectual Property Case Guidance; and (5) representative intellectual property cases published by the SPC's Judicial Case Academy.[7] In addition, specific rules and mechanisms for case

[6] For the purpose of this chapter, the terms prior case, judicial precedents and precedents may be used interchangeably. In addition, the term "typical case", instead of the identical terms "representative case" and "model case", is used in this chapter.

[7] Research Institute for Judicial Cases (司法案例研究院 *sifa anlie yanjiuyuan*), formally affiliated with the Supreme People's Court, was established in September 2016. The aim of

selection, the level of legal force of different types of precedents, the authority of different publishing institutions and the publication methods have been defined accordingly.

The guiding case system does not work effectively as a sort of case law, but this does not mean that it is of no value in other ways. The guiding case system has in fact acted to solidify the national typical-case-selection movement in that a certain number of typical cases, preliminarily selected and submitted mostly by lower courts, are submitted to the SPC for final selection and determination.

It appears that the guiding cases do not arise spontaneously from the trial practice, as opposed to the decentralized model of case law which is binding once rendered by the judges. The guiding cases are artificially selected from lower courts and passed up to the SPC for final determination. In order to make the selection movement run smoothly, there must at least exist some mechanism that ensures a certain number of typical cases are selected and submitted to the SPC periodically.

Interestingly, legally speaking, it is not compulsory for the lower courts to submit a certain number of typical cases to the SPC periodically. Nonetheless, it has been common practice for provincial-level courts to submit a certain number of typical cases from within their own respective jurisdiction to the SPC for final selection and publication. These cases, which are selected and determined by the Research Office of the SPC, have de facto the highest authority among all typical cases for they have gained a clear legal status with a binding force. They are then finally endorsed by the highest judicial decision-making body – the Adjudicative Committee of the SPC. In addition, the SPC has issued a specific official notice to give all provincial-level courts details on the style for compiling, submitting and formatting guiding cases (Research Office of Supreme People's Court 2011). In this regard, owing to the higher political authority of the SPC, it is natural for provincial-level courts to select and submit some preliminarily selected guiding cases to the SPC for final determination.

This type of typical-case-selection movement inside the court system has been running in a bureaucratic manner for decades. Due to the higher political status of the SPC, the SPC or its relevant departments

the academy is to collect and carry out research on China's judicial precedents and build up a comprehensive database of China's precedents to facilitate the adjudication in practice. For more details, see the website of the Judicial Case Academy at http://anli.court.gov.cn/static/web/index.html#/yjygk, accessed 18 August 2017.

are able to issue relevant policies or notices informing and mobilizing lower courts to engage with the typical-case-selection movement. In 1992, the SPC's Training Center for China's Senior Judges (中国高级法官培训中心 *zhongguo gaoji faguan peixun zhongxin*), which is currently called the National Judges College (NJC) (国家法官学院 *guojia faguan xueyuan*), formally established a typical-case-selection mechanism, under which the provincial-level courts, in principle, have a liaison judge who is in charge of selecting a certain number of typical cases from within its jurisdiction to the NJC for the final selection and annual publication of *China Case Trial Highlights* (中国审判案例要览 *zhongguo shenpan anlie yaolan*) (hereinafter "*Highlights*"). The *Highlights* is co-edited by senior judges from SPC tribunals and renowned law professors from China's prestigious law school at Renmin University of China (RUC) in Beijing. The director of the editorial board of the *Highlights* is the SPC's President Zhou Qiang and the editors-in-chief are the vice presidents of the SPC and RUC (National Judges College and Renmin University of China School of Law 2016: 1). The high political authority of the editorial team clearly indicates the importance of the *Highlights* among the courts.

In addition, the China Institute for Applied Jurisprudence (CIAJ) (中国应用法学研究所 *zhongguo yingyong faxue yanjiusuo*), a subordinate institute of the SPC, has selected a certain number of typical cases for the publication of *Selected Cases from the People's Courts* (人民法院案例选 *renmin fayuan anlie xuan*) (hereinafter "*Selected Cases*") since 1991. This became a monthly issue in 2016. It also established a stable typical-case-selection mechanism, under which provincial-level courts, as well as many prefectural-level courts, normally appoint one or two liaison judges who are in charge of periodically selecting a certain number of typical cases for the SPC from within their respective jurisdictions (China Institute for Applied Jurisprudence 2016: 258–260). The advisory board of the *Selected Cases* includes the SPC's executive vice president and vice presidents, and the editors are generally chief judges of the SPC, which to some extent also shows the high authority of the *Selected Cases* among the courts.

As far as the departmental interests are concerned, given that the NJC and CIAJ are not trial divisions of the SPC, the *Highlights* and *Selected Cases* have become extremely significant for the two. Over the past decades, the CIAJ has regularly issued relevant official documents to regulate and fuel its typical-case-selection movement with regard to the submission style, format requirement, criteria, etc. (China Institute for Applied Jurisprudence 2016). The typical-case-selection work of the

CIAJ has been officially stressed and supported by the SPC. For instance, in 2005, the General Office of the SPC issued a specific official notice to all provincial-level courts, stressing the authority of the CIAJ and the importance of its edited *Selected Cases* and asking the courts to establish and improve the mechanism of liaison judges so that they can edit, select and submit quality typical cases regularly to CIAJ for the final selection, determination and publication in *Selected Cases* (General Office of Supreme People's Court 2005). In particular, the importance of *Highlights* has been constantly emphasized by the presidents of the SPC and its work has been appraised by state leaders such as Xi Jinping and Hu Jintao (National Judges College and Renmin University of China School of Law 2016).

Due to this, these two typical case compilation and selection works have gained political significance among the courts and in practice the courts are cooperative. At present, it has become common practice for provincial-level courts to engage with the selection movement and submit a certain number of typical cases to the NJC and CIAJ for their final selection and publication in *Highlights* and *Selected Cases* respectively. For example, the High People's Court of Shandong Province submitted eighty-four typical cases in total from within the province to *Selected Cases* and fifty-seven to *Highlights* between 2013 and 2017.[8]

Apart from these, the *Gazette* of the SPC is also held in high regard by the courts. This is due in no small measure to its editor-in-chief being the executive vice president of the SPC and it being administered by the General Office of the SPC. In practice, the courts normally treat a typical case, if selected and published in the *Gazette*, as more authoritative than those edited by other SPC institutes/tribunals, such as *Highlights* and *Selected Cases* (Interviews 03-16-JS03, 04-16-JS04, 05-16-JS05). For example, the High People's Court of Jiangsu stipulates that, if a typical case is selected as a guiding case or published in the *Gazette*, then both the judge and his or her court or tribunal will be awarded a Citation for Merit (Jiangsu High People's Court Adjudicative Committee 2012). This indicates that the typical cases in the *Gazette* and guiding cases are normally more authoritative than other forms of typical cases, to a large extent owing to the higher political authority of the competent authorities of the SPC.

In addition, mostly for political, policy and even market reasons, the SPC or its tribunals in the name of the SPC may organize some

[8] The information is provided by a Chinese judge (Interview 49-17-JNSD01).

typical-case-selection awarding activities in adjudicative areas across the country. For instance, the Environment and Resources Tribunal of the SPC, in responding to the CCP's new policy with an emphasis on environmental protection, called on all legal professionals to submit quality judicial precedents in this area for the SPC's national award programme of typical/model cases (Qiao 2017). Receiving an award of this type is a title of honour for the trial judges and their court. These kinds of awarding activities are officially noted by the SPC's institutes and the judges/courts normally participate in them on a voluntary basis. Largely due to the SPC's high political authority and the influence of these types of national awarding activities, it has become common practice for the *Selected Cases* to contain a special column in each issue for the publication of the typical cases selected from national awarding activities.

Most tribunals of the SPC play their own role in informing the judiciary by publishing specialist periodicals or book series in their respective areas of expertise, such as the *Book Series of China Trial Guide* (中国审判指导丛书 *zhongguo shenpan zhidao congshu*), which provide judges with newly released policies, judicial interpretations, typical cases, opinions on new or difficult legal issues, etc. For example, the SPC's criminal adjudication tribunals publish *Reference to Criminal Trial* (刑事审判参考 *xingshi shenpan cankao*) bimonthly. Issues of *Reference to Criminal Trial* often contain special columns for publication of some typical/model cases with judges' specialist comments, as well as some representative judgments with a commentary summary of judges' reasoning therein. In addition, the periodicals or books of this type that are edited by the SPC's tribunals often contain some case notes that discuss new or difficult issues in each volume. Because the SPC has not officially recognized the importance of this type of periodical or book, in spite of them being edited by the tribunals of the SPC, they are often treated as significant reference books or periodicals among legal professionals. In practice, the typical cases of this type normally are further selected by SPC's relevant institutes for the publication on the *Selected Cases* periodically.

Furthermore, SPC's publishing agencies, including its newspaper, *People's Court Daily* (人民法院报 *renmin fayuan bao*); the weekly magazine, *The People's Judicature* (人民司法 *renmin sifa*); and the publishing company, People's Court Press (人民法院出版社 *renmin fayuan chubanshe*), also publish some typical cases in their volumes periodically, as well as edited casebooks. For example, the *Collection of the SPC's Judicial*

Rules (最高人民法院司法观点集成 *zuigao renmin fayuan sifa guandian jicheng*), published by the People's Court Press, is in its second edition and has become very popular among judges as a useful reference book for their judicial decision-making. In addition, as only a limited number of submissions can be published in the *Selected Cases*, its editorial committee, to a certain extent motivated by the publishing market, has collaborated with a publishing company to publish the book series *Annual Casebook of China's Courts* (中国法院年度案例 *zhongguo fayuan niandu anli*) in order to publish more submissions on it, which can actually include some published typical cases in the *Selected Cases* (China Case Trial Highlights Editorial Board 2016). For these types of typical cases, they are normally market-oriented with no political importance in the courts, and the purpose is mainly for legal education, rule-of-law propaganda, scholarly research, etc.

Based on this analysis, it can be seen that the SPC has actually created a variety of typical-case-selection movements largely in a bureaucratic manner, and the guiding case has become a legalized form among all of the SPC's typical cases and has largely crystallized the typical-case-selection movement. The variety of SPC typical-case-selection movements is illustrated in Table 6.1.

It is widely accepted as a title of honour for a judge if his or her judgment is selected as a typical case for publication, especially in the first four types mentioned in Table 6.1. Such an honour is often treated as a bonus point for a judge or a court to compete for the SPC-organized national awards, such as "National Model Judges" and "National Model Courts". In addition, some courts may take it as a performance indicator.

The Detailed Rules set out, in article 14, that the people's courts at all levels will reward entities and individuals that have made outstanding contributions to case guidance work in accordance with the Judges Law (法官法 *faguan fa*) and other relevant provisions (Supreme People's Court 2015a). However, strictly speaking, there are no rigid regulations on the typical-case-selection movement. Normally, submitting a certain number of typical cases to the SPC is more like a political task for the lower courts. In this regard, the extent to which the courts are actively engaged with the movement may vary from province to province because it largely depends on the extent to which the provincial-level court has taken effective incentive measures to motivate the courts within its jurisdiction to engage with the selection activities. The High People's Court of Jiangsu is an example of a court that has taken its case guidance work seriously and has issued the Implementation Rules on

Table 6.1 *Variety of typical-case-selection movements of the Supreme People's Court*

Type	Selection institute	Ground	Binding force	Honour	Frequency
1. Guiding cases	SPC's Research Office (endorsed by the Adjudicative Committee)	SPC's statutory rules	Yes	Highest	Periodical on a batch basis
2. Typical cases in SPC's *Gazette*	SPC's General Office	Official document	No	High	Monthly
3. Typical cases in *China Case Trial Highlights*	SPC's NJC	Official document	No	Medium	Yearly
4. Typical cases in *Selection of People's Court Cases*	SPC's China Institute for Applied Jurisprudence	Official document	No	Medium	Yearly
5. Typical cases selected through national contest	SPC's relevant institutes/tribunals	Official document	No	Medium	Occasional
6. Typical cases in SPC tribunals' edited publications	SPC's tribunals	Semi-official	No	Low	Periodical
7. Typical cases in other publications	SPC's publishing agencies and others	Market-oriented	No	Extremely low	Periodical/ aperiodic

Strengthening the Work of Case Guidance (关于加强案例指导工作的实施意见 *guanyu jiaqiang anlie zhidao gongzuo de shishi yijian*) (hereinafter "Implementation Rules") (Jiangsu High People's Court 2012; Jiangsu High People's Court Adjudicative Committee 2012). This encourages the courts of Jiangsu to establish a special fund to make awards to judges whose judgments are ultimately selected as an SPC typical case in the first four types in Table 6.1. Specifically, the judge will be given bonus points towards his or her annual performance score as well as this financial award. In addition, the court to which the judge is affiliated will be rewarded by the High People's Court of Jiangsu. Furthermore, if a judgment is ultimately selected as a guiding case, he or she will be awarded a Citation for Merit Second Class, and if selected and published by the SPC's *Gazette*, a Third Class.[9] In contrast, if a provincial-level court does not adopt relevant policies or offer incentives to motivate lower courts to submit a certain number of quality typical cases to the SPC, the lower courts will obviously have fewer incentives and will not take the task seriously as an important part of their work, for example, in Guangxi (Interviews 21-16-GX02, 22-16-GX03, 23-16-FCG01, 32-16-QZ02). Moreover, as submitting a certain number of typical cases to the SPC has been somehow an assigned "political" task, in order to avoid unnecessary controversies from the public or even political risks from the relevant higher-up authorities, the judges normally follow the principle that the selected typical cases are not controversial and sensitive when considering which precedent falls within the category of "typical cases" (Interviews 01-16-JS01, 03-16-JS03, 05-16-JS05). This means that, submitting a socially controversial judicial precedent, though perhaps satisfying the conditions as a typical case, generally is not a rational choice for judges in the context of China.

A Bureaucratic Model of Judicial Precedents Centred on Guiding Cases

It has been established that the effectiveness of the SPC's typical-case-selection work needs the active participation of the provincial-level courts. In response to this, the SPC has delegated the development of a supplementary system on a formal basis to the provincial-level courts,

[9] In this regard, it is understandable that some courts sometimes invited the editor of the SPC *Gazette* to deliver a lecture on how a precedent could be selected as a representative case by the SPC.

which is officially called the reference case system, as distinguished from the guiding case system, in order to further strengthen its typical-case-selection work nationwide. Specifically, in 2010, the SPC (2010d) issued the Certain Opinions on Regulating Trial Relations Between Courts in a Vertical Relationship, clearly stating in article 9 that the High People's Courts of each province shall guide the trial work of local courts at all levels within their respective jurisdictions by a variety of measures, including establishing a reference case system (Supreme People's Court 2010d). Moreover, for the courts below the provincial level, they may select and publish a certain number of typical cases within their respective jurisdictions but certainly do not have any authority in the reference case system (Hu 2014c).

Although it is not yet common practice for provincial-level courts to establish a formal reference case system, because of the SPC's constant emphasis on case guidance work some provincial-level courts, such as the High People's Court of Jiangsu, have established a reference case system formally according to the SPC's rules on case guidance work. According to the Implementation Rules issued by the High People's Court of Jiangsu, besides the guiding cases two types of typical cases are categorized as reference cases: one is the typical cases published in the SPC's *Gazette*; and the other is those published in the *Gazette* of Jiangsu High People's Court (Jiangsu High People's Court 2012; Jiangsu High People's Court Adjudicative Committee 2012).

The Implementation Rules have provided more details on the selection mechanisms of guiding and reference cases, relevant incentive measures, submission procedures, training programmes on guiding and reference cases, etc. In contrast, it does not provide details concerning the role of reference cases in judicial decision-making and merely states that the courts within the province may take a reference case into consideration when adjudicating similar cases on a voluntary basis (Jiangsu High People's Court 2012), even though such a legal statement to some extent can show that reference cases have more political importance than other general typical cases or judicial precedents. In any case, given the absence of case law in China, the practical effectiveness of the reference cases is not substantially different to other judicial precedents with no binding force. For example, they may occasionally be referred to as a reference implicitly in the judicial decision-making just as other scholarly articles or casebooks are. Nonetheless, politically, once a reference case system is established at the provincial level, it can definitely institutionalize the case guidance work within the

Table 6.2 *Hierarchy of case guidance system in China*

Category	Publishing authority	Nature	Level
Guiding cases	SPC	Formal/binding	National
Reference cases	Provincial-level courts/specialist court	Formal/non-binding	Provincial
Typical cases	All levels of courts	Informal/non-binding	All levels

province, and further strengthen the guiding case system of the SPC and fortify the typical-case-selection movement.

In addition, for the case guidance system of intellectual property law, the SPC has clearly stated in the Outline of the Juridical Protection of Intellectual Property in China (2016–2020) that it will make efforts to build up a dynamic and interactive case guidance system comprising guiding cases and reference cases, with the latter including typical cases published in the SPC's *Gazette*, those published by the SPC's Intellectual Property Tribunal, those published by the SPC's Research Base (Beijing) for Intellectual Property Case Guidance located at Beijing Intellectual Property Court and those published by the SPC's Research Institute for Judicial Cases (Supreme People's Court 2017). To some extent, such a practice has shown that, due to the higher political authority of the SPC, when the typical cases are selected by its tribunals or relevant institutes, they can become a main source for the selection of reference cases.

Based on this analysis, it can be concluded that there has emerged a hierarchy in the case guidance system in China, which includes guiding cases, reference cases and general typical cases. This is illustrated in Table 6.2. Broadly, all these typical cases are selected from the judicial precedents through the national typical-case-selection movement.

There is no strict requirement for a provincial-level court to establish a formal reference case system within its jurisdiction, and there are no fixed and unified standards applicable to all provincial-level courts. In practice, most provincial-level courts have not yet established this kind of system, although such a system with incentive measures to a large extent is able to fortify the bureaucratization of judicial precedents. Moreover, it is understandable that, given the political importance of typical cases, the prefectural and grassroots-level courts are more or less engaged with the typical-case-selection movement. More than that, given the importance of propaganda in authoritarian regimes, the typical case has somehow become an effective way for the courts to propagandize their judicial credibility and build up a good image in society (Interview 01-16-JS01). For example, the Suzhou Intermediate People's Court initiated a series of typical-case-selection activities for the purposes of propaganda that would enhance the court's image by informing the public that they can expect expertise, justice, fairness and impartiality from judges. Since 2015, the court has also published over 8,800 promotional articles to explain and propagandize the law through selected typical cases in state-owned media at the prefectural level and above. In addition, since the establishment of its own press conference system, the Suzhou Intermediate People's Court has held press conferences ninety-four times and released 768 typical cases through this medium as well as through state-owned media (Suzhou Intermediate People's Court 2017). In this regard, typical-case-selection activities at the grassroots level play a unique role in China's legal system politically.

Conclusion

Although China still follows a traditional civil law model, the SPC established a novel guiding case system in 2010. According to the SPC's specific rules, all courts should refer to a guiding case in the reasoning part of a judgment if it is similar to a case at hand. The aim of this is to achieve justice by "treating like cases alike", with the proviso that under no circumstances can a guiding case be treated as a legal basis for judicial decision-making. There has previously been debate about whether China's courts should have a distinctive legislative authority through such a guiding case system. Nevertheless, the SPC formally established and developed the system so that it could interpret the law directly by adding an additional part – the MPA – to its selected guiding cases. The CCP endorsed the SPC's work on case guidance at the fourth plenary session of the 18th CCP Central Committee, which has cleared the way for its further development.

In the literature, much attention has been paid to the guiding case system in terms of its similarities with precedential case systems in both common law and civil law traditions. However, in reality, it was found that guiding cases hardly function as a type of case law – a quality which has been exaggerated in the literature. In fact, the guiding case system is substantially different from case law systems in other rule-of-law jurisdictions – systems which the SPC has officially rejected. Comparative studies can hardly explain the ineffectiveness of the guiding case system and particularly the political dynamics behind it.

Moreover, this chapter reveals that China's judges are generally reluctant to refer to a judicial precedent, including a guiding case, in the process of making a judicial decision. Given the absence of a case law system as opposed to a guiding case system, it would be irrational for China's judges to make a clear and independent statement of the rule of law from a case before them. Instead, they normally hide the understanding or reasoning with which they determined the factual issues and applied the law from the public for fear of being accused of exercising a lawmaking authority. By doing so, judges can continue to cast themselves as "loyal executants" of the will of the legislature while ensuring that they are not held to account by the authorities in the event of legal ambiguities. In line with this, China follows a collective model of judicial decision-making; judges do not normally provide detailed reasoning expressly in judgments to avoid a "dialogue" with the public. As a consequence, judgments are normally technical and brief with no detailed reasoning and are not responsive to the public. It can be noted that responsiveness is the foundation of case law development in a liberal context.

However, the guiding case system is not wholly ineffective. The emergence of a guiding case system has crystallized a bureaucratic system of judicial precedents in which guiding cases are at the top of the pyramid. Such a bureaucratic system is based on a nationwide typical-case-selection movement in which the provincial-level courts are politically responsible for submitting a certain number of typical cases selected from within their respective jurisdictions to the SPC annually. Furthermore, the SPC has been attempting to strengthen such a bureaucratic system through promoting a fluid reference case system which can be formally established and promoted by the provincial-level courts. The extent to which such a bureaucratic system can be implemented at local levels largely depends on the extent to which local-level courts have taken effective measures to achieve this. Given that judges' caseload is heavy, in particular at the grassroots level, and the selection of typical cases is not an indicator used in the assessment of judges' annual performance, judges normally just do the least required of them in the typical-case-selection movement.

As a whole, China has actually formed a vertical hierarchy of typical cases of different types which comprises guiding cases, reference cases and typical cases. The guiding case system has been formally institutionalized by the SPC, while the reference case system has emerged in some provinces under the SPC's policy of emphasizing case guidance work.

The typical cases, mainly selected through the typical-case-selection movement, have been the main source for guiding cases and reference cases. Moreover, given the absence of case law, China appears to have created a bureaucratic model of judicial precedents within which a case can achieve a certain degree of political importance if selected as a typical case.

The operation of such a bureaucratic system is mainly grounded on the political hierarchy of the courts in the context of China. In this regard, it is foreseeable that, provided the courts to some extent remain politically dependent on the authorities, and the judges are reluctant to make an explicit statement of the rule of law out of a case before them, it is unrealistic that China will embrace a vibrant case law system which is responsive to the public and has a tangible effect on judicial decision-making. Rather, stressing the so-called "Chinese characteristics" of the system is merely a way for the SPC or the higher-level courts to strengthen their political authority through the typical-case-selection movement. In this sense, the guiding case system, though not effective in judicial decision-making, has self-empowered the SPC with additional legislative authority and has mostly played a political role in strengthening the SPC's political authority. More importantly, it has crystallized the bureaucratization of judicial precedents in China. Such a bureaucratic theory of judicial precedents centred on guiding cases clearly fits into China's authoritarian context and is substantially different from any other type of case law in a liberal context. Of course, politically, the typical-case-selection movement can also have a positive effect on the propaganda of judicial credibility in an authoritarian regime.

7

Concluding Reflections

Chinese Law, Authoritarian Legality and Legal Instrumentalism

It is evident that the law as perceived in conventional wisdom has been reconfigured to some extent in contemporary China. Undoubtedly, the law does both exist and work distinctively in such an illiberal context. That being said, given the increasing significance of law in China's society, it generates questions for further inquiries in "Chinese law" as *practised in* context, as well as the reconceptualization and theorization of "Chinese law" in the literature.

Understanding "Chinese Law" in Context

Once upon a time, American scholar William Alford (1997: 398, 400, 402) said that for much of the twentieth century, the impact of law on Chinese life was largely neglected in the Western scholarship of Chinese history and society, with law typically being treated as an afterthought. This view was largely ascribed to the worldview of Confucian scholar-officials, in the sense that law was principally considered to be an inferior social instrument; this indicates that the prevailing function of law, if considered in a societal context, was to mitigate failures of the ruler (and by implication, his delegates) to lead people satisfactorily through the moral persuasion and exemplary education of Confucianism. In addition, technically speaking, the difficulty of accessing the "field" or data – due to the political sensitivity of the issue, cultural or language barriers, etc. – also forms part of the reason why the role of Chinese law, particularly at the local level, has been relatively underexplored in Western scholarship. Furthermore, it is perceived that "Chinese lawlessness" stood as something of a globally recognized "fact" in European Orientalist scholarship, as Orientalisms typically posit law as inherently "Western" and "modern", thereby excluding the Chinese from both law and modernity (Ruskola 2013: 42, 56).

Of course, since 1978, this perception of "Chinese law" was increasingly challenged by the increasingly important role of law in China's practice, as its economic rise was accompanied by its rapid legal development. As a result, the discipline of Chinese law has emerged. The focus of this discipline has shifted more towards what the role of Chinese law *is* in society, given the increasingly important role of law for China's Party-state, or alternatively, from a liberal rule-of-law perspective, what legal practices China has *not* implemented (Minzner 2011: 977). Clearly, understanding the role of law in Chinese society entails that the inquiry go beyond the perception in a liberal context, as it would otherwise be relatively easy to argue that China lacks – or at least is largely lacking in – law due to the absence of the Western formal-rational traditions of legalism in the Chinese context (Shklar 1986: 179; Huang 2015). Due to historical and cultural differences between China and the West, it is possible to imagine the "Chinese non-legal nonsubject" in the West, if (for example) the "American legal subject" is taken as a standpoint. Moreover, as Ruskola (2013) pointed out, perceiving Chinese people as being either unable or unwilling to rely on the law to defend their rights is simply inaccurate. Undoubtedly, legal concepts and theories developed in the West may sometimes make very little sense when applied in an attempt to understand the nature and use of law in China's sociopolitical context. As Philip Huang once cautioned, unwittingly approaching China with Western models in mind must be avoided (Huang 1991). As law is not static but dynamic in society, it is almost impossible to understand a written legal doctrine in complete isolation from its social context. It would indeed be accurate to state that China historically lacks Western formal-rational traditions, and that there has often been a "crucial difference between the logicality of theory and the illogicality of practice" (Huang 2015: 33). Nonetheless, understanding the logic of this "illogicality of practice" is an unavoidable intellectual task if one is to conceptualize and theorize Chinese law. It is evident, as discussed in this book, that various forms of positive laws have been created and put into practice within China's legal system. As such, understanding Chinese law is a journey grounded in the Chinese context and involves incorporating law into a broader understanding of contemporary China (Alford 1997: 412).

Legal Instrumentalism in Context

Intellectually, there have been significant efforts made to (re)conceptualize and theorize issues of Chinese law in their sociopolitical context.

For example, "zones of lawlessness" were conceptualized as a part of China's legal order, indicating that "notwithstanding the existence of an emerging sphere of legality, lawlessness remains firmly entrenched" in China's criminal justice system (Sapio 2010: 3). Of course, apart from existing theoretical discussion in relevant specific subfields, or on some specific topics of Chinese law, the question of whether a general theory could be developed to characterize the nature and function of Chinese law remains a scholarly issue that needs to be further addressed.

In Western legal tradition, there have been three competing classical legal theories – namely, natural law theory, legal positivism and the historical school – that each emphasize a different single dimension of law. Harold Berman (1988: 779) summarized these as follows:

> The positivist school treats law essentially as a particular type of political instrument: a body of rules laid down ("posited") by the state, having its own independent self-contained character separate and distinct from both morality and history. The natural-law school, by contrast, treats law essentially as the embodiment in legal rules and concepts of moral principles derived from reason and conscience. Finally, the historical school treats law as a manifestation of the historically developing ethos – the traditional social representations and attitudes – of a people or a society.

Having concluded that each individual dimension of law emphasized by each of these classical theories respectively seems to be indispensable to a general legal theory, Berman (1988) attempted to bring them into common focus by developing a so-called "integrative jurisprudence", which incorporates each apparently indispensable dimension of law as reflected in the classical theories. Notably, these theories were both historically situated in the West and developed largely in a liberal context.

Historically, these traditions and social conditions as they evolved in the Occident are substantially different from those in the Orient. In particular, the development of modern law in the West exhibits transcendent qualities rooted in its religious traditions. As Berman (2000: 335) pointed out, in history, "all the system of West emerged in response to a belief in the lawful character of the universe and in the fundamental purpose of law to guide men and women to salvation", although the sources of Western legal tradition in these ancestral religious beliefs (both Jewish and Christian) are rarely mentioned today. In comparison, China has no such theistic religious tradition, and the natural law theory rooted in Western history barely resonates in China owing to its different legal traditions.

Moreover, legal positivism holds that law is an official rule handed down by a sovereign lawmaker, and claims the separation of morality from law; this stands in contrast to the position of natural law theorists, who explicitly incorporate morality into the law. In a modern context, such a theory may stand out in the normative sense when the sovereign lawmaker has been thoroughly democratized, particularly as demonstrated in well-developed Western liberal democracies with formal-rational traditions, and especially when accompanied with economic success. Furthermore, judicial independence, as an essential constitutional requirement for a liberal rule-of-law order, has made the courts politically independent in a way that sets them apart from other political branches of government (e.g. the legislative and executive bodies). In this way, positive laws are institutionally enforced by judges in a "non-political" way, such that judges are assumed to be just, fair and impartial. Thus, two ways of thinking have formed, namely the political and the legal, although these may sometimes be blurred or mixed in practice. In comparison, illiberal regimes may adopt a basic form of constitutional democracy that is often categorized as substantially "illiberal" (Zakaria 1997). Nonetheless, the operation of the legislature, officially claimed to represent the will of the people, is politically controlled or manipulated by the single ruling party under such regimes and by no means functions as it would in a genuine liberal democracy. Of course, positive laws are formally made by the legislature of the illiberal regime, and this process may incorporate democratic formats to varying degrees. For instance, an illiberal election may adopt a non-competitive form that is politically controllable by the single ruling party, while in other situations, an opposing party may be tolerated while still being dominated by the single ruling party in some way (such as in the case of Singapore). In this regard, the positive law of the illiberal state can hardly be considered as a genuine democratic system of liberal values in a modern sense. It is therefore unsurprising that the legislature of an illiberal regime may have very few (or no) politically deliberative functions. Thus, the theoretical discussion of legal positivism in a liberal context is unlikely to resonate with the nature and function of law in an illiberal context.

Of course, the historical school of law has seemingly gone beyond the boundary of the nature of law as understood by naturalists and legal positivists, which combined the political and moral character of law into the ethos of a nation-state. This has positioned law as part of the historical dynamics – from the past to the present – of a nation-state. Nonetheless, proponents of the historical school, such as Friedrich Karl von Savigny (2002), contend that the law is located in the spirit of the people, and that the enactment of legislation is inferior to the people's expression of its common consciousness; in a modern democratic context, this is mostly premised on people being able to express their will freely through various democratic channels. Furthermore, it should be noted that discovering the ethos of a nation-state is in fact a context-specific task, which means that the nature and function of law needs to be identified in the context of the nation-state. For example, the historical conditions for the development of modern law in the West are not identical with those of non-Western societies.

To speak frankly, in the twentieth century, it has been widely perceived that the historical soil of the Western legal tradition is being washed away, and that traditional beliefs in the structural integrity of law (such as its religious roots and transcendent qualities) are disappearing in the West (Berman 2000: 338–339). Law now seems to have less to do with justice and more with argumentative technique. There has been increasing agreement with the idea that law as a man-made object varies across time and space, as reflected in cultural relativity. This represents a significant departure from most premodern theories of law, which held law to be sacred or natural (i.e. in essence, not man-made). As a result, the legitimacy of modern law has become much more instrumental and pragmatic, with fewer "magic" characteristics than before (Friedman 1986: 764). This is evidenced by the paradigm shift of legal theory towards the increasing prevalence of so-called "legal realism", the pioneers of which include Roscoe Pound (1931) and Karl N. Llewellyn (1931). This paradigm shift has undoubtedly caused the focus of legal theory to turn towards the practical facets of law by considering the social reality in which the law exists. This shift has grounded the theory in experience, representing a substantial difference from metaphysical claims that postulate the existence of a reality beyond human experience (Holmes 1881). In this vein, Western law in the modern context is geared more towards expediency and less towards morality. This tendency has been elaborated upon at length in legal theory; instrumentalism (somewhat akin to realism) has even been referred to as the fourth great tradition of Western legal theory in addition to the three classical ones.[1] Moreover,

[1] Summers (1982: 36–37) points out that it is untrue that instrumentalism has long borne the name "legal realism". Moreover, he specifically offered five main reasons for the use of the terminology "instrumentalism" rather than "legal realism". First, the term "legal realism" is sometimes confusing, as it may have both a broad meaning (including all

the primary task of instrumentalism is the provision of a coherent body of ideas about law that will make law more valuable in the hands of officials and practical men of affairs (Summers 1982: 19–20). This largely follows the philosophical logic of pragmatism, which centres around human beings and their purpose and actions in the universe. It is clear that legal theory has become a political, instrumental or pragmatic discipline as opposed to a religious, moral or historical one. In essence, modern law is treated primarily as an instrument for achieving political, economic and social goals.

In this vein, instrumentalism treats law as being finite and material, rather than articulating objective principles of justice. As Berman (2000: 335) noted, law in itself is not currently understood as a reflection of an objective justice or of the ultimate meaning or purpose of law. By contrast, law is typically thought to reflect, at best, the community sense of what is expedient, and is more commonly thought to express the more or less arbitrary will of the lawmaker. This theory became particularly relevant and vivid as the law came to play a fundamentally instrumental role in achieving specific social goals. Taking the USA as an example, in the progressive era (1896–1916), any theory of law that is articulated would certainly be instrumentalist and pragmatic (Summers 1982: 29). The court even pragmatically adjusted itself to be an essential de facto legislator – substantially repudiating the formalistic concepts of the nature of law – in achieving social reform goals.

Of course, the primary focus of a legal theory is typically inclusive rather than exclusive. For instance, despite differing from integrative jurisprudence (which aims to bring the moral, political and historical dimensions of law together), legal positivism developed to increasingly

pragmatic instrumentalist ideas) and a narrow meaning (such as the ideas expressed by Llewellyn, Frank, et al.). Second, use of the term "legal realism" in a broad sense may give the impression that some earlier theorists (such as Holmes, Gray and Pound) are mere precursors to the most important developments of legal instrumentalism in the US context. In fact, these authors are not mere precursors to instrumentalism; their work is seminal. Third, certain tenets of legal realism – in the narrow sense – are too extreme, such as a radical scepticism and an emphasis on non-rational (and even irrational) factors in the judicial process. Fourth, the term "legal realism" has certain misleading philosophical connotations, as most of the pragmatic legal instrumentalists in the US context were not realists as understood in traditional philosophical usage. Fifth, the expression "pragmatic instrumentalism" in the US context is a descriptively appropriate name. Of course, legal instrumentalism is a type of theory about law and its use. In particular, a Chinese version is approached as the instantiation of legal instrumentalism. The "legal realism" widely used in the US context is not descriptively appropriate.

take the effect of morality on law into account; likewise, naturalists increasingly considered the political elements of law (Berman 1988: 784). In the same vein, legal instrumentalism by no means rejects, but rather considers and integrates, the political, moral and historical elements of law into the enterprise of law, considering them instruments of social engineering. In the political sense, law, as distinguished from other rules, is a set of rules created by the sovereign authority, with sanctions being recognized by the state and enforced (if rules are violated) by state-authorized bodies. In the moral sense, law may be filled or supplemented with relevant moral meaning. Moreover, in the historical-cultural sense, law is both the reflection of and identified in the ethos of a nation-state. Notably, and distinctively, legal instrumentalism has been posited to address the decisive nature of law as an instrument grounded in the society within which it operates.

Given that legal instrumentalism has shifted its focus on the law as "it is", thus separating itself from these Western religious, historical and cultural traditions, it has become far more reflective of a non-Western context. At the general level, the nature of law as an instrument for achieving social goals has found widespread resonance that extends beyond the differences between the West and societies outside the West. In this vein, there are a number of questions that address the pragmatic facet of law but are largely ignored by classical legal theories that may come into play for legal instrumentalists: for example, what complexities are contained in the law's model of operation? To what extent does law serve as a means of achieving social goals? What are the positions of personnel in the law's enterprise? What task is performed when a law is created and enforced in efficacy? (Summers 1982: 11).

This is not to say that the inquiries arising from legal instrumentalism have become completely sociological and concern themselves only with raw facts, and therefore have nothing to do with the value of law in itself. Regarding the theory of value, as Summers (1982: 49) states, instrumentalism inherently incorporates the tenet that it exalts the wants and interests of the many, not the few. Moreover, the maximal satisfaction of wants and interests prevail over the free pursuit of gain when these two principles conflict. The value placed on these principles has gone beyond the religious and historical roots of Western jurisprudence, with the result that they resonate to a certain extent in a non-Western context with no history of Western traditions.

In a different context, of course, the content of legal frameworks may be different (Yu 1989: 30). For instance, legal instrumentalism as situated

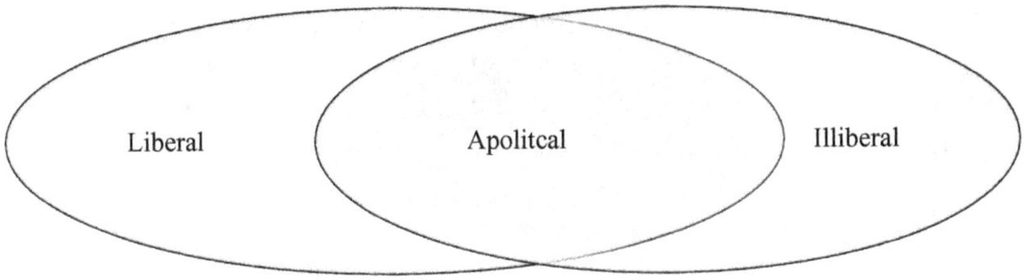

Figure 7.1 Ideological instantiations of legal instrumentalism.

in the USA is premised on American experience and the unique American judicial model. In this vein, the idea that American instrumentalists are "rule-sceptics" is clearly located in an American context, particularly given the United States' "judicial supremacy" model, whereby a Supreme Court's decision on the unconstitutionality of a law may be overruled only by extraordinary (rather than ordinary) political means, such as constitutional amendment, and may not be overruled by legislation enacted by Congress (Perry 2003; Wacks 2015: 167–170). Regarding the fundamental question of what constitutes the law, Oliver Wendell Holmes (1897: 460–461) even claimed that "[t]he prophecies of what the court will do in fact, and nothing more pretentious, are what I mean by the law". Legal instrumentalism in such a US judicial model is clearly distinct from, for example, legal instrumentalism in non-liberal regimes, where courts may function as political subordinates for the sovereign authority.

Therefore, at the general level of description, the primary focus of legal instrumentalism on the pragmatic facets of law extends beyond any particular ideology or tradition. However, if placed in a certain specific context, its instantiation may vary from one ideology to another. In theory, there are three pure types of instantiations of legal instrumentalism, based on the variance of political ideologies: liberal, apolitical and illiberal (see Figure 7.1).

The liberal instantiation means that the instrumental facet of law is aligned with liberal ideologies, while the illiberal instantiation means its alignment with illiberal ideologies. The apolitical dimension means that the law serves as an instrument of achieving social goals without (or at least without a clear) ideological tendency and can be included in both liberal and illiberal instantiations. The conceptual distinction between liberal and illiberal ideology is not absolute for a given regime, notwithstanding that said regime may be labelled as either "liberal" or "illiberal";

this is because, in reality, the regime may be a hybrid, characterized by an ideology that is liberal in some aspects and illiberal in others. In this regard, the categorization of a specific political regime's ideology may sometimes be a matter of degree. In particular, the rise of authoritarianism and developing crisis of traditional liberal democracy has resulted in the emergence of more regimes with hybrid characteristics that may sometimes be difficult to categorize as either purely liberal or purely illiberal. For example, a politically authoritarian regime, such as Singapore, may be pragmatically adapted to the principles of economic liberalism.

Having said this, Marxism and Confucianism – both of which are quite relevant to contemporary China, as noted by Kissinger (2012: 299) – may also be relevant to scholarly inquiry into Chinese legal theory. There is no doubt that contemporary China officially upholds Marxist ideology. However, China has largely deviated from Marxist traditions in many respects, particularly since 1978. It is clear that traditionally Marxist legal theorists in fact paid little attention to law; moreover, there is no doubt that the principal aim of Marxist legal theory was to criticize the centrepiece of liberal political philosophy, namely the ideal known as the rule of law. Marxists regularly questioned the need for law, and further contended that there would be no law in a truly communist society (Collins 1982: 1,94,107). This hostility towards law was evidenced to an extreme in China under Mao during the Cultural Revolution era, when legal nihilism was prevalent in the society. However, since 1978, when Deng Xiaoping initiated the reform era, the law has come to play an increasingly important instrumental role in China's economic development. Chinese legal theorists have even subsequently argued that the Marxist tenet "law is an instrument of class oppression" was no longer suitable for China's practice, as the function of the law had shifted towards facilitating economic development rather than the "diminished" class struggle (Sun 1996: 154–155). According to the logic of "class struggle" as adopted in the era of Mao Zedong, social conflict was ideologically divided into two types: "the antagonistic contradictions between the enemy and the people and the non-antagonistic contradictions among the people" (Fu and Cullen 2011). With the development of positive law in China, this "class struggle" ideology involving an "enemy" hostile to the regime has largely disappeared from domestic political discourse. To some extent, it has been replaced by the ideology of "legality", in the sense that the antagonistic politics of illiberal regimes have been further legalized by law and legal institutions. This means that those exhibiting a politically intolerable hostility or who challenge to the regime – particularly if this challenge is substantiated – may be purged as criminal offenders by legal means. In this regard, with reference to the Marxist tenet that law is an instrument of class oppression (Collins 1982: 17–34), legal instrumentalism does indeed have a place in classical Marxist legal theory, in the sense that law is treated as a political instrument (Yu 1989: 40). However, the increasing importance of law for achieving sociopolitical goals has meant a substantial deviation from classical Marxist theory, which is ideologically hostile to the law, particularly under a liberal political order.

Furthermore, internally, legal instrumentalism has some resonance with historical Chinese legal traditions. In fact, from the perspective of both the Confucian school and the legalist school, law was treated as a secular instrument that by no means has any transcendent meaning as derived from natural law, religion or rights, in contrast to historical tradition in the West. As Ch'ü (1961: 267, 275, 279) points out, in Confucian tradition, *li* (translated as "rites" or "rituals"), which forms the basis of all laws dealing with the family, marriage and inheritance, is a primary means of maintaining the social order with an emphasis on moral education. The fundamental principles of Confucianism were accorded more respect than legal authority under Confucian tradition. Accordingly, to the Confucian, law is largely a means of enforcing *li*, and litigation is traditionally discouraged. Moreover, although the role of law in the legalist school appears more important than in the Confucian school, the law is in fact used merely as an instrument to maintain a legal order ruled over by the emperor (Ch'ü 1961: 267), and by no means operates to exert limits on the powers of rulers, as reflected in the central value of Western civilisation. Traditional Chinese culture idealized and aspired to a harmonious society free of litigation and internal conflicts (Chen 2021: 148). This is in fact consistent with the logic of an authoritarian regime, where political controversy is in principle considered disharmonious and even dangerous, as it is difficult to control, and where consent can be enforced and predefined by the rulers. Accordingly, the media are largely both censored and politically controllable, and the right to political participation in principle is granted to those who support the regime.

Of course, in the twenty-first century, due to the new wave of advanced technological developments, including artificial intelligence (AI), instrumentalist thinking within the law may be further advanced, just as an increase in instrumentalist thinking occurred in conjunction with the technological advances of the later nineteenth and early twentieth centuries (Summers 1982: 30).

Authoritarian Legality and Legitimacy

It has long been perceived that the utility of law for authoritarian regimes is reflected in its functions of social and political control, cultivating "legal" legitimacy for the regime, facilitating and strengthening administrative compliance and accountability within the bureaucratic machinery and encouraging trade and investment (Ginsburg and Moustafa 2008; Moustafa 2014; Solomon 2015; Zhang and Ginsburg 2019). Having realized the importance of law for development, China has clearly learned to integrate the language of the "rule of law" used in liberal democracies into its political discourse. This is reflected by, among other things, China's recent political rhetoric; for example, consider Xi Jinping's "Rule of Law Thoughts", which have been disseminated throughout the country as state propaganda. Moreover, the "fetishism of law" – once criticized by classical Marxists (Collins 1982: 95), in the sense that law is believed to possess supernatural powers in a liberal political order – has now been grafted in some ways onto the scheme of authoritarian legality. Of course, the language of "rule of law", "democracy", "human rights", etc., which has been widely used in genuine liberal democracies, has also been incorporated into China's propaganda (although often with some variation in terms, such as "socialist rule of law", "Chinese rule of law" and "rule of law with Chinese characteristics"). Undoubtedly, the nature and function of law in an illiberal context are not identical to those in liberal democracies but rather represent "ruling by law", given the law's utility for authoritarian regimes. This means that although an illiberal ideology does not uphold the same ethical attitudes as liberal legalism, it may incorporate a certain degree of legalistic aspiration as reflected in legalism.

Needless to say, in a liberal democracy structured around the rule of law, law has to some extent been ideologically deified as a distinctive embodiment of justice and a constraint on power. As Shklar (1986: 111, 223) points out, ideologically speaking, legalism has made politics into not only something apart from law but something inferior to law; the law, aiming at justice, is differentiated from politics, looking only to expediency. This approach has even led to the separation of legal thinking from political thinking, with the latter now permeated with legalistic notions and terms, as reflected in the ideological prevalence of legalism. However, there is no doubt that law in a secular modern society is human-made. The dichotomy between law and non-law is largely grounded in an electorally accountable government, while the court is constitutionally designated as an independent non-political institution with final authority for adjudication in accordance with the law. The prevalence of the legalist tradition has somehow crystallized the line between law and non-law by isolating law from the social context within which it exists. Of course, if society is ideologically disenchanted with the law, and people's belief in law as an embodiment of justice as upheld by naturalists is thereby substantially weakened, the demarcation between "law" and "politics" may sometimes be blurred or even erased in practice. Moreover, the meaning of law – particularly as an instrument for social utility – cannot be locked into the statutes and the courtroom but instead necessarily takes on its full character only in the sociopolitical context.

Nonetheless, the liberal logic of demarcating law from politics is largely not applicable to illiberal situations, in which the law may be utilized as a political means for solidifying authoritarian legality and strengthening the legitimacy of the regime. A crucial difference here is that an illiberal regime is typically not based in a political system characterized by highly competitive democratic elections, like those in liberal democracies. Such a regime does not generally adopt the traditional form of rational-legal authority – a hallmark of modern democracies, where "power is given to people elected by voters, and the rules of wielding that power are usually set forth in a constitution, a charter, or another written document" (Weber 2012: 328). However, with the rise of authoritarianism, the "legal" element as reflected in the rational-legal authority – which is legitimate, according to the classical typology of legitimacy articulated by Max Weber (2012) – may be mixed instrumentally as a source of legitimacy for the authoritarian regime (Zhang and Ginsburg 2019: 375–385; Jia 2020: 1712). This may be illustrated by the authoritarian regime's efforts to establish a rule-based or -oriented system to strengthen people's belief in the "legality" of normative rules.

This approach has been conceptualized to some extent as "authoritarian legality", the definition of which may be briefly summarized as "legal norms of authoritarian states and the process in which those legal norms are implemented" (Fu and Dowdle 2020: 63). Taking China as an example, there is no doubt that tremendous efforts have been made to establish a comprehensive system of positive law in China, which has pragmatically strengthened the "legal" elements as reflected in the rational-legal tradition. In fact, rational-legal authority, as defined by

Weber, entails that superiors are subject to rules that limit their powers (Bendix 1977: 294). In this regard, it may be argued that authoritarian legality is ultimately contradictory, since legality requires institutionalization, predictability and certainty, all of which function to tie the hands of autocrats, while the "rule of law" under autocracies is bounded, limited and unstable (Gallagher 2017: 47; Jia 2020: 1712). Such a view has consciously placed "law" – mostly understood from a liberal rational-legal perspective – as differentiated or substantially separated from "politics". In fact, "authoritarian legality" indicates a hybrid body of law and politics in an authoritarian regime, the meaning of which may be better identified in context. On the one hand, "legality" indicates the "legal" elements that have been incorporated into the authoritarian regime, although it does not signify a degree of predictability and certainty that is identical or comparable to a liberal rule-of-law order. The "legality" entails legal rules being imposed on the exercise of powers by superior authorities, aimed at facilitating the efficiency of state governance. On the other hand, the "authoritarian" element in the term indicates the political condition of "legality", one primary purpose of which is to maintain an authoritarian regime from a political point of view. In other words, although the law applies to all powers in principle, it is in fact subject to and may give way to political expediency in practice, as the entire enterprise of the law is politically controllable by the regime from law-making to final adjudication.

In order to illustrate the dynamics of authoritarian legality, two pure types of authoritarian politics may be delineated: one is normal politics, and the other is exceptional politics, as illustrated in Table 7.1. In normal politics, the law is relatively stable and predictable, particularly as regards relatively apolitical matters (such as regular economic and commercial activities and normal social matters). In this situation, the approach to the law is largely rule-based, although the law itself may be enforced at the discretion of political actors to some extent. Of course, due to the contingent nature of authoritarian politics, the meaning of law as is relevant to dominant politics (in whatever sense) may be practically defined in a contingent way. Moreover, relevant state actors may enforce the law in different ways under different circumstances, arguably at these actors' discretion. In this regard, functionally, law on the one hand may subject political actors to legal rules; for instance, for the purpose of administrative compliance, as is essentially required for normal politics. On the other hand, law may reserve a place for the politically expedient exception that may arise due to sociopolitical reality. This political

Table 7.1 *Dynamics of authoritarian legality*

	Normal politics	Exceptional politics
Law	Literally stable; relatively predictable but with possible exceptions; relatively wide discretion on the part of law enforcement if relevant to politics	Relevant laws temporally defined differently to support specific sociopolitical goals (usually through legal means, such as lawmaking or judicial interpretation); temporally unpredictable
Approach	Routine; discretion to respond to unusual circumstances, as well as new or difficult cases involving politics if arising from social reality; mostly law-based	Abnormal; uniform; very little discretion; law is made, interpreted and enforced in accordance with temporally specific sociopolitical goals; mostly law-based or -oriented
Application	Normal economic and commercial activities; normal trade and investment issues; other relatively apolitical social issues (including normal criminal cases)	Various political campaigns/movements; emergency situations; politically sensitive issues; issues concerning national security; etc.

expediency – which the law is inherently required to respond to under an authoritarian regime – determines the unique nature and structure of law in an illiberal context to a certain extent. As discussed, the more political the matter in question, the more contingent the law may be inherently required to be in order to resolve it.

Of course, exceptional politics has nothing to do with temporal frequency in practice. It is possible that exceptional politics may be more prevalent under some circumstances than others; for example, during periods of nationwide political movements or campaigns or to facilitate consolidation of power immediately after succession in order to subdue potential challenges from rival factions. Accordingly, law may be defined temporally in different ways compared to the situation in normal politics. In exceptional politics, the meaning of relevant laws in normal politics may be adjusted, redefined or even suspended, usually through legal means (such as the SPC's judicial interpretations) in order to accord with specific sociopolitical goals. In principle, legal instrumentalism has enabled both normal and exceptional politics to be incorporated into the broad domain of law on the surface, meaning that the political rhetoric of "law" (such as "rule of law") can still be sustained rhetorically via propaganda during times of exceptional politics. More importantly, the legal means through which normative law can be defined and specified by the powers that be, both spatially and temporally, may be more pragmatically effective than other non-legal means when it comes to achieving certain specific sociopolitical goals. Although law in an illiberal context without a politically independent court system is often inextricable from politics, the law still serves as a crucial instrument for distinguishing "lawful" from "unlawful" issues in such a way that legality can be practically lineated, established and solidified.

It can be seen that authoritarian legality to some extent dictates the ways in which law may work uniquely for an authoritarian regime. Indeed, at least ostensibly, law is considered as an impersonal means of governance that differs from other non-legal means. It is in this sense that the more respectable the law is in the people's minds, the more perceived legality and legitimacy the regime may gain and cultivate. In order for this to occur, periodic nationwide propaganda regarding law and its importance, or the like – whatever form this may take – is a key element of the illiberal political agenda.

More importantly, authoritarian legality is largely institutionalized – from lawmaking to final adjudication – through a politically controllable Congress and court system under authoritarian regimes. The Congress, on the one hand, is described in the official rhetoric as representing the will of the people according to the highest law, usually the Constitution, through non-competitive or minimally competitive elections that are politically controllable by the single ruling party. In practice, such illiberal democratic procedures enable the authoritarian and repressive characteristics of the regime to be ideologically obscured, particularly through propaganda that disseminates this democratic language (widely used in liberal democracies) throughout public discourse through various dominant and politically controllable media. This places authoritarian rulers in a politically favourable position to ideologically defend their own model of "democracy" against any criticism regarding practical "deviation" or "difference" from liberal democracies. When accompanied by economic success, this kind of illiberal democracy may even secure more public legitimacy than other forms of authoritarian regime.

In the same vein, courts under authoritarian regimes are usually rhetorically defined as independent constitutional authorities for adjudication. It is true that the court is assigned the function of resolving disputes through adjudication in accordance with law, and that this function in itself may exhibit little or no difference between various regimes. Moreover, the court is generally considered to be an impartial guardian of law and justice, an idea that may be promoted through political means (such as propaganda regarding selected and/or typical cases of high quality decided by the court). Assuming that there is no thorny political issue involved in the dispute, it is understandable that the court should be able to function as a de facto independent adjudicator in resolving disputes (for example, in civil and commercial cases). Nonetheless, there is no doubt that courts under authoritarian regimes are institutionally not immune from politics, and that their adjudication is subject to varying degrees of political control in practice. More specifically, this may take the form of a politically controllable special tribunal or committee (whatever it is called) either inside or outside the ordinary court system. To a lesser extent, a politically controllable congress may be used to oversee the courts retrospectively via lawmaking that is opposed to the court's ruling. In any event, the courts in an authoritarian regime are hybrid entities with a political function, the channels of which can be manipulated by the dominant political actors either implicitly or explicitly. Having said this, due to the existence of a channel of political penetration – either explicit or implicit – into formal laws, there may exist a sharp discrepancy between formal laws and informal practice under authoritarian regimes (Solomon 2015). This "discrepancy" illustrates the inner logic of authoritarian legality. On the one hand, formal laws with normative expressions are claimed to be impersonal and accessible to the public and function to solidify the regime's "legality" in a way that cultivates its legitimacy through nationwide propaganda or even indoctrination of these normative laws in the community. For example, China has regularly propagandized newly enacted formal laws with a normative expression, with the goal of strengthening people's belief in the regime's achievements and efforts to develop a "rule-of-law" order. This practice could bolster the authoritarian regime's ideological defence against "condemnations" from a liberal ideological perspective, if and when these are levelled. On the other hand, there is no doubt that the actual meaning of law in a given concrete case is determined contextually and specifically by politically controllable authorities, including courts. To some extent, this represents self-enforcement by all relevant politically controlled authorities, from lawmaker to final adjudicator, and usually in a well-organized and centralized way.

Concluding Remarks

As a theory, legal instrumentalism incorporates several descriptive components, focusing primarily on instrumental facets of law in the social context. In a liberal context, it may be argued that the normative components of legal instrumentalism tend to dovetail with and thus reinforce democratic values (Summers 1982: 49). Clearly, this is not to suggest that there is no way to identify a theory of value for legal instrumentalism in a non-Western and non-liberal context.

In a liberal tradition, political controversy – particularly between competing political parties – is typically considered both necessary and productive for achieving agreement and compromise in a politically pluralistic society. A political decision, in principle, is open for critical review by the public, and is usually made through a process of collective learning involving fierce debate. These lively debates over controversies can be supported by free media. Each individual or group has a right to argue and promote its different goals, interests and values before the public. Nonetheless, with the rise of Asia, there have arguably been certain significant values proposed as being distinctive from traditional political values situated in the Western liberal context. For instance, many scholars once considered Confucianism antithetical to modernity. However, the experience of rapid development in East Asia led to the recognition of the possibility that Confucianism's commitments to self-improvement, family ties, education and the social good could facilitate economic and political modernization in East Asian societies, where civil and political liberties are much less central to the moral framework than in Western political traditions (Bell 2010). Some leading political values in China's political culture have been compared and contrasted with their liberal counterparts: for example, meritocracy v. democracy, hierarchy v. equality and harmony v. freedom. Clearly, in a globalized world marked by political polarization, certain other political values may be further identified in non-Western philosophical traditions (Bell 2017). Assuming India's rise as a global dominant power, for example, there may be even more distinctive political values identified in its traditions (Rachman 2016).

Furthermore, in a non-Western illiberal context, the discrepancy between formal laws and informal practice, as illustrated in the inner logic of authoritarian legality, is reflected to some extent in the legal scholarship of these societies. As far as Chinese legal scholarship is concerned, the theoretical shift towards the instrumental function of law in achieving social goals – as evidenced in legal instrumentalism – entails the bridging of law with social sciences in order to investigate the nature and function of law in context. Moreover, law's instrumental elements may be more perceivable through further advances in modern technology, such as AI. As the meaning of law in a given society cannot be completely understood outside of its social context, the trend of considering the "non-legal" elements *within* law itself may continue; in some ways, this may have been demonstrated by the rise of the "law and society movement" (Friedman 1986; Liu and Wang 2015).

Of course, there is no doubt that law as a discipline is still internal to the legal system and may derive its rationale from "legal" autonomous principles. Given that these formal laws with their normative expression are an inherent component of authoritarian legality in practice, the doctrinal approach to law remains a focus of legal scholarship in China's context. Moreover, normative legal analysis in this context is mostly carried out using a comparative law approach. Clearly, if the single ruling party is to maintain ideological control, it is understandable that these politically sensitive issues – particularly if they represent a potential challenge to the official ideology – are prohibited from being discussed (in whatever form) in public or a relatively large sphere. Legal scholarship of this kind is largely normative and interpretative but not critical, at least in the eyes of the regime. In this context, law can continue to be considered – or even propagandized – as a value system in and among the public. In fact, it is clear that authoritarian regimes typically make efforts to propagandize these normative expressions of laws for the purpose of bolstering the belief in the legitimacy of the law among the people, in a way that may in turn benefit the cultivation of the regime's own legitimacy. In the meantime, the illiberal informal practice of law, if it exists, could be obscured to some extent (in certain high-profile and exceptional cases, e.g., the responsibility could be shifted to the "unlawfulness" of the individual(s) involved rather than the law in itself).

Generally speaking, legal instrumentalism primarily offers a theoretical framework for the study of the nature and use of Chinese law in an illiberal context. These concepts and theories about laws in China, including those transplanted from foreign jurisprudence, have their own unique logic and meaning in application to China's sociopolitical context. In order to reflect the nature and use of law in the social reality of an illiberal regime, these theories and concepts may need to be reconceptualized or retheorized in order to describe and explain the legal phenomenon in the context.

Clearly, this discussion of legal instrumentalism and authoritarian legality may be temporarily concluded under certain circumstances but is rarely conclusive. The substance of legal instrumentalism and authoritarian legality may vary according to the varying degrees to which illiberal elements are incorporated into authoritarian regimes. In any event, the function of the law as a crucial instrument for achieving social goals in both liberal and illiberal regimes has resulted in legal scholarship focusing its attention on the nature and use of law in its sociopolitical context. This may be a timely reminder to avoid unsubstantiated speculation regarding "Chinese law" both within and outside China.

Appendix:

Methodology and Data

With the development of China's legislative system in a process of legal transplantation, particularly since the reform era in 1978, it has been intellectually desirable to conduct socio-legal exploration of the dynamics of sources of Chinese law in its sociopolitical context. In this book, the socio-legal exploration is primarily based on interviews and fieldwork conducted mostly from 2016 to 2019. Conducting research in authoritarian settings is methodologically challenging due to the political sensitivity and limited access to data in their relatively "closed contexts" (Koesel 2014: 185; Carlson et al. 2010: 14; Janenova 2019). These "closed contexts" might be referred to as "illiberal", "authoritarian", "non-democratic", "coercive", or even (non) "exceptions" within the prevailing "liberal" system (Koch 2013: 390; Janenova 2019: 1). There are also various methodological challenges for the fieldwork in China's courts, e.g., the difficulty of access to the courts for researchers (Ng and He 2017: 204–206). I was allowed access through personal connections with some judges. And the judges interviewed were recruited through personal connections and the snowball sampling method. Furthermore, I had the opportunity to engage with Chinese judges from different parts of China regularly in Hong Kong; a number of Chinese judges were admitted to attend common law training courses and education programmes at City University of Hong Kong, where I taught.

Specifically, for the component of socio-legal exploration of the judicial documents as mainly discussed in Chapter 4, the data were collected during the fieldwork in an intermediate people's court and a grassroots-level court (in A (a pseudonym) city) in Guangdong Province, and the visits to the SPC in Beijing, and two grassroots-level courts (in B, C (a pseudonym) cities) in Guangdong Province. It has been perceived that there are at least three types of decisions made by China's courts: "(1) decisions too trivial to cover with legal rules; (2) decisions covered by legal rules; and (3) decisions too important to make without being reviewed by the vertical hierarchy" (Ng and He 2017: 9). Nonetheless, in practice, apart from these explicit legal rules in various statutes and the SPC's judicial interpretations, the court may rely on those rules in judicial documents, sometimes implicitly, to adjudicate a dispute.

To better understand the role of judicial documents in the process of adjudicating disputes, particularly the ways in which and the extent to which judges refer, explicitly or implicitly, to these documents when handling cases, I conducted ethnographic observations of sixteen court hearings in A city in June 2019. Moreover, it has been a common practice for the SPC to publish its promulgated judicial documents. These documents, involving the interpretation of statutory laws and the creations of new rules for adjudication, are published through multiple publication outlets, including the SPC Gazette since 1985, and the monthly publication *Selected Judicial Documents of the SPC* (司法文件选 *sifa wenjian xuan*) since 1992.[1] However, judicial documents of this kind produced by subnational courts are, in practice, normally difficult to access by the public. Moreover, it's found that the practice of producing judicial documents by local courts may vary from one to another. For example, B city is a special economic zone with a relatively high level of autonomy, and its intermediate people's court has often produced judicial documents to specify national statutes. In contrast, C city is more akin to a normal local jurisdiction, producing relatively fewer judicial documents. During the visits to the courts, I was granted consent to access relevant unpublished judicial documents produced in B city and C city. This has greatly facilitated the documentary analysis involved in the research.

Furthermore, in order to investigate the dynamics of the SPC's guiding cases system and other judicial precedents in China's context, as mostly discussed in Chapters 6, the data were collected during the visits to three prefecture-level courts in G (a pseudonym) city, H (a pseudonym) city and I (a pseudonym) city in Guangxi Zhuang Autonomous Region, a basic-level court of C city in Guangdong Province and the High People's Court of F Province, respectively. Guangxi, as an Autonomous Region, is in mountainous terrain in the far south of China, bordering Vietnam, and its economy often languishes behind coastal provinces in China. Data from 2020 show that its per capita GDP was 44,309 yuan (about US$6,959), being ranked 29th among thirty-one provinces of mainland China (Statista.com 2021). In contrast, in 2020, the per capita GPD of Guangdong province reached about 88,210 yuan (about US$13,855) (Statista.com 2022). And the professional level of judges from Guangdong is normally higher than that of Guangxi. For example, judges from Guangxi said that the quality of judgments from Guangdong is relatively high, and newly appointed judges from Guangxi often take the judgments of Guangdong courts as a sample to learn how to write a quality judgment (Interviews 40-16-GL03, 30-16-GKFCG01). Also, the judges from Guangdong are quite

[1] *Selected Judicial Documents of the SPC* is a yearly publication edited by the SPC's Research Institute and published by People's Court Press – a public institute of the SPC.

confident about the high quality of their judgments on average when compared with other provinces (Interview 48-16-GZGD01). In addition, F High People's Court is the forerunner with regard to its performance in the typical-case-selection movement and has established its own reference case system. From this, it selects and publishes a certain number of reference cases in its *Gazette* regularly. The number of SPC guiding cases and its *Gazette*-published cases submitted by courts of J Province mean that the province is often top-ranked nationwide. Furthermore, the relevant unpublished documents regarding the local submission and selection of guiding cases and non-guiding cases in these courts were made relatively accessible during the visits.

Apart from ethnographic observations and the collection of the relevant unpublished documents during the visits to the courts, I conducted sixty-three semi-structured and sixteen loosely structured interviews. On average, an interview lasted from thirty minutes to one hour. Table A.1 identifies the interview subjects by level (where relevant), type of institution and occupation.[2]

The interview as mentioned here refers to an explicitly arranged meeting where I asked interviewees questions and took notes (some notes were written up as soon as possible after the interview). This does not include many discussions and informal conversations with Chinese judges, lawyers and government officials in the past when the conditions of interview were absent. There is no doubt that these discussions and conversations are of illuminative significance in clarifying relevant issues.

Moreover, some interviews with the judges were *in situ* during the period of fieldwork, usually after the ethnographic observation of trials in the courtroom, which make them more issue-specific. Usually, the interviews were conducted in workplaces during the visits in mainland China, and sometimes in informal settings – such as restaurants or teahouses – in ways that were more comfortable or convenient for some interviewees than otherwise. In addition, some of the interviews of China's judges were conducted in Hong Kong when they came there for the training programme, while some others were carried out via cell phone along with data analysis. During the interviews, I asked them specific, relevant questions to the research topic, for example how and why judges use judicial documents when making a decision and the extent to which, and why, they view a relevant judicial document as binding,

[2] The two digits after the first hyphen refer to the year the interview was conducted. The capital letters are unidentifiable code for the workplace of interviewee, because specific details of the locality and date risk breaching a protocol that protects human subjects (Manion 2015: 155). The last two digits refer to the number of the interview under the same time period and workplace.

Table A.1 *List of interview subjects*

Code	Level	Institution	Occupation
01-16-JS01	Provincial	Court	Director of the research office
02-16-JS02	Provincial	Court	Judge of judicial supervision division
03-16-JS03	Provincial	Court	Judge of a civil division
04-16-JS04	Provincial	Court	Judge of a civil division
05-16-JS05	Provincial	Court	Judge of a criminal division
06-16-JS06	Provincial	Court	Judge of a criminal division
07-16-JS07	Provincial	Court	Judge of the judges management division
08-16-JS08	Provincial	Court	Judge of the education and training division
09-16-JS09	Provincial	Court	Judge of a civil division
10-16-JSNJ01	Prefectural	Court	Chief judge of the case-filing division
11-16-JSNJ02	Prefectural	Court	Judge of a civil division
12-16-JSYHT01	County/district	Court	Judge of the administrative division
13-16-HZ01	County/district	Court	Judge of a civil division
14-16-HZ02	County/district	Court	Judge of a civil division
15-16-HZ03	County/district	Court	Judge of a criminal division
16-16-HZ04	County/district	Court	Deputy chief judge of a criminal division
17-16-HZ05	County/district	Court	Judge of the enforcement department
18-13-JMJH01	County/district	Court	Judge and vice president
18-13-JMJH01	County/district	Court	Judge and vice president
19-13-JM01	Prefectural	Court	Director of the research office
20-16-GX01	Provincial	Court	Deputy chief judge of a criminal division
21-16-GX02	Provincial	Court	Judge of a criminal division
22-16-GX03	Provincial	Court	Judge of the administrative division
23-16-FCG01	Prefectural	Court	Judge of a criminal division
24-16-FCG02	Prefectural	Court	Judge of a criminal division
25-16-FCG03	Prefectural	Court	Chief judge of the administrative division
26-16-fCG04	Prefectural	Court	Judge of a criminal division
27-16-FCG05	Prefectural	Court	Judge of a criminal division

Table A.1 (*cont.*)

Code	Level	Institution	Occupation
28-16-FCG06	Prefectural	Court	Judge of a civil division
29-16-FCG07	Prefectural	Court	Chief judge of the judicial supervision division
30-16-KFCG01	County/district	Court	Judge of a civil division
31-16-QZ01	Prefectural	Court	Chief judge of a civil division
32-16-QZ02	Prefectural	Court	Deputy chief judge of a civil division
33-16-QZ03	Prefectural	Court	Judge of a criminal division
34-16-QZ04	Prefectural	Court	Judge of a criminal division
35-16-QZ05	Prefectural	Court	Judge of the office of the Adjudication Committee
36-16-QZ06	Prefectural	Court	Judge of a civil division
37-16-QZ07	Prefectural	Court	Judge of a civil division
38-16-GL01	Prefectural	Court	Standing member of the Adjudication Committee
39-16-GL02	Prefectural	Court	Deputy director of the research office
40-16-GL03	Prefectural	Court	Chief judge of a criminal division
41-16-GL04	Prefectural	Court	Deputy chief judge of a criminal division
42-16-GL05	Prefectural	Court	Deputy chief judge of a criminal division
43-16-YSGL01	County/district	Court	Judge of a criminal division
44-16-LCGL01	County/district	Court	Judge of a criminal division
45-16-YGGL01	County/district	Court	Chief judge of a criminal division
46-16-LDGL01	County/district	Court	Chief judge of a criminal division
47-16-SZJS01	Prefectural	Court	Judge and president
48-16-GZGD01	Prefectural	Court	Former judge of a civil division
49-17-JNSD01	Prefectural	Court	Director of the general office
50-17-NSSZ01	County/district	Court	Chief judge of a civil division
51-17-NSSZ02	County/district	Court	Judge and vice president
52-17-NSSZ03	County/district	Court	Judge of a civil division

Table A.1 (*cont.*)

Code	Level	Institution	Occupation
53-17-NSSZ04	County/district	Court	Judicial officer of the research office
54-17-CQ01	Prefectural	Court	Chief judge of a civil division
55-17-JMGD01	Prefectural	Congress	Delegate of the People's Congress standing committee
56-18-HZ01	County/district	Court	Judge of a criminal division
57-18-HZ02	County/district	Court	Chief judge of a civil division
58-18-HZ03	County/district	Court	Chief judge of a criminal division
59-18-HZ04	County/district	Court	Judge and president
60-18-YJJL01	Prefectural	Court	Judge and vice president
61-19-FS01	Prefectural	Court	Chief judge of the judicial supervision division
62-19-FS02	Prefectural	Court	Judge and director of the political department
63-19-FSSD01	County/district	Court	Judge and the vice president
64-19-FSSD02	County/district	Court	Chief judge of a civil division
65-19-FSSD03	County/district	Court	Chief judge of the enforcement department
66-19-ZJWZ01	Township	Government	Government official
67-19-ZJWZ02	Township	Dispatched tribunal	Chief judge
68-19-HB01	Provincial	Court	Deputy chief judge of the case-filing division
69-16-JSJC01	Provincial	Court	Head of a provincial branch of NJC
70-17-GZ01		Law firm	Practising lawyer and a partner
71-17-SZ01		Law firm	Practising lawyer and a partner
72-17-SZ02		Law firm	Practising lawyer and a former judge
73-17-SZ03		Law firm	Practising lawyer and a former government official

Table A.1 (*cont.*)

Code	Level	Institution	Occupation
74-17-SZ04		Law firm	Practising lawyer and a former judge
75-18-SZ05		Law firm	Practising lawyer
76-18-SZ06		Law firm	Practising lawyer
77-18-SZ07		Law firm	Practising lawyer
78-18-BJ01		Law firm	Practising lawyer
79-18-BJ02		Law firm	Practising lawyer and a professor

informal state law. In addition, in order to verify that the data collected were not regionally unique, I tried to interview judges from different parts of China, including those from the provinces of Jiangsu, Hebei, Jilin, Zhejiang, Guangdong and Shandong, Chongqing Municipality and Beijing Municipality, and Guangxi Zhuang Autonomous Region.

BIBLIOGRAPHY

English-Language Literature

Acemoglu, Daron, and James A. Robinson. 2005. *Economic Origins of Dictatorship and Democracy*. New York: Cambridge University Press.

Ahl, Björn. 2014. "Retaining Judicial Professionalism: The New Guiding Cases Mechanism of the Supreme People's Court". *The China Quarterly* 217: 121–139.

Alexy, Robert. 2005. "Balancing, Constitutional Review, and Representation". *International Journal of Constitutional Law* 3(4): 572–581.

Alford, William P. 1997. "Law, Law, What Law? Why Western Scholars of Chinese History and Society Have Not Had More to Say about Its Law". *Modern China* 23(4): 398–419.

Ames, Barry. 1970. "Bases of Support for Mexico's Dominant Party". *The American Political Science Review* 64(1): 153–167.

Backer, Larry Catá. 2014. "Toward a Robust Theory of the Chinese Constitutional State: Between Formalism and Legitimacy in Jiang Shigong's Constitutionalism". *Modern China* 40(2): 168–195.

Barwick, Sir Garfield. 1980. "Judiciary Law: Some Observations Thereon". *Current Legal Problems* 33(1): 239–240.

Baum, Richard. 1969. "Revolution and Reaction in the Chinese Countryside: The Socialist Education Movement in Cultural Revolutionary Perspective". *The China Quarterly* 38: 92–119.

Beissinger, Jason. 2007. *Authoritarianism in an Age of Democratization*. Cambridge: Cambridge University Press.

Bell, Daniel A. 2010. "Preface". In *Confucian Political Ethics*, ed. Daniel A. Bell, viiii–xii. Princeton: Princeton University Press.

2017. "Comparing Political Values in China and the West: What Can Be Learned and Why It Matters". *Annual Review of Political Science* 20: 93–110.

Bell, John. 2006. *Judiciaries within Europe: A Comparative Review*. New York: Cambridge University Press.

Bendix, Reinhard. 1977. *Max Weber: An Intellectual Portrait*. Berkeley: University of California Press.

Berman, Harold J. 1988. "Toward an Integrative Jurisprudence: Politics, Morality, History". *California Law Review* 76(4): 779–801.

2000. *Faith and Order: The Reconciliation of Law and Religion*. Grand Rapids: Wm. B. Eerdmans Publishing Co.

Berman, Harold J., and Charles J. Reid. 1996. "The Transformation of English Legal Science: From Hale to Blackstone". *Emory Law Journal* 45(2): 446–448.

Bodenheimer, Edgar. 1974. *Jurisprudence: The Philosophy and Method of the Law*. Cambridge, MA: Harvard University Press.

Brown, Stephen. 2001. "Authoritarian Leaders and Multiparty Elections in Africa: How Foreign Donors Help to Keep Kenya's Daniel Arap Moi in Power". *Third World Quarterly* 22(5): 725–739.

Brownlee, Jason. 2007. *Authoritarianism in an Age of Democratization*. New York: Cambridge University Press.

Bunce, Valerie J., and Sharon L. Wolchik. 2010. "Defeating Dictators: Electoral Change and Stability in Competitive Authoritarian Regimes". *World Politics* 62(1): 43–86.

Cai, Yongshun. 2018. "Grid Management and Social Control in China". *The Asia Dialogue*, 27 April. https://theasiadialogue.com/2018/04/27/grid-management-and-social-control-in-china/.

Cappelletti, Mauro. 1981. "The Law-Making Power of the Judge and Its Limits: A Comparative Analysis". *Monash University Law Review* 8(1): 15–67.

Carlson, Allen, Mary E. Gallagher and Melanie Manion. 2010. "Introduction". In *Contemporary Chinese Politics: New Sources, Methods, and Field Strategies*, eds. Allen Carlson, Mary E. Gallagher, Kenneth Lieberthal and Melanie Manion, 1–12. New York: Cambridge University Press.

Carter, Liz. 2012. "Whom Should the Chinese Army Serve: The Party or the State?" *The Atlantic*, 25 October. www.theatlantic.com/international/archive/2012/10/whom-should-the-chinese-army-serve-the-party-or-the-state/264104/.

Chen, Albert H. Y. 2021. *The Changing Legal Orders in Hong Kong and Mainland China: Essays on "One Country, Two Systems"*. Hong Kong: City University of Hong Kong Press.

Chen, Jianfu. 2013. *Criminal Law and Criminal Procedural Law in the People's Republic of China*. Leiden: Brill.

Chen, Xingliang. 2010. "Chinese Criminal Jurisprudence (1979–2009)" *Frontier of Law in China* 5(4): 485–509.

2014. "China's Guiding Case System". *Peking University Law Journal* 1(2): 215–258.

Cho, Young Nam. 2002. "From 'Rubber Stamps' to 'Iron Stamps': The Emergence of Chinese Local People's Congress as Supervisory Powerhouse". *China Quarterly* 171: 724–740.

Ch'ü, T'ung-Tsu. 1961. *Law and Society in Traditional China*. Connecticut: Hyperion Press, Inc.

Clarke, Donald. 2020. "Anti Anti-Orientalism, or Is Chinese Law Different?" *The American Journal of Comparative Law* 68(1): 55–94.

Cohen, Jerome. 1968. *The Criminal Process in the People's Republic of China, 1949–1963: An Introduction*. Cambridge, MA: Harvard University Press.

Cohen, Mark. 2017. "Spring Time for IPR Case Law in China?" *China IPR*, March 12. https://chinaipr.com/2017/03/12/spring-time-for-ipr-case-law-in-china/.

Collins, Hugh. 1982. *Marxism and Law*. Oxford: Oxford University Press.

Corne, Peter Howard. 2002. "Creation and Application of Law in the PRC". *The American Journal of Comparative Law* 50(2): 369–443.

Cox, Gary W. 2009. "Authoritarian Elections and Leadership Succession: 1975–2004". *APSA 2009 Toronto Meeting Paper*, 21 August. https://ssrn.com/abstract=1449034.

David, René. 1972. *French Law: Its Structure, Sources and Methodology*. Baton Rouge: Louisiana State University Press.

Deng, Jinting. 2015. "The Guiding Case System in China's Mainland". *Frontiers of Law in China* 10(3): 449–474.

2016. "Functional Analysis of China's Guiding Cases". *China: An International Journal* 14(2): 44–70.

Devlin, Lord. 1976. "Judges and Lawmakers". *Modern Law Review* 39(1): 1–16.

Dicey, A. V. 1915. *Law of the Constitution*. London: Macmillan and Co., Ltd.

1959. *Law of the Constitution*. London: Macmillan Education Ltd.

1982. *Law of the Constitution*, 8th edition. Indianapolis: Liberty Fund Inc.

Dickson, Bruce J. 2014. "Who Wants to Be a Communist? Career Incentives and Mobilized Loyalty in China". *The China Quarterly* 217: 42–68.

Diplock, Kenneth. 1978. "The Courts as Legislator". In *The Lawyer and Justice*, ed. B. W. Harvey, 266–280. London: Sweet & Maxwell.

Dowdle, Michael. 1997. "The Constitutional Development and Operations of the National People's Congress". *Columbia Journal of Asian Law* 11(8): 1–125.

2002. "Of Parliaments, Pragmatism, and the Dynamics of Constitutional Development: The Curious Case of China". *New York University Journal of International Law and Politics* 35(1): 1–200.

Dworkin, Ronald. 1998. *Law's Empire*. London: Hart Publishing.

Eulau, Heinz, and Paul D. Karps. 1977. "The Puzzle of Representation: Specifying Components of Responsiveness". *Legislative Studies Quarterly* 2(3): 233–254.

Evans, Jim. 1987. "Change in the Doctrine of Precedent during the Nineteenth Century". In *Precedent in Law*, ed. Laurence Goldstein, 35–72. Oxford: Clarendon Press.

Fairbank, John King. 1983. *The United States and China*. Cambridge, MA: Harvard University Press.

Feng, Yang. 2017. "The Legislation in Autonomous Areas of China: Progress, Limitations and Recommendations". *Asian-Pacific Law & Policy Journal* 18(2): 46–82.

Finder, Susan. 1993. "The Supreme People's Court of the People's Republic of China". *Journal of Chinese Law* 7(2): 145–223.

2017a. "China's Evolving Case Law System in Practice". *Tsinghua China Law Review* 9(2): 245–259.

2017b. "Signals in Zhou Qiang's 2017 NPC Report". *Supreme People's Court Monitor*, 18 March. https://supremepeoplescourtmonitor.com/2017/03/18/signals-in-zhou-qiangs-2017-npc-report-part-1/.

2019. "How the SPC Serves National Strategy and 'Makes Law': The Pilot FTZ's Opinion and Its Implications". In *International Economic Law and the Challenges of the Free Zones*, eds. Julien Chaisse and Jiaxiang Hu, 277–297. Alphen aan den Rijn: Kluwer Law International B.V.

Fon, Vincy, and Francesco Parisi. 2006. "Judicial Precedents in Civil Law System: A Dynamic Analysis". *International Review of Law and Economics* 26(4): 519–535.

Freeman, Edward A. 1876. *The Growth of the English Constitution: From the Earliest Times*. London: Macmillan and Co.

Friedland, M. L. 1974. "Prospective and Retrospective Judicial Lawmaking". *University of Toronto Law Review* 24(2): 170–190.

Friedman, Lawrence M. 1986. "The Law and Society Movement". *Stanford Law Review* 38(3): 763–780.

1998. *American Law: An Introduction*. New York and London: W.W. Norton & Company.

Friedmann, Wolfgang. 1966. "Limits of Judicial Lawmaking and Prospective Overruling". *Modern Law Review* 29(6): 593–607.

Fu, Hualing. 2016. "Building Judicial Integrity in China". *Hastings International and Comparative Law* 39(1): 167–181.

Fu, Hualing, and Richard Cullen. 2011. "From Mediatory to Adjudicatory Justice: The Limits of Civil Justice Reform in China". In *Chinese Justice: Civil Dispute Resolution in Contemporary China*, eds. Margaret Y. K. Woo and Mary E. Gallagher, 25–57. New York: Cambridge University Press.

Fu, Hualing, and Michael Dowdle. 2020. "The Concept of Authoritarian Legality: The Chinese Case". In *Authoritarian Legality in Asia: Formation, Development and Transition*, eds. Weitseng Chen and Hualing Fu, 63–89. Cambridge: Cambridge University Press.

Fyrnys, Markus. 2011. "Expanding Competences by Judicial Lawmaking: The Pilot Judgment Procedure of the European Court of Human Rights". *German Law Journal* 12(5): 1231–1260.

Gallagher, Mary E. 2017. *Authoritarian Legality in China: Law, Workers, and the State*. Cambridge: Cambridge University Press.

Gandhi, Jennifer. 2008. *Political Institutions under Dictatorship*. New York: Cambridge University Press.

Gandhi, Jennifer, and Ellen Lust-Okar. 2009. "Elections under Authoritarianism". *Annual Review of Political Science* 12: 403–422.

Gasper, Donald. 1982. "The Chinese National People's Congress". In *Communist Legislatures in Comparative Perspective*, eds. Daniel Nelson and Stephen White, 160–169. London: The Macmillan Press.

Geddes, Barbara. 1999. "Authoritarian Breakdown: Empirical Test of a Game Theoretic Argument". Paper presented at the Annual Meeting of the American Political Science Association, 2 September. https://eppam.weebly.com/uploads/5/5/6/2/5562069/authoritarianbreakdown_geddes.pdf.

Ghazi-Tehrani, Adam Kavon and Henry N. Pontell. 2015. "Corporate Crime and State Legitimacy: The 2008 Chinese Melamine Milk Scandal". *Crime, Law and Social Change* 63(5): 247–267.

Ginsburg, Tom, and Moustafa Tamir. 2008. "Introduction: The Functions of Courts in Authoritarian Politics". In *Rule by Law: The Politics of Courts in Authoritarian Regimes*, eds. Tom Ginsburg and Moustafa Tamir, 1–22. Cambridge: Cambridge University Press.

He, Xin. 2007. "Why Do They Not Take the Disputes? Law, Power, Politics in the Decision-Making of Chinese Courts". *International Journal of Law in Context* 3(3): 203–225.

2012a. "Black Hole of Responsibility: The Adjudication Committee's Role in a Chinese Court". *Law & Society Review* 46(4): 681–712.

2012b. "The Party's Leadership as a Living Constitution in China". *Hong Kong Law Journal* 42(1): 73–94.

2013. "Judicial Innovation and Local Politics: Judicialization of Administrative Governance in East China". *The China Journal* 69(1): 20–42.

Ho, Norman P. 2010. "'Stare Decisis' in Han China? Dong Zhongshu, the Chunqiu, and the Systematization of Law". *Tufts Historical Review* 3(1): 153–169.

Holmes, Oliver Wendell. 1881. *The Common Law*. Boston: Little Brown and Company.

1897. "The Path of the Law". *Harvard Law Review* 10(8): 457–479.

Hu, Shikai. 1993. "Representation without Democratization: 'Signature Incident' and China's National People's Congress". *Journal of Contemporary China* 2 (2): 3–34.

Huang, Philip C. C. 1991. "The Paradigmatic Crisis in Chinese Studies: Paradoxes in Social and Economic History". *Modern China* 17(3): 299–341.

2006a. "Civil Adjudication in China, Past and Present". *Modern China* 32(2): 135–180.

2006b. "Court Mediation in China, Past and Present". *Modern China* 32(3): 275–314.

2015. "Morality and Law in China, Past and Present". *Modern China* 41(1): 3–39.

Janenova, Saltanat. 2019. "The Boundaries of Research in an Authoritarian State". *International Journal of Qualitative Methods* 18: 1–8.

Ip, Eric C. 2010. "The Supreme People's Court and the Making of Public Policy in Contemporary China". *The Michigan Journal of Public Affairs* 7(1): 1–15.

Jia, Mark. 2016. "Chinese Common Law? Guiding Cases and Judicial Reform". *Harvard Law Review* 129(8): 2213–2234.

2020. "Illiberal Law in American Courts". *University of Pennsylvania Law Review* 168(6): 1685–1744.

Jiang, Shigong. 2009. "Written and Unwritten Constitutions: A New Approach to the Study of Constitutional Government in China". *Modern China* 36(1): 12–46.

2014. "Chinese-Style Constitutionalism: On Backer's Chinese Party-State Constitutionalism". *Modern China* 40(2): 133–167.

Jiang, Xiaoyi, and Ling Shao. 2013. "The Guiding Case System in China". *China Legal Science* 1(3): 106–130.

Keith, Donald C., and Zhiqiu Lin. 2009. "Judicial Interpretation of China's Supreme People's Court as 'Secondary Law' with Special Reference to Criminal Law". *China Information* 23(2): 223–256.

Keller, Perry. 1989. "Legislation in People's Republic of China". *University of British Columbia Law Review* 23(3): 653–688.

1994. "Sources of Order in Chinese Law". *American Journal of Comparative Law* 42(4): 711–760.

Kellogg, Thomas. 2007. "Courageous Explorers: Education Litigation and Judicial Innovation in China". *Harvard Human Rights Journal* 20: 141–188.

Kinkel, Jonathan J., and William J. Hurst. 2015. "The Judicial Cadre Evaluation System in China: From Quantification to Intra-State Legibility". *China Quarterly* 224: 933–954.

Kirk, Russell. 2003. *The Roots of American Order*, 4th edition. Wilmington: ISI Books.

Kissinger, Henry. 2012. *On China*. New York: Penguin Group.

Koch, Natalie. 2013. "Introduction – Field Methods in 'Closed Contexts': Undertaking Research in Authoritarian State and Places". *Area* 45: 390–395.

Koesel, Karrie J. 2014. *Religion and Authoritarianism: Cooperation, Conflict, and the Consequences*. New York: Cambridge University Press.

Kong, Xiaohong. 1991. "Legal Interpretation in China". *Connecticut Journal of International Law* 6(2): 491–506.

Lam, Oiwan. 2011. "China: Update on the Independent Candidate Campaigns". *Global Voices*, 26 June. http://globalvoicesonline.org/2011/06/26/china-update-on-the-independent-candidate-campaigns.

Lambert, Enouann, and Max J Wasserman. 1929. "The Case Method in Canada and the Possibilities of Its Adaptation to the Civil Law". *Yale Law Journal* 39 (1): 1–21.

Lehavi, Amnon. 2011. "Judicial Review of Judicial Lawmaking". *Minnesota Law Review* 96(2): 520–583.

Levi, Edward H. 1948. "An Introduction to Legal Reasoning". *University of Chicago Law Review* 15(3): 501–574.

Li, Cheng. 2010. "Intra-Party Democracy in China: Should We Take It Seriously?" *China Leadership Monitor* 30, 20 January. www.brookings.edu/wp-content/uploads/2016/06/fall_china_democracy_li.pdf.

Li, Hongbin, and Li-An Zhou. 2005. "Political Turnover and Economic Performance: The Incentive Role of Personnel Control in China". *Journal of Public Economics* 89(9): 1743–1762.

Li, Ling. 2019. "Political-Legal Order and the Curious Double Character of China's Courts". *Asian Journal of Law and Society* 6(1): 19–29.

Li, Wei. 1997. "Judicial Interpretation in China". *Willamette Journal of International Law and Dispute Resolution* 5(1): 87–112.

Li, Yang. 2016. "Practice and Theory of the Guiding Case System in China". *Hong Kong Law Journal* 46(1): 307–338.

Liebman, Benjamin. 2007a. "China's Courts: Restricted Reform". *China Quarterly* 191: 620–638.

2007b. "China's Courts: Restricted Reforms" *Columbia Journal of Asian Law* 21 (1): 1–44.

Limmer, Jocelyn E. H. 2013. "China's New 'Common Law': Using China's Guiding Cases to Understand How to Do Business in the People's Republic of China". *Willamette Journal of International Law and Dispute Resolution* 21(2): 96–133.

Lin, Yan. 2015. "Constitutional Evolution through Legislation: The Quiet Transformation of China's Constitution". *International Journal of Constitutional Law* 13(1): 61–89.

Lindberg, Staffan I. 2006. "Opposition Parties and Democratization in Sub-Saharan Africa". *Journal of Contemporary African Studies* 24(1): 123–138.

Liu, Nanping. 1997. *Opinions of the Supreme People's Court: Judicial Interpretation in China*. Hong Kong: Sweet & Maxwell Asian.

Liu, Sida, and Zhizhou Wang. 2015. "The Fall and Rise of Law and Social Science in China". *Annual Review of Law and Social Science* 11: 373–394.

Llewellyn, Karl N. 1931. "Some Realism about Realism: Responding to Dean Pound". *Harvard Law Review* 44(8): 1222–1264.

Lo, Vai Lo. 2016. "Towards the Rule of Law: Judicial Lawmaking in China". *Bond Law Review* 28(2): 149–168.

Long, Cheryl Xiaoning, and Jun Wang. 2015. "Judicial Local Protectionism in China: An Empirical Study of IP Cases". *International Review of Law and Economics* 42: 48–59.

Lubman, Stanley B. 1999. *Bird in a Cage: Legal Reform in China after Mao*. Stanford: Stanford University Press.

2015. "China's Exodus of Judges". *The Wall Street Journal*, 3 May. www.wsj.com/articles/BL-CJB-26697.

McGregor, Richard. 2010. *The Party: The Secret World of China's Communist Rulers*. London: Penguin Group.

Mackerras, Colin, Donald McMillen and Andrew Watson. 2001. *Dictionary of the Politics of the People's Republic of China*. London: Routledge.

Magaloni, Beatriz. 2006. *Voting for Autocracy: Hegemonic Party Survival and Its Demise in Mexico*. New York: Cambridge University Press.

Malesky, Edmund, and Paul Schuler. 2011. "The Single-Party Dictator's Dilemma: Information in Elections without Opposition". *Legislative Studies Quarterly* 36(4): 491–530.

Manion, Melanie. 2015. *Information for Autocrats: Representation in Chinese Local Congresses*. New York: Cambridge University Press.

Merryman, John H. 1985. *The Civil Law Tradition: An Introduction to the Legal System of Western Europe and Latin America*. Stanford: Stanford University Press.

Miller, Michael K. 2013. "Electoral Authoritarianism and Democracy: A Formal Model of Regime Transitions". *Journal of Theoretical Politics* 25(2): 153–181.

Minzner, Carl. 2009. "Judicial Disciplinary Systems for Incorrectly Decided Cases: The Imperial Chinese Heritage Lives on". *New Mexico Law Review* 39(1): 63–87.

2011. "China's Turn against Law". *American Journal of Comparative Law* 59(4): 935–984.

Moens, Gabriel. 1992. "Judicial Lawmaking in the European Court of Justice". *University of Queensland Law Journal* 17(1): 76–110.

Montrose, James L. 1968. *Precedent in English Law and Other Essays*. Shannon: Irish University Press.

Moustafa, Tamir. 2007. *The Struggle for Constitutional Power: Law, Politics, and Economic Development in Egypt*. Cambridge and New York: Cambridge University Press.

2014. "Law and Courts in Authoritarian Regimes". *Annual Review of Law and Social Science* 10: 281–299.

Ng, Kwai Hang, and Xin He. 2017. *Embedded Courts: Judicial Decision-Making in China*. New York: Cambridge University Press.

O'Brien, Kevin. 1990. *Reform without Liberalization: China's National People's Congress and the Politics of Institutional Change*. Cambridge: Cambridge University Press.

Oliveira, Maria Angela Jardim de Santa Cruz, and Nuno Garoupa. 2012. "Stare Decisis and Certiorari Arrive to Brazil: A Comparative Law and Economics Approach". *Emory International Law Review* 26(2): 555–598.

Parisi, Francesco, and Ben Depoorter. 2003. "Legal Precedents and Judicial Discretion". In *Encyclopedia of Public Choice*, eds. Charles K Rowley and Friderich Schneider, 667–671. Amsterdam: Kluwer.

Peerenboom, Randall. 2002. *China's Long March toward Rule of Law*. Cambridge: Cambridge University Press.

2003. "Beyond Universalism and Relativism: The Evolving Debates about Values in Asia". *Indiana International Comparative Law Review* 14(1): 1–85.

2007. "Courts as Legislators: Supreme People's Court Interpretations and Procedural Reforms". *The Foundation for Law, Justice and Society*, 30 August. www.fljs.org/sites/www.fljs.org/files/publications/Peerenboom.pdf.

2010. "Introduction". In *Judicial Independence in China*, ed. Randall Peerenboom, 1–22. Cambridge: Cambridge University Press.

2012. "Social Foundations of China's Living Constitution". In *Comparative Constitutional Design*, ed. Tom Ginsburg, 155–159. Cambridge: Cambridge University Press.

Perry, Elizabeth J. 2008. "Chinese Conceptions of 'Rights': From Mencius to Mao – and Now". *Perspectives on Politics* 6(1): 37–50.

Perry, Michael J. 2003. "Protecting Human Rights in a Democracy: What Role for the Courts?" *Wake Forest Law Review* 38(2): 635–696.

Pitkin, Hanna F. 1967. *The Concept of Representation*. Berkeley: University of California Press.

Posner, Richard A. 2008. *How Judges Think*. Cambridge, MA: Harvard University Press.

Pound, Roscoe. 1931. "The Call for a Realist Jurisprudence". *Harvard Law Review* 44(5): 697–711.

Rachman, Gideon. 2016. *Easternization: War and Peace in the Asian Century*. London: Bodley Head.

Roessler, Philip G., and Marc M. Howard. 2009. "Post-Cold War Political Regimes: When Do Elections Matter?" In *Democratization by Elections: A New Mode of Transition*, ed. Staffan I. Lindberg, 101–127. Baltimore: The Johns Hopkins University Press.

Ruskola, Teemu. 2013. *Legal Orientalism: China, the United States, and Modern Law*. Cambridge, MA: Harvard University Press.

Sapio, Flora. 2008. "*Shuanggui* and Extralegal Detention in China". *China Information* 22(1): 7–33.

2010. *Sovereign Power and the Law in China: Zones of Exception in the Criminal Justice System*. Leiden: Brill.

Savigny, Friedrich Karl von. 2002. *The Vocation of Our Age for Legislation and Jurisprudence*. Clark, NJ: The Lawbook Exchange, Ltd.

Scheppele, Kim Lane. 2018. "Autocratic Legalism". *The University of Chicago Law Review* 85(2): 545–583.

Schoenhals, Michael. 1999. "Political Movements, Change and Stability: The Chinese Communist Party in Power". *China Quarterly* 159: 595–605.

Seppänen, Samuli. 2018. "Anti-formalism and the Preordained Birth of Chinese Jurisprudence". *China Perspectives* 4(115): 31–38.

Shen, Wei, and Shang Shu. 2020. "Tackling Local Protectionism in Enforcing Foreign Arbitral Awards in China: An Empirical Study of the Supreme People's Court's Review Decisions, 1995–2015". *China Quarterly* 241: 144–168.

Shklar, Judith N. 1986. *Legalism: Law, Morals and Political Trials*. Cambridge, MA: Harvard University Press.

Sidel, Mark. 2009. *The Constitution of Vietnam: A Contextual Analysis*. Oxford: Hart Publishing.

Simpser, Alberto. 2005. "Making Votes Not Count: Strategic Incentives for Electoral Corruption". PhD dissertation, Department of Political Science, Stanford University.

Smith, Gordon B. 1988. *Soviet Politics: Continuity and Contradiction*. Hampshire and London: Macmillan Education Ltd.

Solomon, Peter H. Jr. 2007. "Courts and Judges in Authoritarian Regimes". *World Politics* 60(1): 122–145.

2015. "Law and Courts in Authoritarian States". In *International Encyclopedia of the Social and Behavioral Sciences*, 2nd edition, ed. James D. Wright, 427–434. Oxford: Elsevier.

South China Morning Post. 2014. "China Ratifies Constitution Day Holiday to Enhance Rule-of-Law Campaign". *South China Morning Post*, 1 November. www.scmp.com/news/china/article/1629919/china-ratifies-constitution-day-holiday-enhance-rule-law-campaign.

Statista.com. 2021. "Per Capita Gross Domestic Product (GDP) in China in 2020, by Province or Region". *Statistia Website*. 23 November. https://www.statista.com/statistics/1093666/china-per-capita-gross-domestic-product-gdp-by-province/.

Statista.com. 2022. "Per Capita Gross Domestic Product (GDP) of Guangdong Province, China from 2011 to 2021". 22 March. https://www.statista.com/statistics/1093860/china-per-capita-gross-domestic-product-gdp-of-guangdong-province/.

Steinbeck, John. 1962. *Travels with Charley: In Search of America*. New York: Viking Press.

Steiner, Eva. 2015. "Judicial Rulings with Prospective Effect: From Comparison to Systematisation". In *Comparing the Prospective Effect of Judicial Rulings across Jurisdictions*, ed. Eva Steiner, 1–23. Switzerland: Springer.

Steinman, Adam. 2004. "A Constitution of Judicial Lawmaking". *University of Pittsburgh Law Review* 65(3): 545–596.

Stephan, Paul. 2018. "Inferences of Judicial Lawmaking Power and the Law of Nations". *Georgetown Law Journal* 106(6): 1793–1824.

Strauss, David. 2002. "Must Like Cases be Treated Alike?" University of Chicago Public Law and Legal Theory Working Paper No. 24, 18 May. https://papers.ssrn.com/sol3/papers.cfm?abstract_id=312180.

Summers, Robert Samuel. 1982. *Instrumentalism and American Legal Theory*. Ithaca, NY and London: Cornell University Press.

Tanner, Murray Scot. 1994. "The Erosion of Communist Party Control over Lawmaking in China". *The China Quarterly* 138: 381–403.

Thompson, Mark R., and Philipp Kuntz. 2004. "Stolen Elections: The Case of the Serbian October". *Journal of Democracy* 15(4): 159–172.

Tomlinson, Edward. 1997. "Judicial Lawmaking in a Code Jurisdiction: A French Saga on Certainty of Price in Contract Law". *Louisiana Law Review* 58(1): 101–144.

Tong, Zhiwei. 2010. "A Comment on the Rise and Fall of the Supreme People's Court's Reply to Qi Yuling's Case". *Suffolk University Law Review* 43(3): 669–679.

Tóth, Gábor Attila. 2017. "Authoritarianism". In *Max Plank Encyclopedia of Comparative Constitutional Law*. http://oxcon.ouplaw.com/view/10.1093/law-mpeccol/law-mpeccol-e205?prd=MPECCOL.

Troper, Michel, and Christophe Grzegorczyk. 1997. "Precedent in France". In *Interpreting Precedents: A Comparative Study*, eds. Donald N. MacCormick and Robert S. Summers, 115–119. Dartmouth: Dartmouth Publishing Co.

Tushnet, Mark. 2003. *The New Constitutional Order*. Princeton: Princeton University Press.

2014. *Comparative Constitutional Law*. Cheltenham: Edward Elgar.

2015. "Authoritarian Constitutionalism". *Cornell Law Review* 100(2): 391–461.

Ursin, Edmund. 2014. "California Supreme Court and Judicial Lawmaking: The Jurisprudence of the California Supreme Court". *California Legal History* 9: 383–392.

Wacks, Raymond. 2015. *Understanding Jurisprudence*. Oxford: Oxford University Press.

Wang, Chenguang. 2010. "From the Rule of Man to the Rule of Law". In *China's Journey toward the Rule of Law: Legal Reform (1978–2008)*, eds. Cai Dingjian and Wang Chenguang, 1–50. Leiden and Boston: Brill.

Wang, Juan, and Sida Liu. 2019. "Ordering Power under the Party: A Relational Approach to Law and Politics in China." *Asian Journal of Law and Society* 6 (1): 1–18.

Wang, Peng. 2019. "Politics of Crime Control: How Campaign-Style Law Enforcement Sustains Authoritarian Rule in China". *British Journal of Criminology* 60(2): 422–443.

Wang, Shizhou. 1995. "The Judicial Explanation in Chinese Criminal Law". *American Journal of Comparative Law* 43(4): 569–579.

Wang, Shucheng. 2017. "Tripartite Freedom of Religion in China: An Illiberal Perspective". *Human Rights Quarterly* 39(4): 783–810.

2018. "Guiding Cases as a Form of Statutory Interpretation: Expansion of Supreme People's Court's Judicial Lawmaking Authority in China". *Hong Kong Law Journal* 48(3): 1067–1096.

Wang, Yuhua. 2016. "Beyond Local Protectionism: China's State–Business Relations in the Last Two Decades". *China Quarterly* 226: 319–341.

2018. "Can the Chinese Communist Party Learn from Chinese Emperors?" *Los Angeles Review of Books: The China Channel*, 22 March. https://chinachannel.org/2018/03/22/chinese-emperors/.

Wang, Zhiqiang. 2005. "Case Precedent in Qing China: Rethinking Traditional Case Law". *Columbia Journal of Asian Law* 19(1): 323–344.

Weber, Max. 2012. *The Theory of Social and Economic Organization*. Eastford: Martino Publishing.

Wheare, K. C. 1951. *Modern Constitution*. London: Oxford University Press.

Wight, Teresa. 2015. *Party and State in post-Mao China*. Cambridge: Polity Press, 2015.

Wu, Guoguang. 1995. "Documentary Politics: Hypotheses, Process, and Case Studies". In *Decision-Making in Deng's China*, eds. Carol Lee Hamarin and Shuisheng Zhao, 24–38. New York: M.E. Sharpe.

Xi, Chao. 2013. "Local Courts as Legislators: Judicial Lawmaking by Subnational Courts in China". *Statute Law Review* 34(1): 39–57.

Xie, Qingtao. 2016. "An Empirical Study of the Application of China Guiding Cases in Trial". Masters thesis, Stanford University.

Xinhua News Agency. 2004. "Chronology of China's Constitutional Amendments". China.org.cn, 8 March. www.china.org.cn/english/MATERIAL/89687.htm.

Yan, Xiaojun. 2011. "Regime Inclusion and the Resilience of Authoritarianism: The Local People's Political Consultative Conference in post-Mao Chinese Politics". *The China Journal* 66: 53–75.

Yang, Fan. 2019. "The Role of CPC Regulations in Chinese Judicial Decisions: An Empirical Study based on Published Judgments". *The China Review* 19(2): 69–97.

Yang, Li. 2016. "Practice and Theory of the Guiding Case System in China". *Hong Kong Law Journal* 46(1): 307–337.

Yu, Ping and Seth Gurgel. 2012. "Stare Decisis in China? The Newly Enacted Guiding Case System". In *Reading the Legal Case: Cross-Currents between Law and the Humanities*, ed. Marco Wan, 142–158. New York: Routledge.

Yu, Xingzhong. 1989. "Legal Pragmatism in the People's Republic of China". *Columbia Journal of Asian Law* 3(1): 28–51.

Zakaria, Fareed. 1997. "The Rise of Illiberal Democracy". *Foreign Affairs* 76(6): 22–43.

Zhang, Mo. 2017. “Pushing the Envelope: Application of Guiding Cases in Chinese Courts and Development of Case Law”. *Washington International Law Journal* 26(2): 269–306.

Zhang, Qianfan. 2010. “A Constitution without Constitutionalism? The Paths of Constitutional Development in China”. *International Journal of Constitutional Law* 8(4): 950–976.

Zhang, Taisu. 2012. “The Pragmatic Court: Reinterpreting the Supreme People’s Court of China”. *Columbia Journal of Asian Law* 25(1): 1–61.

Zhang, Taisu, and Tom Ginsburg. 2019. “China’s Turn toward Law”. *Virginia Journal of International Law* 59(2): 306–389.

Zhang, Wenxiong. 2016. “Prospective Judicial Pronouncement and Limits to Judicial Lawmaking”. *Singapore Academy of Law Journal* 28(2): 611–630.

Zhao, Xiaoli. 2012. “On the Composition of the Deputies in the National People’s Congress of China”. *Tsinghua China Law Review* 5(1): 2–27.

Zheng, Shiping. 1997. *Party vs. State in post-1949 China: The Institutional Dilemma*. New York: Cambridge University Press.

Chinese-Language Literature

Cai, Dingjian. 1998. *Zhongguo renmin daibiao dahui zhidu* (People’s Congress System in China). Beijing: Law Press.

Caixinglobal.com. 2017. *Duowei quanguo renda changweihui weiyuan fandui, tezhong shebei xiufa beifou* (Many Members of the NPCSC Object to Amend the Special Equipment Safety Law). *Caixin wang* (Caixin Website). 24 April. http://china.caixin.com/2017-2004-24/101082504.html.

Chen, Duanhong. 2008. *Lun xiangfa zuowei guojia de genbenfa yu gaojifa* (The Constitution as the Basic Law and the Higher Law in China). *Zhongwai faxue* (Peking University Law Journal) 20(4): 485–511.

Chen, Sixi. 2010. *Xin zhongguo lifa liushinian huigu yu zhanwang* (The Legislative Development over the past Sixty Years in China). *Shanghai zhengfa xueyuan xuebao* (Journal of Shanghai University of Political Science and Law) 25(2): 1–8.

China Discipline Inspection and State Supervision Newspaper. 2018. *Jiancha weiyuanhui shi zhengzhi jiguan* (Supervision Commission Is a Political Organ). *Zhongguo jijian jiancha bao* (China Discipline Inspection and State Supervision Newspaper). 8 March. www.ccdi.gov.cn/yaowen/201803/t20180308_165743.html.

China Institute for Applied Jurisprudence. ed. 2016. *Renmin fayuan anli xuan* (Selected Cases from the People’s Courts). Beijing: People’s Court’s Press.

Chinalawinfo. 2015. *Zuigao renmin fayuan zhidaoxing anli sifa yingyong niandu baogao* (Annual Report on the Judicial Application of Guiding Cases of the

SPC 2015). 24 December. www.chinalawinfo.com/AdHtml/20151224/fulltext.html.

Chu, Bailiang. 2015. *Henan renda daibiao kangyi gaodeng jiaoyu difang qishi* (Henan Delegates Protest Inequality in University Admissions). *New York Times (Chinese) Website.* 11 March. https://cn.nytimes.com/china/20150311/c11university/zh-hant/.

Deng, Xiaoping. 2008 [1978]. *Jiefang sixiang shishi qiushi tuanjie yizhi xiangqiankan* (Revolutionary Ideology, Seeking Truth from Facts, and Uniting for the Future). *Fenghuang Wang* (IFeng Website). 6 October. http://news.ifeng.com/mainland/special/zgsqjszqh/others/200810/1006_4778_818636.shtml.

Du, Qiangqiang. 2009. *Hunan renda changweihui bupizhun xu qingsheng danren chenzhou shi jiachanzhang* (People's Congress Standing Committee of Hunan Province Disapproves the Appointment of Xu Qingsheng to be the Chief Procurator of Chenzhou City). In *Zhongguo xianfa anshilie pingxi* (Comments on Constitutional Incidents in China), ed. Han Dayuan, 310–325. Beijing: Law Press.

Han, Dayuan. 2012. *Jianshe shehui zhuyi xianzheng* (Construct a Socialist Constitutionalism). *Xin chanjing* (New Industrial Economy) 4: 40–43.

Hong, Hao. 2017. *Falü jieshi de zhongguo fanshi* (The Chinese Paradigm of Legal Interpretation). Beijing: Peking University Press.

Hu, Yunteng. 2014a. *Guanyu anli zhidao zhidu de jige wenti* (Several Issues on Case Guidance System). *Guangming ribao* (Guang Ming Daily). 29 January. http://theory.people.com.cn/n/2014/0129/c107503-24256964.html.

2014b. *Renmin fayuan anli zhidao zhidu de goujian* (Construction of the Case Guidance System). *Ai sixiang wang* (Ai Sixiang Website). 2 May. www.aisixiang.com/data/74445.html.

2014c. *Zhongguo tese de anli zhidao zhidu yu zhidaoxing anli* (Case Guidance System with Chinese Characteristics and Guiding Case System). *Renmin sifa* (People's Judicature) 6: 1.

Huang, Xiaoyun. 2011. *Anli zhidao zhidu de lishi yan'ge* (History of Guiding Case System). *Zhongguo shenpan xinwen yuekan* (China Trial) 59(4): 17.

Institute for Recording and Review of the Law Committee of the National People's Congress Standing Committee, ed. 2020. *Fagui sifa jieshi beian shencha gongzuo banfa daodu* (Introduction to the Working Methods of Record and Review of Regulations and Judicial Interpretations). Beijing: China Democracy and Legal Publishing House.

International Herald Leader. 2011. *Yuenan gongchandang zhengzhi gaige dabu zou* (Communist Party of Vietnam: A Big Step Forward). *Xinlang wang* (Sina Website).24 June. http://news.sina.com.cn/w/sd/2011-2006-24/111522698677_2.shtml.

Ji, Chen. 2007. *Zuigao renmin fayuan sifa jieshi* (Judicial Interpretations of the SPC). Beijing: China University of Political Science and Law Press.

Jin, Hao. 2015. *Yuan e zhi huo yin anduo renshao zhuanjia kaichu chufang* (Quota System May Lead to "More Cases but Less Judges" Experts Gave out a "Prescription"). *Shanghai fazhi bao* (Shanghai Law Journal). 1 December. www.shzfzz.net/node2/zzb/shzfzz2013/yw/u1ai936111.html.

Jing, Yuejin. 2016. *Zhongguo de wenjian zhengzhi* (China's Documentary Politics). *Ai sixiang wang* (Ai Sixiang Website). 28 October. www.aisixiang.com/data/101883.html.

Ju, Jing. 2007. *Renda daibiao foujue fayuan baogao shimo* (Delegates Veto the Work Report of People's Court). *Nanfang zhoumo* (Southern Weekly). 18 December. www.infzm.com/content/2085.

Legal Daily. 2018. *Jiuzheng difang fayuan yuequan zhiding sifa jieshi xingzhi wenjian* (Correcting the Local Courts' Wrongdoing in Making Judicial Documents). *Fazhi ribao* (Legal Daily). 14 August. www.legaldaily.com.cn/index/content/2018–2008/14/content_7617629.htm?node=20908.

Li, Min. 2010. *Sifa jieshi de quanwei jiedu-fang zuigao renmin fayuan yanjiushi zhuren hu yunteng* (Authoritative Understanding of Judicial Interpretations: Interview with Hu Yunteng the Director of the Research Office of the SPC). *Zhongguo shenpan* (China Trial) 9: 72–73.

Li, Shichun. 2009. *Anli zhidao zhidu de lingyitiao silu* (Another Approach to Case Guidance System). *Faxue* (Legal Science Monthly) 6: 59–77.

Ling, Bin. 2015. *Faguan ruhe shuoli zhongguo jingyan yu pubian yuanli* (How Judges Reason: A Chinese Story and Principles). *Zhongguo faxue* (China Legal Science) 5: 99–117.

Liu, Hongjian, Shiyong An and Yuanyuan Cao. 2004. *Dui zhengzhoushi zhongyuanqu renmin fayuan shixing xianli panjue de diaocha yu sikao* (Investigating and Thinking the Precedent System of Zhongyuan District Court at Zhengzhou City). *Henan gaoji renmin fayuan wang* (The Website of Henan High People's Court). 27 February. www.hncourt.gov.cn/public/detail.php?id=28171.

Liu, Zuoxiang. 2011. *Anli zhidao zhidu de dingwei ji xiangguan wenti* (Nature of Guiding Cases and Other Relevant Issues). *Suzhou daxue xuebao* (Journal of Suzhou University) 4: 54–56.

National Judges College, and Renmin University of China School of Law, eds. 2016. *Zhongguo shenpan anlie yaolan* (China Case Trial Highlights). Beijing: Renmin University Press.

Npc.gov.cn. 2021. *Guojia falü fagui shujuku zhengshi kaitong le* (The Database of Statutory Laws and Regulations Launched). *Zhongguo renda wang* (Website of the NPC of the PRC). 24 February. www.npc.gov.cn/npc/c30834/202102/152d893e1c8445fba91a5192bd035f0b.shtml.

Pkulaw.com. 2018. *Zuigao renmin fayuan zhidaoxing anlie sifa yingyong niandu bijiao fenxi baogao* (Annual Report on the Application of SPC's Guiding

Cases). 17 May. http://weekly.pkulaw.cn/Admin/Content/Static/47c5757c-54c8-4543-bc40-1f14040a50e7.html.

Qiao, Wenxin. 2017. *Zuigao fa gongbu huanjing ziyuan xingshi minshi xingzheng dianxing anli* (The SPC Releases Typical Cases Concerning Environmental Law). *Zuigao renmin fayuan wang* (The SPC Website). 22 June. www.court.gov.cn/zixun-xiangqing-48782.html.

Regulation Editorial Center of People's Court Press, ed. 2014. *Jiedu zuigao renmin fayuan sifa jieshi* (Understanding Judicial Interpretations of the SPC) [volume 2013]. Beijing: People's Court Press.

Research Office of the Supreme People's Court, ed. 1994. *Zhonghua renmin gongheguo zuigao renmin fayuan sifa jieshi quanji* (Collections of the Judicial Interpretations of the SPC of the PRC) [volume 1]. Beijing: People's Court Press.

1997. *Zhonghua renmin gongheguo zuigao renmin fayuan sifa jieshi quanji* (Collections of the Judicial Interpretations of the SPC of the PRC) [volume 2]. Beijing: People's Court Press.

2002. *Zhonghua renmin gongheguo zuigao renmin fayuan sifa jieshi quanji* (Collections of the Judicial Interpretations of the Supreme People's Court of the PRC) [volume 3]. Beijing: People's Court Press.

Shangguan, Piliang. 2010. *Faguan falü jieshiquan chuyi* (On Judicial Construction in China). *Jianghai xuekan* (Jianghai Academic Journal) 3: 149–153.

Shen, Xinwang, and Xue Wang. 2011. *Jiang bikun: qingli diyibu xianfa* (Jiang Bikun: the Experience with the First Constitution in China). *Zhongguo xinwen zhoukan* (News Weekly) 514(16): 76–78.

Shi, Congmei. 2008. *Wenjian zhengzhi: dangxia zhongguo xiangcun zhili yanjiu de xin shijiao* (Documentary Politics: A New Perspective for the Study of China's Rural Governance). *Jiangsu shehui kexue* (Jiangsu Social Science Journal) 236(1): 96–102.

Sichuan High People's Court, and Sichuan University Collective Project. 2013. *Anli zhidao zhidu de tansuo yu shijian* (Experiment and Practice of the Typical Case System). *Zhongguo faxue* (Chinese Legal Science) 3: 34–45.

Sohu.com. 2017. *Quanguo faguan renshu shao sicheng jinnian shang bannian jiean liang tongbi sheng jin yicheng* (The Number of Judges Reducing by 40 per cent, the Number of Cases Closed Increasing by 10 per cent). 31 July. www.sohu.com/a/161092121_260616.

Sun, Zhe. 2004. *Quanguo renda zhidu yanjiu (1979–2000)* (A Study of the National People's Congress of China (1979–2000)). Beijing: Law Press.

Sun, Guohua. 1996. *Dangdai zhongguo faxuejie guanyu fa de gainian he benzhi zhi zheng* (Debate over the Concept and Nature of Law in Contemporary China). In *Makesi zhuyi faxue yanjiu* (Research on Marxist Jurisprudence), ed. Guohua Sun, 145–156. Beijing: Qunzhong Publishing House.

Suzhou Intermedia People's Court. 2017. *Suzhou zhongyuan yi an shi fa zhutui suzhou jianshe xin fazhan* (Explain the Law to the Public through Typical Cases: A Way to Promote Suzhou's New Achievements of Rule-of-Law Construction). *Jiangsu fazhi bao* (Jiangsu Law Journal). 14 July.

Tao, Kaiyuan. 2015. *Tansuo wanshan juyou zhongguo tese de zhishi chanquan anlie zhidao zhidu* (Explore Intellectual Property Guiding Case System with Chinese Characteristics). *Zuigao renmin fayuan wang* (The SPC Website). 24 April. www.court.gov.cn/zixun-xiangqing-14266.html.

The Beijing News. 2013. *Ershisi shengfen shuji jianren renda zhuren* (Party Secretaries of 24 Provinces Assume the Chairmans of Local People's Congress Standing Committee). Xinjing bao (The Beijing News). 7 February. www.chinanews.com/gn/2013/02–07/4554599.shtml.

Tong, Zhiwei. 2014. *Sifa zhongli: gaishan dang de lingdao de guanjian* (Judicial Neutrality: A Key Point to Improve Party's Leadership). *Yanhuang chunqiu* (Journal on China) 9: 1–8.

Tsou, Tang. 2012. *Er shi shijie zhongguo zhengzhi: cong hongguan lishi yu weiguan xingdong jiaodu kan* (Twentieth Century Chinese Politics: From the Perspective of Macro-History and Micro-Mechanism Analysis). Hong Kong: Oxford University Press.

Wang, Jian. 2009. *Anli zhidao qidai zhongjie tongan butong pan* (Guiding Cases Is a Way to End the Case: Like Cases Treated Differently). *Minzhu yu fazhi* (Democracy and Law) 9: 22–24.

Wang, Weiguo. 2010. *Zuigao renmin fayuan minshangshi lei sifa jieshi yanjiu* (Judicial Interpretation of Civil and Commercial Laws of the SPC). Beijing: China Renmin University Press.

Xi, Jinping. 2017. *Juesheng quanmian jiancheng xiaokang shehui duoqu xinshidai zhongguo tese shehuizhuyi weida shengli – zai zhongguo gongchandan di shijiuci quanguo daibiao dahui shang de baogao* (Secure a Decisive Victory in Building a Moderately Prosperous Society in All Respects and Strive for the Great Success of Socialism with Chinese Characteristics for a New Era – Delivered at the 19th National Congress of the CCP). 18 October. www.chinadaily.com.cn/interface/flipboard/1142846/2017–2011–06/cd_34188086.html.

Xie, Yue. 2006. *Dangdai zhongguo zhengzhi goutong* (Political Communication in Contemporary China). Shanghai: Shanghai People Press.

Yang, Jing. 2017. *Anlie zhidao zhidu zai zhishi chanquan lingyu de shijian tansuo* (The Pilot Practice of Case Guidance System in the Field of Intellectual Property). *Renming fayuan bao* (People's Court Daily). 26 July. www.chinacourt.org/article/detail/2017/07/id/2935072.shtml.

Yang, Youjiong. 1936. *Jindai zhongguo lifashi* (Legislative History of Modern China). Shanghai: The Commercial Press.

Yang, Xiaoqing. 2013. Xianzheng yu renmin minzhu zhidu zhi bijiao (Compare Constitutionalism with People's Democratic System). *Hongqi wengao* (Red Flag Manuscript) 10: 4–10.

You, Le. 2008. *Zhengzhou shi zhengfu zhuanxiang gongzuo baogao bei renda changweihui foujue* (Work Report of Zhengzhou Government was Vetoed at the Session of the Standing Committee of Local Pepople's Congress). In *Zhongguo xianfa anshilie pingxi* (Comments on Constitutional Incidents in China) [volume 2], ed. Han Dayuan, 300–320. Beijing: Law Press.

Zhang, Youyu. 1983. *Renmin daibiao dahui zhidu de xin fazhan* (New Developments of the People's Congress System). *Renmin ribao* (People's Daily). 14 January.

Zhang, Zhiming. 2012. *Zhongguo fayuan anli zhidao zhidu jiazhi gongneng zhi renzhi* (Values of China's Guiding Case System). *Xuexi yu tansuo* (Study & Exploration) 200(3): 65–70.

Zhao, Chunfeng. 2010. *Cong zuigao renmin fayuan gongzuo baogao kan sifa jieshi* (A Review of Judicial Interpretation from the Work Report of the SPC). *Guojia jianchaguan xueyuan xuebao* (Journal of National Prosecutors College) 3: 131–138.

Zhao, Xiaohai, and Ye Guo. 2017. *Zuigao renmin fayuan minshangshi zhidaoxing anlie de sifa yingyong yanjiu* (Judicial Application of SPC's Guiding Civil and Commercial Cases). *Falü shiyong* (Journal of Legal Application) 1: 56–64.

Zheng, Zhixue. 2013. *Renqing xianzheng de benzhi* (Clarify the Essence of Constitutionalism). *Dang jian* (Party Construction) 29(6): 29–31.

Zheng, Yongnian. 2013a. *Zhongguo de xianzheng zhizheng shuoming le shime* (What Can Be Reflected from the Controversial Issue over the Constitutionalism) *Lianhe Zaobao* (Joint Morning Paper) 18 June. www.rujiazg.com/article/3378.

2013b. *Xinshiqi de zhongguo gongchandang: tiaozhan yu jiyu* (Chinese Communist Party in New Era: Opportunities and Challenges). *Wuhan daxue xuebao* (Wuhan University Journal) 66(3): 10–18.

Zhou, Bin. 2017. *Zhong jiceng fayuan yuanzhang jun you shengji dangwei guanli* (Court Presidents at Grassroots and Prefectural Levels Managed by CCP Committee of Provincial Level). *Fazhi ribao* (Legal Daily). 3 July. www.legaldaily.com.cn/index/content/2017-2007/03/content_7229420.htm?node=20908.

Zhou, Daoluan. 1994. *Xinzhongguo sifa jieshi gongzuo de huigu yu wanshan sifa jieshi gongzuo de sikao daixu* (Review of the Work of Judicial Interpretations and the Thoughts on Improving the Work of Judicial Interpretations [a Preface]). In *Zhonghua renmin gongheguo zuigao renmin fayuan sifa jieshi quanji* (Collections of the Judicial Interpretations of the SPC of the PRC), ed. Research Office of the Supreme People's Court [volume 1] (October 1949–June 1993). Beijing: People's Court Press.

Zhou, Qiang, ed. 2015. *Zuigao renmin fayuan sifa jieshi huibian* (Compilation of SPC's Judicial Interpretations) [1949–2013]. Beijing: People's Court Press.

Zhou, Yongkun. 2011. Bu chengwen xianfa yanjiu de jige wenti (Several Issues on Unwritten Constitution). *Fa xue* (Legal Science Monthly) 3: 26–33.

Zhu, Jingwen, ed. 2007. *Zhongguo falü fazhan baogao* (Report on China Law Development: Database and Indicators). Beijing: Renmin University of China Press.

Statutes, Documents, Judicial Decisions and CCP Regulations Cited

Adjudication Committee of the Supreme People's Court [最高人民法院审判委员会]. 1984. *Guanyu guanche zhixing minshi susong fa shixing ruogan wenti de yijian* [关于贯彻执行<民事诉讼法(试行)>若干问题的意见] (Opinions on the implementation of Civil Procedural Law [Interim]), effective 30 August 1984.

Central Committee of the Chinese Communist Party [中国共产党中央委员会]. 1950. *Guanyu zhenya fangeming de zhishi* [关于镇压反革命活动的指示] (The Directive on Suppressing Counterrevolutionary Activities), effective, 18 March 1950.

1991. *Guanyu jiaqiang dui guojia lifa gongzuo lingdao de ruogan yijian* [关于加强对国家立法工作领导的若干意见] (Several Opinions of the Central Committee on Strengthening Leadership over Lawmaking Work), effective February 1991.

1998. *Zhonggong zhongyan guanyu nongye he nongcun gongzuo ruogan wenti de jueding* [中共中央关于农业和农村工作若干重大问题的决定] (Decision on Major Issues of Agriculture and Rural Work), effective 14 October 1998.

2004. *Zhonggong zhongyan guanyu jiaqiang dang de zhizheng nengli jianshe de jihua* [中共中央关于加强党的执政能力建设的决定] (Resolution on Improving Party's Governing Capacity), effective 19 September 2004.

2014. *Zhonggong zhongyang guanyu quanmian tuijin yifa zhiguo ruogan zhongda wenti de jueding* [中共中央关于全面推进依法治国若干重大问题的决定] (CCP Central Committee Decision Concerning Several Major Issues in Comprehensively Advancing Governance according to Law), effective 23 October 2014.

2017. *Zhongguo gongchandang dangwu gongkai tiaoli [shixing]* [中国共产党党务公开条例(试行)] (Regulation of the CCP on Open Party Affairs [For Trial Implementation]), effective 20 December 2017.

2019. *Zhongguo gongchandang dangnei fagui zhiding tiaoli* [中国共产党党内法规制定条例] (Regulation on the Formation of Intraparty Regulations), effective 30 August 2019.

Central Committee of the Chinese Communist Party, and State Council [国务院]. 2018. *Xiangcun zhengxing zhanlue jihua* [乡村振兴战略规划] (Plan for

Strategic Revitalization of the Countryside) [2018–2022], effective 26 September 2018.

Central Committee of the Chinese Communist Party, and Central Military Commission of the Chinese Communist Party [中共中央军事委员会]. 2010. *Zhongguo renmin jiefangjun zhengzhi gongzuo tiaoli* [中国人民解放军政治工作条例] (Regulations for the Chinese People's Liberation Army on Political Work), effective 9 August 2010.

Central Discipline Inspection Commission of the Chinese Communist Party [中央中央纪律检查委员会]. 1994. *Zhongguo gongchandang jilv jiancha jiguan anjian jiancha gongzuo tiaoli* [中国共产党纪律检查机关案件检查工作条例] (CCP Regulation on the Work of Case Investigation by the DIC), effective 1 May 1994.

China Case Trial Highlights Editorial Board [<中国审判案例要览>编审委员会]. 2016. *Guanyu zhengji zhongguo fayuan 2018 niandu anli gaojian de tongzhi* [关于征集<中国法院2018年度案例>稿件的通知] (Notice on Calling for Representative Cases of 2018), effective 5 December 2016.

China Institute for Applied Jurisprudence [中国应用法学研究所]. 2016. *Guanyu yinfa renmin fayuan anlie xuan anli bianxie tili yu baosong guifan de tongzhi* [关于印发<人民法院案例选>案例编写体例与报送规范的通知] (Notice on How to Edit and Submit Prior Cases to the *Selected Cases from the People's Courts*), effective 1 April 2016.

General Office of the Central Committee of the Chinese Communist Party [中共中央办公厅]. 2019a. *Zhongguo gongchandang dangnei fagui he guifanxing wenjian beian shencha guiding* [中国共产党党内法规和规范性文件备案审查规定] (Provisions for Filing and Reviewing Party Regulations and Normative Documents), effective 30 August 2019.

2019b. *Zhongguo gongchandang jilv jiancha jiguan jiandu zhiji gognzuo guize* [中国共产党纪律检查机关监督执纪工作规则] (CCP Rules on the Work of Monitoring DIC's Enforcement of Disciplines), effective 1 January 2019.

General Office of the Central Committee of the Chinese Communist Party and the State Council [国务院]. 2012. *Dangzheng jiguan gongwen chuli gongzuo tiaoli* [党政机关公文处理工作条例] (Regulations on the Work of Party and Government Organs on the Handling of Official Documents), effective 1 July 2012.

General Office of Supreme People's Court [最高人民法院办公厅]. 2005. *Zuigao renmin fayuan bangongting guanyu jiaqiang renmin fayuan anli xuan bianji gongzuo de tongzhi* [最高人民法院办公厅关于加强<人民法院案例选>编辑工作的通知] (Notice on the Editorial Work of the *Selected Cases from the People's Courts*), effective 23 June 2005.

Government Administrative Council of Central People's Government [中央人民政府政务院], and Supreme People's Court [最高人民法院]. 1950. *Guanyu zhenya fangeming huodong de zhishi* [关于镇压反革命活动的指示] (The

Directive on Suppressing Counterrevolutionary Activities), effective 23 July 1950.

Heilongjiang High People's Court [黑龙江省高级人民法院]. 2016. Wang zhong su jiage daqi linyeju [王忠诉加格达奇林业局] (Wang Zhong v. Jia Ge Da Qi Forestry Bureau). *Hei Min Shen Zi* [黑民申字] (Civil Judgement of Judicial Complaint) No. 451.

Jiangsu High People's Court [江苏省高级人民法院]. 2011. *Guanyu shenpan yewu guifangxing wenjian shiyong yu jieshi gongzuo de ruogan guiding* [关于审判业务规范性文件适用与解释工作的若干规定] (Provisions on the application and interpretation of judicial documents in respect of trial), effective 24 November 2011.

2012. *Jiangsu sheng gaoji renmin fayuan guangyu jiaqiang anli zhidao gongzuo de shishi yijian* [江苏省高级人民法院关于加强案例指导工作的实施意见] (Implementation Rules on Strengthening the Work of Case Guidance), effective 25 December 2012.

Jiangsu High People's Court Adjudicative Committee [江苏省高级人民法院审判委员会]. 2012. *Jiangsu sheng gaoji renmin fayuan shenpan weiyuanhui huiyi jiyao* [江苏省高级人民法院审判委员会会议纪要] (Conference Brief of Adjudicative Committee of Jiangsu High People's Court) No. 15 (internal document, on file with author).

Jiangyan District Court of Taizhou City of Jiangsu Provinice [江苏省泰州市姜堰区人民法院]. 2014. *Mei min su zhang dexiu deng jidongche jiaotong shigu zeren jiufen an* [梅敏诉张德修等机动车交通事故责任纠纷案] (Mei Min v. Zhang Dexiu et al.). *Tai Jiang Min Chu Zi* [泰姜民初字] (Civil Judgment of First Instance) No. 943.

National Health and Family Planning Commission [国家卫生和计划生育委员会], State Administration for Industry and Commerce [国家工商行政管理总局] and State Food and Drug Administration [国家食品药品监督管理总局]. 2016. *Jinzhi fei yixue xuyao de taier xingbie jianding he xuanze xingbie rengong zhongzhi rencheng de guiding* [禁止非医学需要的胎儿性别鉴定和选择性别人工终止妊娠的规定] (Prohibition on Gender Determination for Non-medical Purposes and Selection of Termination of Pregnancy), effective 1 May 2016.

National Congress of the Chinese Communist Party [中国共产党全国代表大会]. 2017. *Zhongguo gongchnadang dangzhang* [中国共产党党章] (Constitution of the CCP), effective 24 October 2017.

National People's Congress [全国人民代表大会]. 1954. *Zhonghua renmin gongheguo xian fa* [中华人民共和国宪法] (The Constitution of the PRC), effective 20 September 1954.

1979. *Zhonghua renmin gongheguo renmin fayuan zuzhi fa* [中华人民共和国人民法院组织法] (Organic Law of the People's Courts of the PRC), effective 1 January 1980.

2015. *Zhonghua renmin gongheguo lifa fa* [中华人民共和国立法法] (Legislation Law of the PRC), effective 15 March 2015.

2018a. *Zhonghua renmin gongheguo xian fa xiuzhengan* [中华人民共和国宪法修正案] (Constitutional Amendments of the PRC), effective 11 March 2018.

2018b. *Zhonghua renmin gongheguo jiancha fa* [中华人民共和国监察法] (Supervision Law of the PRC), effective 20 March 2018.

2018c. *Zhonghua renmin gongheguo renmin fayuan zuzhi fa* [中华人民共和国人民法院组织法] (Organic Law of the People's Courts), effective 1 January 2019.

Ningbo Intermediate People's Court of Zhejiang Province [浙江省宁波市中级人民法院]. 2014. *Ningbo pujie chuzuche youxian gongsi yu zhou xiuqing chuzu qiche yunshu hetong jiufen shangsu an* [宁波普捷出租车有限公司与周秀琴出租汽车运输合同纠纷上诉案] (Ningbo Pujie Taxi Co Ltd v. Zhou Xiuqing Taxi Co Ltd). *Zhe Yong Shang Zhong Zi* [浙甬商终字] (Civil Judgment of Second Instance) No. 474.

Organisation Department of the Central Committee of the Chinese Communist Party [中共中央组织部]. 2019. *Gongwuyuan fanwei guiding* [公务员范围规定] (Rules on the Scope of Civil Servants), effective 3 March 2020.

Research Office of the Supreme People's Court [最高人民法院研究室]. 2011. *Zuigao renmin fayuan yanjiushi guanyu yinfa guanyu bianxie baosong zhidaoxing anli tili de yijian zhidaoxing anli yangshi de tongzhi* [最高人民法院研究室关于印发"关于编写报送指导性案例体例的意见"，"指导性案例样式"的通知] (Notice of the Research Office of the SPC on Issuing the Opinions on Style for Compiling and Submitting Guiding Cases and the Format for Guiding Cases), effective 30 December 2011.

Shandong High People's Court [山东省高级人民法院]. 2001. *Qi yuling su chen xiaoqi deng yi qinfan xingmingquan de shouduan qinfan xianfa baohu de gongmin shoujiaoyu de jiben quanli jiufen an* [齐玉苓诉陈晓琪等以侵犯姓名权的手段侵犯宪法保护的公民受教育的基本权利纠纷案] (Qi Yuling v. Chen Xiaoqi et al). *Zuigao renmin fayuan gongbao* (Gazette of Supreme People's Court) [Issue 5]. 13 August.

Shanghai High People's Court [上海市高级人民法院]. 2006. *Guanyu shenpan yewu zhidaoxing wenjian zhiding fabu he shiyong de yijian* [关于审判业务指导性文件制定、发布和适用的意见] (Opinions on the Formulation, Promulgation, and Application of Judicial Documents in Respect of Trial), effective 11 December 2006.

Standing Committee of the National People's Congress [全国人民代表大会常务委员会]. 1955. *Guanyu jieshi falü wenti de jueyi* [关于解释法律问题的决议] (Resolution on Matters of Legal Interpretation), effective 23 June 1955.

1981. *Guangyu jianqiang falü jieshi gongzuo de jueyi* [关于加强法律解释工作的决议] (Resolutions on Strengthening the Work of Interpretation of Law), effective 10 June 1981.

1982. *Zhonghua renmin gongheguo minshi susongfa shixing* [中华人民共和国民事诉讼法(试行)] (Civil Procedural Law of the PRC [Interim]), effective 1 October 1982.

2005. *Sifa jieshi beian shencha gongzuo chengxu* [司法解释备案审查工作程序] (Working Procedures on the Record and Review of Judicial Interpretations), effective 19 December 2005.

2006. *Zhonghua renmin gonghe guo geji renmin dabiao dahui changwu weiyuanhui jiandufa* [中华人民共和国各级人民代表大会常务委员会监督法] (Law of the PRC on the Supervision of Standing Committees of People's Congresses at Various Levels), effective 1 January 2007.

2015. *Zhonghua renmin gongheguo difang geji renmin daibiao dahui he difang geji renmin zhengfu zuzhi fa* [中华人民共和国地方各级人民代表大会和地方各级人民政府组织法] (Organic Law of the Local People's Congresses and Local People's Governments of the PRC [2015 Amendment]), effective 29 August 2015.

2018a. *Zhonghua renmin gongheguo xingshi susong fa* [中华人民共和国刑事诉讼法] (Criminal Procedural Law of the PRC), effective 26 October 2018.

2018b. *Zhonghua renmin gongheguo gongwuyuan fa* [中华人民共和国公务员法] (Civil Servant Law of the PRC), effective 1 June 2019.

2019. *Fagui sifa jieshi beian shencha gongzuo banfa* [法规、司法解释备案审查工作办法] (Working Measures for the Recording and Review of Regulations and Judicial Interpretations), effective 16 December 2019.

2020. *Zhonghua renmin gongheguo guofang fa* [中华人民共和国国防法] (PRC Law on National Defence), effective 1 January 2021.

State Council [国务院]. 2019. *Zhengfu xinxi gongkai tiaolie* [政府信息公开条例] (Regulation on the Disclosure of Government Information), effective 15 May 2019.

Supreme People's Court [最高人民法院]. 1952. *Guanyu tanwufan yingfou huanxing ji huanxing qixian wenti de fuhan* [关于贪污犯应否缓刑及缓刑期限问题的复函] (Reply regarding the Application of a Suspended Sentence and the Probationary Period of Sentence to Offenders in Corruption), effective 22 May 1952.

1986. *Guanyu renmin fayuan zhizuo de falü wenshu ruhe yinyong falü guifanxing wenjian de pifu* [关于人民法院制作的法律文书应如何引用法律规范性文件的批复] (Reply on How Courts Should Cite Statutes and Normative Documents when Producing Formal Legal Documents), effective 28 October 1986.

1989. *Guanyu renmin fayuan shenli lihun anjian ruhe rending fuqi ganqing yi polie de ruogan yijian* [关于人民法院审理离婚案件如何认定夫妻感情确已破裂的若干具体意见] (Several Specific Opinions on How to Define the Breakdown of Marital Relations in Adjudicating Divorce Cases), effective 13 December 1989.

1993. *Quanguo jingji shenpan gongzuo zuotanhui jiyao* [全国经济审判工作座谈会纪要] (Minutes of Meeting on National Trial Work of Economic Cases), effective 6 May 1993.

1997. *Guanyu sifa jieshi gongzuo de ruogan guiding* [关于司法解释工作的若干规定] (Rules on the Work of Judicial Interpretation), effective 23 June 1997.

1999a. *Guanyu shenli nongye chengbao hetong jiufen anjian ruogan wenti de guiding shixing* [关于审理农业承包合同纠纷案件若干问题的规定(试行)] (Regulation on Several Issues of Adjudicating Disputes over Agriculture Contract [interim]), effective 8 July 1999.

1999b. *Zuigao renmin fayuan guanyu guanche quanguo renda changweihui guanyu qudi xiejiao zuzhi fangfan he chengzhi xiejiao huodong de guiding* [最高人民法院关于贯彻全国人大常委会<关于取缔邪教组织防范和惩治邪教活动的决定>和"两院"司法解释的通知] (Notice of the SPC on the Implementation of the Decision of the NPCSC on the Ban on Evil Organizations, and Prevention and Suppression of Evil Religious Activity, and the Judicial Interpretations of the SPC and the SPP), effective 5 November 1999.

1999c. *Renmin fayuan wunian gaige gangyao* [人民法院五年改革纲要] (Five-Year Reform Outline for the People's Courts) [1999–2003], effective 20 October 1999.

2000. *Guanyu zhixing zhonghua renmin gongheguo xingzheng susongfa ruogan wenti de jieshi* [关于执行<中华人民共和国行政诉讼法>若干问题的解释] (Interpretations on Several Issues concerning the Application of the Administrative Procedure Law of the People's Republic of China), effective 10 March 2000.

2005. *Renmin fayuan di er ge wunian gaige gangyao* [人民法院第二个五年改革纲要] (Second Five-Year Reform Outline for People's Courts) [2004–2008], effective 26 October 2005.

2006. *Guanyu chongfen fahui shenpan zhineng zuoyong qishi zuohao zhili shangye huilu zhuanxiang gongzuo de tongzhi* [关于充分发挥审判职能作用切实做好治理商业贿赂专项工作的通知] (Notice on Bringing into Full Play the Functional Role of Adjudication and Properly Handling the Special Work for Combating Commercial Bribery), effective 5 April 2006.

2007a. *Guanyu sifa jieshi gongzuo de guiding* [关于司法解释工作的规定] (Provisions on the Work Concerning Judicial Interpretation), effective 1 April 2007.

2007b. *Guanyu fuhe sixing anjian ruogan wenti de guiding* [关于复核死刑案件若干问题的规定] (Provisions on Certain Issues Concerning Review of Death Penalty Cases), effective 28 February 2007.

2008. *Zuigao renmin fayuan guanyu feizhi 2007 niandi yiqian fabu de youguan sifa jieshi diqipi de jueding* [最高人民法院关于废止2007年底以前发布的有关司法解释(第七批)的决定] (The 7th Decision of the SPC to Repeal

Relevant Judicial Interpretations Released before 2007), effective 24 December 2008.

2009. *Guanyu caipan wenshu yinyong falü fagui deng guifangxing falü wenjian de guiding* [关于裁判文书引用法律、法规等规范性法律文件的规定] (Provisions on Citation of Laws, Regulations and Other Normative Legal Documents in Adjudicative Documents), effective 4 November 2009.

2010a. *Guanyu gaige he wanshan renmin fayuan shenpan weiyuanhui zhidu de shishi yijian* [关于改革和完善人民法院审判委员会制度的实施意见] (Notice of the SPC on Issuing the Implementation Opinions on Reforming and Improving the Adjudication Committee System of the People's Court], effective 11 January 2010.

2010b. *Guanyu anlie zhidao gongzuo de guiding* [关于案例指导工作的规定] (Provisions concerning Work on Guiding Cases), effective 26 November 2010.

2010c. *Guanyu shenli zhengfu xinxi gongkai xingzheng anjian ruogan wenti de guiding* [关于审理政府信息公开行政案件若干问题的规定] (Provisions of the SPC on Several Issues concerning the Trial of Administrative Cases about Open Government Information), effective 13 August 2011.

2010d. *Guanyu guifan shangxiaji renmin fayuan shenpan yewu guanxi de ruogan yijian* [关于规范上下级人民法院审判业务关系的若干意见] (Certain Opinions on Regulating Trial Relations between Courts in a Vertical Relationship), effective 28 December 2010.

2012. *Zuigao renmin fayuan guanyu yinfa renmin fayuan gongwen chuli banfa de tongzhi* [最高人民法院关于印发<人民法院公文处理办法>的通知] (Notice of the SPC on Issuing the Measures for the Handling of People's Court's Documents), effective 1 January 2013.

2015a. *Zuigao renmin fayuan guanyu anlie zhidao gongzuo de guiding shishi xize* [<最高人民法院关于案例指导工作的规定>实施细则] (Detailed Rules for the Implementation of the Provisions of the SPC on Case Guidance), effective 13 May 2015.

2015b. *Guanyu renmin fayuan wei yidai yilu jianshe tigong sifa fuwu he baozhang de ruogan yijian* [关于人民法院为"一带一路"建设提供司法服务和保障的若干意见] (Several Opinions on Providing Judicial Services and Safeguards for the Implementation of One Belt and One Road), effective 16 June 2015.

2015c. *Zuigao renmin fayuan guanyu wanshan renmin fayuan sifa zeren zhi de ruogan yijian* [最高人民法院关于完善人民法院司法责任制的若干意见] (SPC's Opinion on How to Improve the Judicial Responsibility of the People's Courts), effective 21 September 2015.

2016. *Zuigao renmin fayuan guanyu yinfa renmin fayuan minshi caipan wenshu zhizuo guifan minshi susong wenshu yangshi de tongzhi* [最高人民法院关于印发<人民法院民事裁判文书制作规范><民事诉讼文书样式>的通知]

(Notice of the SPC on Issuing the Specifications for Preparing Civil Judgments by the People's Courts and the Style of Civil Litigation Documents), effective 1 August 2016.

2017. *Zhongguo zhishi chanquan sifa baohu gangyao* [中国知识产权司法保护纲要] (Outline of the Juridical Protection of Intellectual Property in China) [2016–2020], effective 20 April 2017.

2018. *Zuigao renmin fayuan guanyu shiyong zhonghua renmin gongheguo xingzheng susong fa de jieshi* [最高人民法院关于适用<中华人民共和国行政诉讼法>的解释] (Interpretations of the SPC on the Application of the Administrative Procedure Law of the PRC), effective 8 February 2018.

2019. *Guanyu jianshe yizhanshi duoyuan jiufen jiejue jizhi yizhanshi susong fuwu zhongxin de yjian* [关于建设一站式多元解纷机制一站式诉讼服务中心的意见] (Opinions of the SPC on Building the One-Stop Diversified Dispute Resolution Mechanism and the One-Stop Litigation Service Center), effective 31 July 2019.

2021. *Guanyu sifa jieshi gongzuo de guiding* [关于司法解释工作的规定] (Provisions on the Work concerning Judicial Interpretation), effective 16 June 2021.

Supreme People's Court and Supreme People's Procuratorate [最高人民检察院]. 2012. *Zuigao renmin fayuan zuigao renmin jianchayuan guanyu difang renmin fayuan renmin jianchayuan bude zhiding sifa jieshi xingzhi wenjian de tongzhi* [关于地方人民法院、人民检察院不得制定司法解释性质文件的通知] (Notice on Prohibiting Local People's Courts and People's Procuratorates from Formulating Judicial Documents), effective 18 January 2012.

Supreme People's Court, Supreme People's Procuratorate and Ministry of Public Security [公安部]. 1957. *Guanyu zhixing quanguo renmin daibiao dahui changwu weiyuanhui guanyu dui fangeming fenzi de guanzhi yilv you renmin fayuan panjue de jueding zhong ruogan juti wenti de lianhe zhishi* [关于执行全国人民代表大会常务委员会<关于对反革命分子的管制一律由人民法院判决的决定>中若干具体问题的联合指示] (The Joint Directive on the Implementation of NPCSC's Resolution on Adjudicating Cases concerning Anti-revolutionaries by the People's Courts), effective 6 February 1957.

Supreme People's Court, Supreme People's Procuratorate, Ministry of Public Security, Ministry of Justice [司法部], and National Health and Family Planning Commission. 2014. *Zuigao renmin fayuan zuigao renmin jianchayuan gong'anbu sifabu guojia weisheng he jihua shengyue weiyuanhui yinfa guanyu yifa chengchu sheyi weifa fanzui weihu zhengchang yiliao zhixu de yijian* [最高人民法院、最高人民检察院、公安部、司法部、国家卫生和计划生育委员会印发<关于依法惩处涉医违法犯罪维护正常医疗秩序的意见>的通知] (Notice of the SPC, the SPP, the Ministry of Public Security, the Ministry of Justice, and the National Health and Family Planning Commission on Printing and Distributing the "Opinions on Punishing Doctor-related Illegal and Criminal Activities according to Law and Maintaining Normal Medical Order"), effective 22 April 2014.

Supreme People's Procuratorate. 2018. *Guanyu renmin jianchayuan lian zhencha sifa gongzuo renyuan xiangguan zhiwu fanzui wenti de guiding* [关于人民检察院立案侦查司法工作人员相关职务犯罪案件若干问题的规定] (Rules on the Various Matters concerning Procuratorate's Filing a Case for Investigating the Occupation-Related Crimes Committed by Judicial Offices), effective 24 November 2018.

Xi'an Intermediate People's Court of Shaanxi Province [陕西省西安市中级人民法院]. 2014. *Xi'an mou fangchan xinxi zixun youxian gongsi yu lu mou jujian hetong jiufen shangsu an* [西安某房产信息咨询有限公司与卢某某居间合同纠纷上诉案] (Xi'an X Property Co Ltd and Lu XX Appealing Case). *Xi Zhong Min Yi Zhong Zi* [西中民一终字] (Civil Judgment of Second Instance) No. 498.

INDEX

Footnotes are indicated by n., figures by *f*, and tables by *t* after the page number.

The index uses the abbreviations CCP for Chinese Communist Party; NPC for National People's Congress; NPCSC for National People's Congress Standing Committee; and SPC for Supreme People's Court.

www.ingramcontent.com/pod-product-compliance
Lightning Source LLC
LaVergne TN
LVHW011813200926
848484LV00005B/1170
9781009152563